The Russian Lab

CONCISE HISTORIES
OF INTELLIGENCE
SERIES

Series Editors
Christopher Moran, Mark Phythian, and Mark Stout

THE RUSSIAN FSB

A CONCISE HISTORY OF THE FEDERAL SECURITY SERVICE

KEVIN P. RIEHLE

Georgetown University Press / Washington, DC

© 2024 Georgetown University Press. All rights reserved. No part of this book may be reproduced or utilized in any form or by any means, electronic or mechanical, including photocopying and recording, or by any information storage and retrieval system, without permission in writing from the publisher.

The publisher is not responsible for third-party websites or their content. URL links were active at time of publication.

Library of Congress Cataloging-in-Publication Data

Names: Riehle, Kevin P., 1963– author.
Title: The Russian FSB : a concise history of the Federal Security Service / Kevin P. Riehle.
Description: Washington, DC : Georgetown University Press, 2024. | Series: Concise histories of intelligence | Includes bibliographical references and index.
Identifiers: LCCN 2023013159 | ISBN 9781647124083 (hardcover) | ISBN 9781647124090 (paperback) | ISBN 9781647124106 (ebook)
Subjects: LCSH: Federal′naiā sluzhba bezopasnosti Rossii—History. Intelligence service—Russia (Federation) | Secret service—Russia (Federation)
Classification: LCC JN6695.A55 I672 2024 | DDC 327.1247009—dc23/eng/20230330
LC record available at https://lccn.loc.gov/2023013159

∞ This paper meets the requirements of ANSI/NISO Z39.48-1992 (Permanence of Paper).

25 24   9 8 7 6 5 4 3 2 First printing

Printed in the United States of America

Cover design by Jeremy John Parker
Interior design by Paul Hotvedt

Contents

List of Illustrations		*vii*
List of Abbreviations		*ix*
	Introduction	1
1	Foundation	5
2	Organization and Culture	29
3	Activities—Including Operations, Analysis, and Technology Development	69
4	Leaders	105
5	International Partners	129
6	Cultural Representations of the FSB	136
7	Legacy, Impact, and Future	154
Bibliography		*161*
Index		*191*
About the Author		*197*

Illustrations

Figures

1.1 Early 1990s genealogy of Russian state security   17
1.2 Correlation of KGB subelements to post-Soviet state security services   20
1.3 Postage stamps commemorating the 100th anniversary of Russian state security in 2017   22
1.4 Postage stamps commemorating the 100th anniversary of Russian counterintelligence in 2022   23
3.1 FBI "wanted" poster for indicted Center 16 officers   94
3.2 FSB Border Guard locations   95
7.1 Photo of FSB Academy graduates from a 2016 video   156

Tables

2.1 FSB Personnel from the List Released by the Ukrainian Government   63
4.1 Senior FSB Leadership as of May 2022   117

Abbreviations

AFB	Federal Security Agency (*Агентство Федеральной Безопасности*)
APS	Seconded Personnel Section (*Аппарат прикомандированных сотрудников*)
DKRO	Department for Counterintelligence Operations (*Департамент контрразведывательных операций*)
DOI	Operational Information Department (*Департамент оперативной информации*)
DPK	Border Control Department (*Департамент пограничного контроля*)
DVKR	Department of Military Counterintelligence (*Департамент военной контрразведки*); Third Service
FAPSI	Federal Agency for Government Communications and Information (*Федеральное Агентство Правительственной Связи и Информации*)
FSB	Federal Security Service (*Федеральная Служба Безопасности*)
FSK	Federal Counterintelligence Service (*Федеральная Служба Контрразведки*)
FSO	Federal Protection Service (*Федеральная Служба Охраны*)

GRU	Main Directorate of the General Staff of the Armed Forces of the Russian Federation, formerly the Main Intelligence Directorate
GUO	Main Directorate for Protection (*Главное управление охраны*)
KGB	Committee of State Security (*Комитет Государственной Безопасности*)
KRO	Counterintelligence Section (*Контрразведывательный Отдел*)
MB	Ministry of Security (*Министерство Безопасности*)
MVD	Ministry of Internal Affairs (*Министерство Внутренних Дел*)
NII	Science and Research Institute (*Научно-исследовательский институт*)
NKVD	People's Commissariat of State Security (*Народный Комиссариат Внутренних Дел*)
NTS	Science and Technology Service (*Научно-техническая служба*)
OO	Special Section (*Особый отдел*)
PS	Border Guard Service (*Пограничная Служба*)
RSFSR	Russian Soviet Federated Socialist Republic (*Российская Советская Федеративная Социалистическая Республика*)
SEB	Economic Counterintelligence Service (*Служба экономической безопасности*); Fourth Service
SIGINT	signals intelligence
SKR	Counterintelligence Service (*Служба Контрразведки*); First Service
SOD	Activity Support Service (*Служба обеспечения деятельности*); Seventh Service
SOIiMS	Service for Operational Information and International Relations (*Служба оперативной информации и международных связей*); Fifth Service
SOKR	Organizational and Personnel Service (*Служба организационно-кадровой работы*); Sixth Service
SORM	System of Operational-Investigative Measures (*Система оперативно-розыскных мероприятий*)

SSBO	Social Welfare Service (*Служба социально-бытового обеспечения*)
SU	Investigative Directorate (*Следственное управление*)
SVR	Foreign Intelligence Service (*Служба Внешней Разведки*)
TsIB	Center for Information Security (*Центр информационной безопасности*); Center 18
TsSN	Special Operations Center (*Центр специального назначения*)
UA	Aviation Directorate (*Управление авиации*)
UFSB	Federal Security Service Directorate (*Управление Федеральной Службы безопасности*)
UIOORD	Directorate of Information Support for Operational-Investigative Activities (*Управление информационного обеспечения оперативно-розыскной деятельности*)
UKAKD	Directorate for Coordination of Analysis and Counterintelligence Activities (*Управление координации и анализа контрразведывательной деятельности*)
UKR Smersh	Counterintelligence Directorate Smersh (*Управление контрразведки СМЕРШ*)
UPS	Directorate for Support Programs (*Управление программ содействия*)
USB	Internal Security Directorate (*Управление собственной безопасности*)
UZKS	Directorate for Protecting the Constitutional Order (*Управление по защите конституционного строя*)
VChK	All-Russian Extraordinary Commission for Combating Counterrevolution and Sabotage under the Council of People's Commissars of the RSFSR (*Всероссийская чрезвычайная комиссия по борьбе с контрреволюцией и саботажем при Совете народных комиссаров РСФСР*)

Introduction

This book discusses the history, missions, and organization of the Russian Federal Security Service (FSB). Although a relatively new organization—the name FSB was instituted only in 1995—the organization inherited a long history of Russian and Soviet powers and institutions, along with many officers who began their careers in the Soviet era. This heritage endows the FSB with the aura and operational mind-set of the Soviet Committee of State Security (KGB), which still-active former KGB officers embrace by honoring the sobriquet "chekist." Yet, the return of a pre-Soviet heritage in today's Russia and more recent memories of the chaotic 1990s modify this aura to give the FSB its twenty-first-century character. Chapter 1 discusses the FSB's historical foundations that connect it with the Russian imperial, Soviet, and 1990s past.

Despite being one of the most powerful organizations in Russia, the FSB is covered in the West only superficially, often only in relation to its activities against Western countries, such as computer-based intelligence operations. However, the FSB is, in fact, primarily a domestic security and law enforcement service that permeates much of Russian society. It accomplishes its domestic missions through its enforcement of a wide range of laws and its authorization to conduct electronic and physical surveillance throughout Russia with little restraint. Those authorities allow the FSB to monitor and neutralize any embryonic manifestations of internal opposition or dissent within the country or their presence elsewhere in the world. The FSB has even resurrected a version of the KGB's Fifth Directorate, which was tasked with what the Soviet Communist Party called "ideological counterintelligence." Chapters 2, 3, and 4 discuss the organization of the FSB; its intelligence, counterintelligence, counterterrorism, and law enforcement missions; and the backgrounds of the leaders who direct those missions.

Although primarily a domestic security service, the FSB also has external missions. Those missions include being Russia's primary clandestine service within the former Soviet space, where the FSB conducts a variety of intelligence collection and covert action operations. The FSB serves as the Russian government's declared liaison with the security services of Russia's allies, through which the FSB influences those countries by sharing selected, ideologically driven intelligence. The Russian government also uses the FSB's role as a counterterrorism service to extend Russia's intelligence, especially its signals intelligence. Chapter 5 discusses the FSB's international missions.

The FSB's reputation inside Russia is founded on respect and patriotism, mixed with a growing perception of corruption. The FSB conducts a concerted campaign to encourage the former, with awards ceremonies, glossy publications, films, and public marketing that portray the FSB as the protector of Russia against spies and terrorists sponsored by nefarious foreign powers. Conversely, Russian media and opposition groups, such as followers of the jailed Russian political activist Aleksey Navalny, often highlight the latter. A series of corruption incidents in the past decade has supplied plentiful material for the opposition's perspective. Chapter 6 discusses cultural representations of the FSB.

One of the FSB's most potent levers of influence inside Russia is the patronage of Russian Federation president Vladimir Putin. Putin led the FSB for a year in 1998–99, and he has since overseen the gradual reaccumulation into the FSB of many powers previously housed in the Soviet-era KGB. This patronage gives the FSB the power to ensure that Putin faces no credible threats to his ruling position in the country. Nevertheless, as time passes, younger officers are replacing the retiring older generation, many of whom are in senior positions, including Putin himself. Chapter 7 discusses the FSB's future, which will depend on how the Russian government promotes or sidelines future FSB leaders.

The data in this book come from a variety of Russian- and English-language sources. However, part of the reason for the lack of depth that often characterizes Western treatments of the FSB is a lack of source material in Western languages. Consequently, most sources cited in this book were originally published in Russian. Relying on Russian-language sources has both advantages and potential disadvantages.

Two Russian sources are particularly foundational. Andrey Soldatov and Irina Borogan's website, Agentura.ru, contains a comprehensive compilation of material about the FSB and its suborganizations. Their information is especially useful for its insights into the FSB's foreign operations within the former Soviet space, including in Ukraine, based on Russian media reports. Another valuable Russian source is a web-published work by the Dossier Center, a Russian dissident organization financed by an exiled former oligarch, Mikhail Khodorkovsky. The Dossier Center makes no secret of its goal to reveal the FSB's criminal activities, and it tends to emphasize negative stories about the FSB, demonstrating its ideological leaning against the organization. Nevertheless, despite the dissident nature of the Dossier Center's material, it provides original content, including interviews with FSB officers, that casts significant light onto the missions and functions of the agency.

Sources also include Russian laws describing the FSB's missions and organization. These form the foundation for and set the limits of FSB operations and provide a public veneer of authority and restraint. Other Russian sources include numerous national and local news articles that, based on the restricted media environment in Russia, often communicate a government-inspired narrative of the FSB's heroics and patriotism. They also report changes in FSB leadership, along with FSB activities and perceived threats that the FSB chooses to publicize to maintain its intrepid reputation. However, the Russian media also frequently focus on conspiracies and scandals that communicate unconfirmed rumors or paint the FSB as corrupt. Much of the reporting about prosecutions of FSB officers caught embezzling or extorting money comes from Russian media.

The advantage of Russian sources is the volume of material they offer that is unavailable in Western languages. They fill many information gaps. The disadvantage is their often questionable objectivity, either in their slavish support for the Putin regime or their inexorable opposition to it, along with their tendency toward salacious stories. This lack of objectivity and conspiracy-mindedness requires careful use of Russian sources.

Nevertheless, no study of the FSB could be complete without them. This book attempts to compile this information, supplemented by English-language data, to describe the FSB's history, missions, and organization as completely and credibly as possible.

1

Foundation

The Russian Federal Security Service (*Федеральная Служба Безопасности*; FSB) is Russia's primary internal security service. Its foremost mission is to protect the ruling Russian regime. Its authorities in counterintelligence, law enforcement, intelligence, and border security give it a pervasive presence throughout Russia and in the rest of the former Soviet space. The FSB is built on the foundation of the Soviet Committee of State Security (KGB) and retains much of the KGB's philosophy and operational mind-set and even some of the same people. In fact, some Western commentators have claimed that the FSB is simply a return of the KGB.[1] Even most Russian intelligence and security service personnel themselves date the organization's founding to 1917, the year the Bolshevik regime established its first state security service, the All-Russian Extraordinary Commission for Combating Counterrevolution and Sabotage under the Council of People's Commissars of the RSFSR (VChK), colloquially called by its acronym, Cheka. The chekist label, which Russian intelligence and security personnel proudly embrace, is a remnant of that first service.[2] The KGB of the past is unquestionably an essential basis for the FSB today.

However, reference to the KGB alone is insufficient to describe the FSB. It is inaccurate to say that nothing changed in the state security apparatus of the independent Russian Federation. Yet these changes, rather than being in personnel or major missions, have been in the FSB's place in Russian history and Russia's government structure. The FSB is more accurately an amalgamation of pre-Soviet, post-Soviet, and Soviet-era forces. Some Western observers and Russian politicians concur about the indispensable role that a strong state security service plays in Russia. Robert Berls of the Nuclear Threat Initiative wrote, "History has shown, whether during Tsarist Russia, the Soviet Union, or Putin's Russia, that a strong central government that maintains a powerful internal political and security apparatus has been the only successful way to restrain the numerous centrifugal forces that seek to drive power away from the center and weaken central authority."[3] Nikolay Kovalev, the FSB's director in 1997 and 1998, affirmed that "a strong state needs a strong special service."[4] Conversely, a weak special service engenders internal conflicts, disunity, civil war, and other states' attempts to degrade the country, which bring about ruin and casualties among the people and a loss of national identity. Kovalev's statement originated not with him but with Boris Yeltsin, who stated more explicitly as early as 1994 that a "strong Russia needs strong special services."[5] Yeltsin's opponent in the 1996 presidential election, the ultrarightist politician Vladimir Zhirinovskiy, wrote similarly, "Strong state—strong special services."[6]

The theme that Russia must have a strong security service threads through the entire existence of the FSB. Rather than being Soviet, however, the FSB is a Russian entity based on a Russian sociocultural foundation, which in Jolanta Darczewska's analysis includes "the Russian spirit, the Russian Orthodox community, conservative values, the mission of uniting a multinational and multi-confessional society, the community of experiences, the experiences of wartime, the spirit of service to the state, the dictatorship of law, etc."[7]

Pre-Soviet Foundations

Soviet-era state security services publicly made a clean ideological break from their tsarist-era predecessors, claiming to have eliminated all bourgeois characteristics of the services that had repressed the Russian people. However, with the return of many Russian imperial symbols and cultural vestiges under Putin's leadership, the Soviet-era ideological antipathy toward the tsarist-era security services has been abandoned. The Russian historian Mikhail Burenkov wrote about the tsarist foundations of the FSB in the agency's own journal, *ФСБ: За и Против* (*FSB: For and Against*): "As is known, VChK elements actively used many normative documents and operational materials of the [tsarist-era] Police Department in the first years of Soviet power not only for the purpose of legal regulation of official activities but also when organizing and conducting operational-investigative, counterintelligence, and intelligence measures."[8]

Such a public statement would have been blasphemous during the Soviet era. However, despite the Soviet Union's superficial ideological purity, the Soviet security services quietly assimilated many operational techniques from the tsarist security services—including the use of agents provocateurs, double agents, and disinformation methods—which then were passed down to post-Soviet services.[9] Former KGB officers Oleg Gordievsky and Oleg Kalugin both noted that the KGB used pre-revolutionary Okhrana materials to train its officers in the 1950s and 1960s.[10] Burenkov writes that it is important to learn lessons from the pre-Bolshevik period to avoid repeating problems that Russia solved in the nineteenth and early twentieth centuries.[11] Although the tsarist-era security services clearly did not solve every problem—they did not prevent the fall of the tsar—they are now portrayed as examples worthy of emulation.

Focused on internal threats, both the prerevolutionary Okhrana and the KGB conducted similar domestic intelligence activities and recruited domestic sources for population control and counterintelligence purposes.[12] Burenkov highlighted several tsarist-era police investigators—such as Nikolay Batyushin, a senior Russian military counterintelligence officer during World War I; Stepan Beletskiy, director of the tsarist Police Department from 1912 to 1914; and Petr Zavarzin, who served in the tsarist police for eighteen years—who all argued for the necessity of domestic agent networks to protect the regime from internal threats. The penetration of domestic opposition groups was aimed at reducing the threat to the regime, often presupposing a link between domestic groups and foreign powers. The Okhrana's emphasis on internal security was founded on an unwavering assumption that foreign powers were meddling in Russian affairs, and this assumption continued into the Soviet era. A 1977 KGB manual used in training new KGB employees made the same point regarding external forces destabilizing the Soviet Union, using Soviet ideological rhetoric without tying it to the pre-Soviet era:

By organizing sabotage of state workers, the exploiting class wanted to force the Soviet government to abandon the decisive path toward breaking the old bourgeois-landowner state apparatus: by encouraging speculation, they tried to exacerbate economic ruin to drown the revolution in famine; with conspiracies and armed revolts, inspired by the participation of the imperialist West, the domestic counterrevolution tried to crush the power of the workers and peasants.[13]

Domestic surveillance networks, in which Russian imperial security services excelled, became a hallmark of the KGB and continued to be used heavily in both the physical and electronic domains in post-Soviet Russia.

Since Putin's ascent to the presidency, Russian publishers have released multiple books that recount the history of tsarist-era security services. Petr Zavarzin's book *The Work of the Secret Police*, originally published in Paris in 1924 after Zavarzin was exiled from Russia, has been republished at least three times in Russia, in 2004, 2018, and 2020.[14] Nikolay Batyushin's writings on counterintelligence were also published in 2007.[15] Aleksandr Shirokorad, in his 2016 book *Secret Operations of Tsarist Special Services, 1877–1917*, explores the question: why did the great Russian Empire experience such a complete downfall in 1917 when it possessed the best security service in the world?[16] Other books—like Aleksandr Kolpakidi's *Special Services of the Russian Empire: A Unique Encyclopedia*; Boris Starkov's *Spy Hunters: Counterintelligence in the Russian Empire 1903–1914*; Ivan Tarasov's *Police of Russia: History, Laws, and Reforms*; and Borisov, Malygin, and Mulukayev's *Three Centuries of Russian Police*—trace the beginning of Russian security services from the tsarist empire through the Soviet era to today.[17] Similarly, Vitaliy Karavashkin's 2008 book *Who Betrayed Russia?* lists individuals accused of being traitors to Russia beginning from ancient Kievan Rus through the Soviet era and into post-Soviet Russia.[18]

Tsarist-era anniversaries have also crept into the FSB's historical memory. In 2012, the Russian government issued a postage stamp honoring the 500th anniversary of the Russian Border Guard Service. That stamp commemorated the "Order to the Ugrian Voevods," a document signed by Grand Duke Vasiliy III of Moscow, father of Ivan IV "The Terrible," on May 16, 1512, to establish a force of Ugrian warlords on the eastern border of the Moscow state to protect it from Siberian hordes. Although dating the establishment of the Russian border guards to that document is historically questionable, Russian border guards openly celebrated their tsarist roots in 2012.[19] Nevertheless, the FSB Border Guard Service, along with the border guard services of other former Soviet states, officially celebrates Border Guards Day on May 28, the day the first Soviet-era border guards were established in 1918.[20]

Vladimir Putin has publicly recognized the prerevolutionary heritage of the Russian intelligence services. In his 2020 speech commemorating the 100th anniversary of Russian foreign intelligence, he noted that Russian intelligence and state security employees today are continuing the traditions not only of their Bolshevik predecessors but also of those that served prerevolutionary Russia.[21] Such statements and publications would not have been possible in the ideologically restricted atmosphere of the Soviet Union. However, respect for Russian imperial security services is now encouraged.

Post-Soviet Drivers

During the Soviet era, the KGB was subordinated to the Communist Party of the Soviet Union, and the security of the party was the KGB's primary responsibility. The most conspicuous change in post-Soviet state security is the removal of the party and the communist ideology's pursuit of world socialism as the ideological force behind state security activities. That allowed for discussion of prerevolutionary state security precursors but also led to a period of chaos, corruption, and politicization during the 1990s. Putin is sometimes accused of remaking the FSB in the image of the KGB, and to an extent, that is true. However, while Putin's experience in the KGB was formative, he also experienced other formative moments, particularly related to Russia's military, political, and economic weakness of the 1990s. The 1990s were a time when Russia tried to build a new governing structure based on Western democracy and capitalism rather than on Soviet communism and centralized economic principles. That attempt was largely unsuccessful and revealed numerous cracks in Russian society. Those cracks often involved the security services, which now bear the scars of Russia's 1990s weakness.

In the first five years after the dissolution of the Soviet Union, several notable works appeared in the West that analyzed the structures, missions, and strategies of the intelligence and security services of the newly independent Russian Federation. J. Michael Waller completed a dissertation for Boston University in 1993 in which he assessed that the intelligence and security services were the only institutions of Russia that did not undergo real reforms due to Gorbachev's perestroika. Instead, the Yeltsin administration harnessed them for its own political purposes rather than reforming or curbing the power they had possessed during the Soviet era.[22] Waller published a book in 1994, *Secret Empire*, based on his dissertation.[23]

Amy Knight gave a similar assessment in her 1996 book *Spies Without Cloaks*. Knight also asserted that Gorbachev himself was complicit in the August 1991 coup attempt in the USSR, and that he had collaborated with the coup plotters to prevent the signing of a new Union Treaty, which would have transferred some power from Moscow to Soviet republic capitals.[24] In her analysis, the KGB never reformed at all, and Gorbachev agreed to retain it unchanged. Yevgenia Albats went further, saying that former intelligence and state security employees' violations of human rights had continued unabated in the post-Soviet era.[25] Martin Ebon took a more sympathetic stance toward the Yeltsin administration, claiming that Yeltsin had been the target of a KGB assassination attempt and that he had tried to work with the new services to maintain Russia's security.[26]

The reality is that, while some aspects of the KGB translated well into the post-Soviet era, others did not. The KGB's human resources remained to a great extent, although there were significant personnel cuts just before the dissolution of the Soviet Union. One element that did not survive was the public reputation of the Russian state security services as the incorruptible protectors of Russia's security. Many in Russia viewed the KGB as an honest, noncorrupt organization. Yuriy Andropov, KGB chief from 1967 to 1982, cultivated an image of the KGB officer as a selfless, upright servant of the state. Andropov himself contrasted with other Soviet Communist Party leaders by living a publicly irreproachable life with no rumor of personal enriching surfacing during his time as KGB chief.[27] The post-Soviet services did not inherit this reputation, because they became enmeshed in political infighting among the corrupt oligarchs who wielded political power in the country during the 1990s.

Another concept that did not survive the dissolution of the Soviet Union was the ideological basis for state security activities. That included the main ideological pillars of the Soviet state, such as glorification of revolution and the communist ideological insistence that revolution was inevitable. That has been replaced by a rejection of revolution as a threat to a legitimate state, characterized by "color revolutions," which, in the Russian state security interpretation, are perpetrated by nefarious foreign states to destroy Russia. The celebration of the 100th anniversary of the VChK's founding in 2017 focused mainly on the agency's role in protecting the state from foreign invasion rather than as its place as "sword of the revolution." The Bolshevik ideological foundation also led the VChK to pursue any manifestation of capitalism or religion in the country as antistate activities. That is the opposite of today's state security services, which are heavily involved with Russian megacorporations, both to support their profit-taking and to embezzle money from them, and emphasize their connection to the Russian Orthodox Church.

The FSB's relationship with the Orthodox Church is a particularly significant break from the Soviet era. Putin reportedly became active in the Church in the 1990s and befriended Metropolitan Tikhon, an Orthodox priest who ran the Sretensky Monastery near the FSB's Lubyanka headquarters. Tikhon states that Putin "makes confession, takes communion, and understands his responsibility before God for the high service entrusted to him and for his immortal soul."[28] Patriarch Kirill of the Russian Orthodox Church laid the foundation for a church on the grounds of the FSB Academy in 2012.[29] The connection to the Church represents a strong trend toward more conservativism in social issues within Russian society in general, and in the FSB in particular. During the formal blessing of the new church's cornerstone in 2013, the director of the FSB Academy, Colonel General Viktor Ostroukhov, stated that the academy's staff was concerned about what he called "the increasing number of attacks on the Christian way of life. . . . Together we can oppose these dangerous threats to modernity and preserve a great and indivisible Russia."[30] The return of the Russian Orthodox philosophical foundation to the Russian security services differs noticeably from the official atheism of the Soviet era.

Another post-Soviet driver in the FSB is the demand for political loyalty to the president rather than to the party. As the Soviet Union was collapsing, the Soviet, and then Russian, security services went through five years of instability and reorganization. The instability began in earnest on June 12, 1990, when the Congress of People's Deputies of the Russian Soviet Federated Socialist Republic (RSFSR) adopted a declaration of sovereignty, initiating a struggle for power over the organs of government control. It accelerated after the KGB director, Vladimir Kryuchkov, participated directly in the attempted coup against Mikhail Gorbachev in August 1991, damaging the KGB's reputation.

That led the newly emboldened president of the Russian Federation, Boris Yeltsin, to make demands on the KGB, including creating for the first time a Russian republic-level KGB in May 1991. The RSFSR, the Russian portion of the Soviet Union, did not have a republic-level state security service, unlike the other fourteen republics. The center–periphery relationship between Moscow and the Soviet republics meant that republic-level KGBs existed more to keep the republics in line with Moscow than to give them an independent security capability. As the Soviet Union's largest, most powerful, and central republic, with Moscow Center at its disposal, the RSFSR did not require a separate security service. However, after the August coup attempt, Yeltsin started to establish his own.

The Soviet central authorities did not immediately acquiesce to Yeltsin's demands. Vladimir Kryuchkov was arrested after the failed coup attempt and replaced with Vadim Bakatin, the former Soviet minister of internal affairs, whom Gorbachev tasked with dismantling the KGB and purging Kryuchkov loyalists. Assigning a former minister of internal affairs as KGB director was culturally repulsive to KGB personnel, as they viewed the MVD with condescension. Consequently, Bakatin met deep-seated resistance to change in the KGB. He later stated in an interview, in answer to a question about his opinion of KGB officers viewing themselves as "chekists": "Ideological dogmatists will have to be sent to rest. . . . The traditions of chekism must be eradicated and chekism as an ideology must terminate its existence. We must comply with the law, but not ideology."[31]

His efforts met with little success, and most KGB functions continued; nevertheless, the USSR's KGB was dissolved by an order signed by Gorbachev dated December 3, 1991, titled "On the Reorganization of Organs of State Security." The order divided the Union KGB into three agencies: the Central Intelligence Service of the USSR, which inherited the KGB's First Chief Directorate (Foreign Intelligence); the Committee for Defending the USSR State Border and Unified Command of Border Forces, which housed the KGB's Chief Directorate for Border Guards; and the Interrepublic Security Service (MSB) of the USSR, which housed the rest of the KGB. The one primary element that did not survive was the Fifth Directorate (Ideological Counterintelligence), which was dissolved altogether (see chapter 2). Bakatin then served briefly as the director of the MSB, until it was disbanded in mid-January 1992 and its resources were shifted to the Russian Federation.

Just before Gorbachev's law "On the Reorganization of Organs of State Security," the Russian Federation created a separate, short-lived Federal Security Agency (AFB). Yeltsin chose his longtime friend from the RSFSR Ministry of Internal Affairs (MVD), Victor Barannikov, to lead it. Yeltsin then named Barannikov the Russian Federation's minister of internal affairs immediately after the August coup attempt.[32] Founded on November 26, 1991, the AFB existed in parallel with the MSB and vied with it for power until the Soviet Union was dissolved on December 25, 1991.

Even before the end of the Soviet Union, Yeltsin issued another order on December 19, creating the Ministry of Security and Internal Affairs, combining most of the former KGB (minus foreign intelligence and border guards) with the MVD to create a superministry responsible for all security and law enforcement in the country, with Barannikov as the new minister. A similar entity had existed several times previously in the Soviet Union, such as from 1934 to 1941, when it was called the People's Commissariat of State Security (NKVD) and was responsible for enforcing Stalin's purges. State security and internal affairs separated again during World War II, but Lavrentiy Beriya recombined them briefly in 1953 after Stalin's death into what was then called the MVD. Those occasions carried ominous memories, which, compounded by the reputational damage to the KGB from the August 1991 coup attempt and an increased urgency among democratic Russian politicians to disband the KGB altogether, led to a Russian Constitutional Court decision in mid-January 1992 ruling that the new superministry violated the constitution.[33]

Still, with the USSR gone, the Russian Federation was faced with the challenge of providing security for itself while also confronting challenges that existed in the fourteen other former Soviet states, such as crime, safe control of nuclear materials, internal corruption, and civil war. To address these challenges, the Russian Federation created the Ministry of Security (MB) on January 24, 1992, recombining most of the components of the former KGB, except for the First Chief Directorate, which the Foreign Intelligence Service (SVR) inherited, and the Ninth Directorate, which transferred to the Main Directorate for Protection (later the Federal Protection Service, FSO). In July 1992, the Yeltsin team pushed through a law that governed the MB's activities, giving it many of the same missions and responsibilities the KGB had, sometimes verbatim.[34] According to Gennadiy Burbulis, a political ally of Yeltsin, the president believed that "the CPSU had been the country's brain and the KGB was its spinal cord. . . . Yeltsin clearly did not want to rupture the spinal cord now that the head had been lopped off."[35] Most personnel remained, including Barannikov, who was named the first minister of security.

Barannikov's tenure was short. As political instability grew within Russia and the economic reforms enacted by Yeltsin's team began to yield high unemployment accompanied by a rise in superrich oligarchs, Barannikov got caught between opposing political camps. In 1993, Yeltsin clashed with members of the Russian parliament who opposed shock therapy economic reforms. Barannikov declined to become involved in March 1993, when Yeltsin threatened to use the "power ministries" (Ministries of Security, Defense, and Internal Affairs) to back up a decree by which Yeltsin imposed "special rule," giving him veto powers over the Supreme Soviet.

Barannikov responded by saying in a speech that he would remain neutral in political confrontations. Yeltsin described his opponents in the Supreme Soviet as political extremists, labeling them communists and fascists, but Barannikov disclaimed any responsibility for combating political extremism.[36] The MB did not crack down on anti-Yeltsin demonstrators in May 1993. Further, Barannikov, by no means free of all corruption allegations himself, reportedly began collecting information about corruption among Yeltsin's entourage rather than targeting Yeltsin's political opponents. By July 1993, Yeltsin had had enough of Barannikov's disloyalty and fired him. The proximate reason for his dismissal was a border clash on the Afghanistan-Tajikistan border, where Russian border guards took heavy losses when a group of Afghan soldiers and Tajik rebels attacked a border post. Yeltsin also accused Barannikov of financially benefiting from criminal activities. The deeper reason was Barannikov's unwillingness to take Yeltsin's side in political battles.[37] Yeltsin was establishing the new norm the Russian state security—that it be politically loyal to the president.

Barannikov's dismissal did not end Yeltsin's conflict with the legislative bodies. Nikolay Golushko, a longtime KGB officer who had gained a reputation for fighting nationalism and dissent in the Soviet Union, replaced Barannikov. Golushko had led the Ukrainian republic's KGB during the late 1980s up to the dissolution of the Soviet Union, and his appointment showed that Yeltsin planned to use the MB powers to pursue his political enemies. In September, Yeltsin dissolved the two legislative branches, the Congress of People's Deputies and the Supreme Soviet, although those bodies refused to disband, citing the president's lack of constitutional authority. Parliament responded by impeaching Yeltsin and naming Yeltsin's opponent, Aleksandr Rutskoy, as acting president. Rutskoy then dismissed Golushko, along with other power ministers.

In October 1993, Yeltsin's clash with the Supreme Soviet reached the point of violence, with mass demonstrations surrounding the Ostankino television station and army troops ordered to forcibly disband the Supreme Soviet, resulting in tanks firing on the White House, where the Supreme Soviet met. Nearly 150 people died in the violence. Although the army responded to Yeltsin's order, the MB provided little aid.[38]

In response to the lack of political support from the MB, Yeltsin issued a decree on December 21, 1993, reorganizing Russia's security structure. The decree began with this statement:

> The system of organs of the VChK-OGPU-NKVD-NKGB-MGB-KGB-MB has proved to be unreformable. Attempts at reorganization made in the past years have been, in general, superficial and cosmetic. Up to now, the Russian Federation Ministry of Security has lacked a strategic concept for ensuring the state security of the Russian Federation. Counterintelligence work is weakened. The system of political investigations has been mothballed but could easily be reconstituted.
>
> Against the background of the democratic and constitutional transformation taking place in Russia, the existing system of providing security for the Russian Federation has outlived itself, is ineffective, is a burden

on the state budget, and is a restraining factor in the implementation of political and economic reforms.[39]

This decree dissolved the MB and replaced it with a new organization, the Federal Counterintelligence Service (FSK), bureaucratically downgrading it from a ministry to a service and placing it more firmly under presidential control. Golushko remained as the FSK director until February 1994, when Sergey Stepashin, who was initially viewed as a potential reformer, was appointed. Like Barannikov, Stepashin had an MVD background, but had led the State Commission to Investigate the Activities of the Committee for State Security and the State Committee for the State of Emergency, which investigated the KGB's role in the August coup attempt. From 1991 to 1993, Stepashin led the Supreme Soviet's defense and security committee.[40] Once appointed to lead the FSK, however, he did not reduce its power but instead emphasized the threats that Russia faced and the urgency needed to address them. Soon after his appointment, Stepashin said that Russia's path to reforming the state security apparatus had not "repeated the Eastern European option and has not completely destroyed Russian special services."[41] (See figure 1.1.)

The FSK was renamed the FSB in a law dated April 12, 1995; that law has subsequently been amended numerous times to broaden the FSB's mandate and strengthen its powers. Thus, what eventually became the FSB underwent multiple reorganizations and name changes through the early 1990s. Those changes were influenced heavily by political conflict within Russia and by the perceived need to retain Russia's strength amid political chaos. Some of the reforms of Russia's governing structure in the post-Soviet era necessitated, in the eyes of Russian political leaders, the continuation of the powerful state security service to prevent the country from disintegrating. In the late 1990s, three prime ministers in quick succession—Yevgeniy Primakov, Sergey Stepashin, and Vladimir Putin—had all led chekist organizations. The fervor to maintain Russia's viability amid post-Soviet political instability while remaining fiercely loyal to the president became a pillar of the FSB's existence.

The 1990s' politicization of the state security service replaced the communist ideology of the Soviet era. However, the requirement for political loyalty to a president whose reputation was badly tarnished and for whom many state security officers had little respect left an impression on the

KGB
  ↳ **AFB** (Russian Federation), November 26, 1991, and MSB (USSR), December 3, 1991
    ↳ **MB**, January 24, 1992
      ↳ **FSK**, December 21, 1993
        ↳ **FSB**, April 12, 1995

Figure 1.1   Early 1990s genealogy of Russian state security

FSB. Both Stepashin and Putin protected Yeltsin's corrupt family members as FSB directors in the late 1990s, deepening the FSB's relationship with corruption and weakening the morale and motivation of FSB employees to perform their work.

Although the KGB was never completely free of all corruption, it had been a relatively clean institution within the Soviet structure. The Soviet Union's dissolution tore away the ideological driver of communism, leaving little impetus for the post-Soviet state security services to operate effectively and for the greater good. Without this external ideological driver, state security employees resorted to working for their personal interests, leading to corruption and business deals on the side.

Putin stepped into this morass of ideological ambiguity when he became the FSB director in 1998. He came from the KGB culture and had witnessed firsthand the confusion that had arisen in the service due to the absence of a coalescing purpose. He also retained no love for the communist past, so there was no likelihood that he would reinstate the communist ideology. In his millennium speech the day before Yeltsin's resignation, Putin said,

> For almost three-fourths of the outgoing century Russia lived under the sign of the implementation of the communist doctrine. It would be a mistake not to see and, even more so, to deny the unquestionable achievements of those times. But it would be an even bigger mistake not to realize the outrageous price our country and its people had to pay for that Bolshevist experiment. What is more, [it would be a mistake] not to understand that Soviet power did not make Russia a prosperous country or a dynamically developing society and free people.[42]

In its place, he installed patriotic pride in Russian history, culture, and power. This patriotism has become the ideological driver for state security activities during the Putin era, although it does not constitute an ideology per se. The complication has been that state security employees have not separated themselves from either the Soviet-era chekist mind-set regarding threats or the 1990s mind-set of working for their own interests. Rather than replacing those drivers, Putin-era state security services have built onto them and encouraged patriotism, which is closely related to the Soviet-era chekist mind-set, while tolerating 1990s self-interest.

Soviet-Era Remnants

Even with the renewed influence of pre-Soviet ideas and the politicization and malaise of the 1990s, the FSB's foundation in the Soviet-era KGB is the agency's most potent driving force. The historian J. Michael Waller points out that the Russian Federation had a more difficult task to reform its state security apparatus than even post–World War II Germany, Italy, or Japan. Their political systems were rebuilt after the war, not by themselves, but by occupying powers. Even postcommunist East Germany is not a perfect analogy because the Bonn government imposed many of the reforms there. The Russian Federation was left to reform itself without outside force, and that left the many personnel who continued in state security service past the end of the Soviet Union to fall back on what they knew—the KGB.[43]

With Putin's support, the FSB is intent on reproducing the Soviet-era popular perception of state security. According to a survey of Soviet citizens between November 1991 and January 1992, the Soviet population had a generally positive view of KGB employees. Most ascribed to them characteristics such as "professional," "intelligent," and "strong. Fewer used terms such as "devious" and "careerist." Only about one in ten thought the KGB should be abolished altogether.[44] These positive perceptions changed across the Yeltsin years. In December 1999, then–prime minister Vladimir Putin said, "Bodies of state security have always defended the national interests of Russia. They must not be separated from the state and turned into some kind of monster. . . . We nearly overdid it when we exposed the crimes committed by the security services, for there were not only dark periods, but also glorious episodes in their history, of which one may really be proud."[45] Those glorious periods of the Soviet era are what the FSB wants people to remember.

Despite the reorganizations and name changes that characterized the four years after the dissolution of the Soviet Union, most primary structures that made up Soviet security services remained. Most initially resided in the MB; however, the break-up of the MB in 1993 left the KGB's heirs in five different organizations. Subsequently, most KGB subelements have been restored to the FSB (see figure 1.2).

The KGB structure consisted of main directorates, directorates, and departments responsible for a specific operational or headquarters mission. The four primary operational elements were

- First Chief Directorate (foreign intelligence), founded December 19, 1920;
- Second Chief Directorate (counterintelligence), founded May 6, 1922;
- Third Chief Directorate (military counterintelligence), founded December 20, 1918; and
- Chief Directorate of Border Guards, founded May 28, 1918.

Each was founded in the first five years of the Bolshevik regime, although initially under different names. With the exception of foreign intelligence, which was spun off into an independent agency as the SVR in 1991, the other three KGB main directorates now reside in the FSB. Between 2017 and 2022, each marked its 100th anniversary, providing opportunities for the Russian government to rhapsodize about state security personnel being the finest representatives of Russian society. On the tenth anniversary of the founding of the Soviet Union's first Counterintelligence Section (KRO), the FSB provided a public affairs statement: "The abbreviation KRO has survived a century and, among the employees and veterans of Russia's FSB, a recognizable symbol of reliability, professionalism, deep understanding of the operational situation, quick reaction to its changes, optimized thinking, selfless devotion to one's duty, decency, and honesty."[46] The same TASS article also referred to prerevolutionary counterintelligence predecessors, noting that the founding of the KRO did not mean that was the first time Russia had an organization that protected the country from spies. But it focused most attention on the various configurations of counterintelligence during the Soviet era, continuing into the post-Soviet era as if it was just another series of reorganizations.

		90	91	92	93	94	95	96	97	98	99	00	01	02	03	04	05	06
1st Chief Directorate	Foreign Intelligence	KGB	SVR															
2nd Chief Directorate	Counterintelligence	KGB	MB		FSK		FSB											
3rd Chief Directorate	Military Counterintelligence	KGB	MB		FSK		FSB											
4th Directorate	CI Support to Transport and Comms	KGB	MB		FSK		FSB											
5th Directorate	Ideological CI	KGB																
6th Directorate	Economic CI	KGB	MB		FSK		FSB											
7th Directorate	Surveillance	KGB	MB		FSK		FSB											
10th Department	Archive	KGB	MB		FSK		FSB											
12th Department	Electronic Surveillance	KGB	MB		FSK		FSB											
Directorate "OP"	Counter-Organized Crime	KGB	MB		FSK		FSB											
Directorate "SCh"	KGB Special Forces	KGB	MB		FSK		FSB											
Main Dir for Border Troops		KGB	MB		FSK		FPS							FSB				
8th Chief Directorate	Cryptography/InfoSec	KGB	MB		FSK	FAPSI								FSB*				
16th Directorate	SIGINT	KGB	MB		FSK	FAPSI								FSB*				
9th Directorate	Senior Leader Protection	KGB	GUO					FSO										
15th Directorate	Sec of Gov Facilities	KGB	GUO					FSO										

Figure 1.2 Correlation of KGB subelements to post-Soviet state security services

*Most FAPSI capabilities were transferred to the FSB, but some went to the FSO and SVR.

In addition to these main directorates, the KGB had the Eighth Chief Directorate, which was originally responsible for signals intelligence (SIGINT) and information security within the Soviet Union. In 1973, the directorate split into two, leaving information security in the Eighth Chief Directorate and creating the new Sixteenth Directorate for SIGINT. These two directorates remained for the rest of the Soviet era. In 1993, they reunited into the newly created Federal Agency for Government Communications and Information (FAPSI). FAPSI existed for ten years as Russia's only separate SIGINT agency in history until the reorganization of Russian state security in 2003, at which time the FSB took control of most of FAPSI as well as the Border Guard Service. The FSB celebrated the 100th anniversary of Russian SIGINT in 2018.

No other country celebrates its "special services" as vigorously as Russia does, and anniversaries are important moments in these celebrations. In the post-Soviet era, most of these anniversaries point to the early Bolshevik period, when the elements that now make up the FSB and the other Russian security services were established. Lenin ordered the creation of the Soviet Union's first state security service, the VChK, on December 20, 1917. Yeltsin signed a decree in 1995 establishing a holiday on December 20 to commemorate "State Security Workers' Day," colloquially known as "Chekists' Day."[47] Although Yeltsin's decree was to a great extent intended to co-opt state security workers politically, it has stood since then. On State Security Workers' Day in 2014, Vladimir Putin said, "The history of special services is rich with brilliant deeds and legendary names. In Russia, we respect all generations of people who have protected our country from external and internal threats, and we bow before the heroism and steadfastness of our veterans."[48] Historical celebrations offer opportunities to bolster morale and highlight the criticality of state security in Russia's existence (see chapter 6) (see figures 1.3 and 1.4).

Retired KGB colonel Vladimir Sychev wrote an article commemorating the hundredth anniversary of Russian state security, stating, "of course there were structures in Russia that were responsible for intelligence, counterintelligence, and border security before 1917. But they were not unified into a single system."[49] They were not unified on the first day of the VChK's founding either. But over the following several years, all the elements that eventually made up Soviet state security came into existence.

Figure 1.3 Postage stamps commemorating the 100th anniversary of Russian state security in 2017

Russia's Chekist Mind-Set

Putin's 2014 State Security Workers' Day statement noted that state security protects Russia "from external and internal threats." This statement manifests an approach to security that has permeated Russia for generations and deepened during the Soviet era. It reflects the KGB's "chekist mind-set," which views threats to Russia as emanating from both internal and external sources, compounded by the perception that internal threats invariably have external connections and sponsorship. After the humiliation Russia experienced in the 1990s, the FSB as an organization perceives Russian security as being under constant threat from the inside and siege from the outside, especially from the United States.

Figure 1.4 Postage stamps commemorating the 100th anniversary of Russian counterintelligence in 2022

Russian security leaders and writers, like Putin and retired KGB officer memoirists, constantly articulate this mind-set, directing their views toward the Russian population to maintain constant vigilance against foreign spies. This mind-set is epitomized by a fictitious plot that circulates around Russian security circles, known as the "Dulles Plan." The Dulles Plan was purportedly proposed by Allen Dulles, director of the US Central Intelligence Agency (CIA) during the Eisenhower administration, in a speech in 1945.[50] The plot envisions destroying the Soviet Union from the inside, using a covert US hand to feed information and support to "likeminded people" inside the Soviet Union, planting chaos, replacing Russian values with falsehoods, and then convincing the Russian population to believe them.

Although proponents of this "plan" assert that it originated with Dulles, who is a particularly nefarious actor in Russians' minds, it actually originated in a work of fiction, the 1972 novel *Eternal Call* by the Soviet author Anatoliy Ivanov, who attributed the plan to a German SS officer near the end of World War II. The German officer character, Lakhunovskiy, claimed that the real war was about to begin, the war for the minds of the Russian people.⁵¹ Ivanov's novel was turned into a television series that ran in the USSR from 1976 to 1983. The Russian journalist Vitaliy Ryumshin notes that the concept of the "Dulles Plan" appeared in public in Russia first in 1993 in the newspaper *Sovetskaya Pravda*; and later the same year, it reappeared in the newspaper *Molodaya Gvardiya*, where coincidentally, Anatoliy Ivanov, the author whose novel the Dulles Plan echoes, was working at the time.⁵²

Some Russians, especially those with state security backgrounds, continue to cite the Dulles Plan as an authentic American plot. Among them is Oleg Khlobustov, who served in the KGB-FSB from 1971 to 2006, ending his career at the FSB Academy. Representing the "chekist" perspective, Khlobustov argued that America's actions align with the Dulles Plan (in Russia's view); ergo, the plan must be real.⁵³ Other former KGB personnel also accept the Dulles Plan as genuine, such as Vyacheslav Shironin, a retired KGB officer who has published several books claiming that Gorbachev's perestroika was a CIA-inspired plot to destroy the Soviet Union. The Dulles Plan factors into that supposed plot.⁵⁴ More recently, a former Russian illegal intelligence officer, Yelena Vavilova, who was arrested in the United States along with nine other Russian illegals and exchanged for arrested Russians in 2010, published a book in 2020 that portrays a similar plot. The book follows a husband-and-wife couple of intelligence illegals who uncover an American scheme to destroy the Russian economy and society with the help of a Russian traitor. The story generally follows the careers of Vavilova and her husband Andrey Bezrukov as intelligence illegals but embellishes it with fictitious elements, most prominently a nefarious American plan.⁵⁵

The British academic Julie Fedor asserts that the plots imagined by chekists serve several functions: to provide an external explanation for why Russian society has deteriorated, to absolve the KGB of responsibility for the dissolution of the Soviet Union, and to present a case for a powerful security service to combat America's purported covert information war against Russia.⁵⁶

That mind-set manifests itself across the FSB's operations, such as in its pursuit of oppositionists and counterterrorism operations. For example, Putin and other government leaders espouse a narrative that any terrorist action inside Russia is sponsored from abroad, including by foreign powers, especially the United States. In an interview with the film producer Oliver Stone in 2015, Vladimir Putin claimed: "You don't have to be a great analyst to see the United States supported financially, provided information, supported them [Chechen terrorists] politically. They supported the separatists and terrorists in the North Caucasus."[57] Putin gained prominence initially and was first elected president thanks to the reputation he built for being tough on terrorism and crime. His reputation for toughness is a foundation for his current popularity and translates today into rhetoric that ties foreign powers, especially the United States, to Russia's domestic terrorism problem.

FSB leaders who began their careers in the KGB also preserve Soviet-era thinking as represented in the "chekist mind-set." Although the Soviet Union dissolved over thirty years ago, most senior FSB leaders entered the KGB in the 1970s and 1980s. This is discussed in greater detail in chapter 4, but the continued leadership of personnel who worked during the Soviet era reinforces the "chekist" influence in the FSB today.

The presence of former KGB officers in FSB leadership positions also perpetuates another Soviet-era factor—rivalry between state security and the MVD. The appointment of MVD officers like Bakatin, Barannikov, and Stepashin to lead state security organizations in the early 1990s was particularly repugnant for many former KGB officers. As real "chekists" returned to the FSB's leadership in the mid-1990s, the FSB began to retake its place of precedence over the MVD. The FSB created Department M in 1999 with the responsibility of providing counterintelligence support to law enforcement agencies, including the MVD.

The most significant remnant of the Soviet era, as well as being a continuation from pre-Soviet times, is state security agencies' loyalty to state unity. In tsarist Russia, the state was the tsar, and state security agencies' reason for existence was to protect the tsar. In 1917, that security system failed, and a Bolshevik coup swept away the tsarist regime. The new Bolshevik regime quickly implemented a state security system, which used violent methods to help the fledgling government establish control over the former imperial territory. By the 1930s, the state security apparatus was firmly in the hands of the Communist Party leader, Stalin, who used it for his own purposes. Stalin kept the state security apparatus under tight supervision for two reasons: to neutralize any flicker of opposition to his regime, similar to the tsar; and to prevent it from becoming an independent power center itself. Beriya attempted to use his control over state security and law enforcement organizations to take control of the country after Stalin's death. However, by the time Nikita Khrushchev read his "secret speech" in 1956 denouncing Stalin's "cult of personality," state security was firmly subordinated to the party rather than to any single leader.

As Gorbachev's reforms laid bare the cracks in Soviet power, leading to the party losing control, state security allegiance transferred from the party to the unified state. KGB chairman Vladimir Kryuchkov reportedly said in 1991, "If each of us does not do everything in his power to avert the disintegration of the Union, history will not forgive us."[58] However, the Soviet state did disintegrate, partly due to Kryuchkov's own actions as a member of the State Committee on the State of Emergency that attempted to remove Gorbachev. When the Soviet Union dissolved, state security officers mourned the loss of power and control over state functions, not the collapse of the party.

When Putin famously called "the collapse of the Soviet Union . . . the greatest geopolitical disaster of the century" (*крупнейшая геополитическая катастрофа века*) in 2005, he was not lamenting the collapse of party leadership but the disunity that replaced the once-strong Soviet Union. He was referring to the resulting "genuine drama" that left "tens of millions of our co-citizens and compatriots . . . outside Russian territory." In his words, that was followed by "the epidemic of disintegration infect[ing] Russia itself." He continued: "Many thought or seemed to think at the time that our young democracy was not a continuation of Russian statehood, but its ultimate collapse, the prolonged agony of the Soviet system. But they were mistaken."[59] He reiterated this in 2012 as he was transitioning back from being prime minister to the presidency: "We should not tempt anyone by allowing ourselves to be weak."[60] Although Putin's 2012 statement referred to military power, for him, unanimity is strength and division is weakness. The state security services enforce unity, and thus not only support the Russian system but also legitimize it. The FSB's primary mission is to maintain the state's strength through unity, and anything that threatens Putin's plan for state unity falls within the FSB's purview, whether it be dissent, terrorism, unsanctioned corruption, disobedient former Soviet states, or the foreign intelligence services.

Conclusion

The FSB today is founded on a mix of forces from the tsarist era, the post-Soviet era, and the Soviet era, all combined to make it a major force in Russian society. It is distinctly a Russian entity, building on Russia's long history of state security structures that serve the ruling elite and protect the unity of the state. Because of the return of pre-Soviet drivers to the foundation of the FSB, constituting a break from the Soviet era, the only way that amalgamation can have meaning is by describing Russia's existence as a constant struggle against internal and external enemies, which only the security services can repel. This constant struggle is at the foundation of Russia's security thinking. Despite the greater ideological freedom that Russian state security gained in the post-Soviet era, FSB officers look to the 1990s as a period of weakness and chaos. The president of the Russian Federation directly oversees the FSB's activity. Under a chekist president, the Russian government holds up the FSB as a patriotic organization empowered to prevent Russia from disintegrating again, as it did in 1917 and 1991.

Notes

1. Goldfarb and Litvinenko, *Death*; Anderson, "Chekist Takeover"; Soldatov, "Putin Has Finally Reincarnated the KGB."
2. Riehle, "Post-KGB Lives."
3. Berls, *Roots*.
4. Interview with Kovalev in *Komsomolskaya Pravda*, February 1997, quoted by Yarovoy, *Farewell, KGB*.
5. Sokolov, "Colonel Yushekov."
6. Zhirinovskiy, *Порядок, достаток, безопасность!*
7. Darczewska, *Defenders of the Besieged Fortress*, 6.
8. Burenkov, "Lessons."
9. Riehle, *Russian Intelligence*, 24–29.
10. Andrew and Gordievsky, *KGB*, 22; Kalugin, *View*.
11. Burenkov, "Lessons."
12. Fischer, *Okhrana*.
13. Chebrikov, *History*, 14.
14. Zavarzin, *"Okhranka"*; Zavarzin, *Work*.
15. Batyushin, *At the Origins*.
16. Shirokorad, *Secret Operations*.
17. Kolpakidi, *Special Services*; Starkov, *Spy Hunters*; Tarasov, *Police*; Borisov, Malygin, and Mulukayev, *Three Centuries*.
18. Karavashkin, *Who Betrayed Russia?*

19. Terentyev, "'Order to the Ugrian Voevods.'"
20. Ivashkina, "Border Guards."
21. Putin, "Congratulations."
22. Waller, *KGB*.
23. Waller, *Secret Empire*.
24. Knight, *Spies*.
25. Albats, *State*.
26. Ebon, *KGB*.
27. Duhamel, *KGB Campaign*, 55.
28. Seddon, "Putin."
29. Bratersky, "Patriarch Plants Church."
30. Coalson, "Close Ties."
31. Bakatin, *Disposing*, 145.
32. "Yeltsin Humiliates Gorbachev."
33. Bennett, *Ministry of Internal Affairs*.
34. Lezina, "Dismantling," 12.
35. Colton, *Yeltsin*, 259.
36. Bennett, *Federal Security Service*, 10.
37. Knight, *Spies*, 63–69.
38. Waller, *Secret Empire*, 118–19.
39. President of Russia, Order 2233.
40. "Fatal KGB Rank."
41. Varyvdin, "Counterintelligence."
42. Putin, "Russia."
43. Waller, *KGB*, 23–24.
44. White and Kryshtanovskaya, "Public Attitudes," 169–75.
45. Quoted by Berman and Waller, *Dismantling Tyranny*, 23.
46. "Russian Counterintelligence."
47. President of Russia, Order 1280.
48. Putin, "Gala."
49. Sychev, "One Hundredth Anniversary."
50. Fedor, "Chekists Look Back," 842–63.
51. Ivanov, *Eternal Call*.
52. Ryumshin, "Pervert and Destroy."
53. Khlobustov, "Once Again," 215–20.
54. Shironin, *Under the Cover*; Shironin, *KGB-CIA*; Shironin, *Agents*.
55. Vavilova and Bronnikov, *Woman*.
56. Fedor, "Chekists Look Back," 842–63.
57. Stone, *Putin Interviews*, 36.
58. Ebon, *KGB*, 55.
59. Putin, "Annual Address."
60. Putin, "Being Strong."

2

Organization and Culture

The FSB emerged during the post-Soviet era of chaos, weakness, and fragmentation for the Russian security services. Over its nearly thirty years of existence, it has gradually reaccumulated the powers that were splintered into multiple organizations in the immediate aftermath of the Soviet Union's dissolution, including organizational elements that trace back directly to their Soviet predecessors.

Many aspects of the FSB are established in Russian law. The Russian legislature adopted a law establishing an entity with the title Federal Security Service on April 3, 1995, and it has amended it over twenty times since then. The FSB's activities are designed to counter threats to Russia's state security, including in the military, political, economic, and even environmental sectors. At the heart of this mission is protecting Vladimir Putin's government and policies. To accomplish this, the FSB's founding law identifies these primary FSB activities:

- counterintelligence
- combating terrorism
- combating crime
- intelligence
- border activity
- safeguarding information security

This foundational law states that the FSB's activities are based primarily on the Russian constitution, Russian federal laws, and international treaties. According to the law, the FSB's operating principles are

- lawfulness;
- respect for and observance of human and civil rights and freedoms
- humanism;
- a unified system of federal security service organs and centralization of administration; and
- secrecy, using a combination of overt and clandestine methods and means of activity.

The law supposedly holds the FSB accountable for violations of these rights and freedoms. It even contains paragraphs addressing appeals by Russian Federation citizens who feel their rights have been violated. Several sections—especially those governing counterintelligence and counterterrorism—stipulate the rules governing actions that "restrict the rights of citizens." Nevertheless, as noted below, the number of FSB officials authorized to order operations that restrict Russian citizens' rights has grown, and violations of Russian citizens' human rights occur routinely. The FSB's commitment to lawfulness is also questionable, although its dedication to legalism—meaning using laws to its advantage—is deep-seated.

This chapter provides descriptions of the FSB's organizational elements that reflect its primary missions, as well as others that are variations on these missions. Since a reorganization of the FSB's structure in 2004, the FSB's primary elements have been called "services," composed of subordinate centers, directorates, and departments. Most have direct predecessors in the KGB. The descriptions given here provide an English translation of elements' names, along with Russian-language acronyms, because FSB elements are seldom referred to by a translated acronym. The next chapter describes in greater detail these activities divided along the FSB's major operational directions.

There are occasionally duplicate unit designators under different services, such as both the Fourth Service and the Special Purpose Center having directorates K and T, although they are not related in function or organization. Similarly, the Organizational and Personnel Service, known as the Sixth Service, has no special connection to the Sixth Service within the Internal Security (Ninth) Directorate, which, despite their confusingly identical names, perform different functions.

The Counterintelligence Service

The Counterintelligence Service (SKR), or First Service, is one of the core elements of the FSB. It is the service charged with countering foreign spies in Russia, which the Russian government trumpets as a significant threat. The SKR is the direct heir to the KGB's Second Chief Directorate (SCD), which was the KGB's organization for monitoring foreign embassies, foreign visitors, and Soviet citizens who had contact with foreigners, using both human and technical means. The SCD's predecessor organization, the Counterintelligence Section (KRO), was founded in 1922, and the SKR dates its beginning to that year. Thus, the FSB celebrated the 100th anniversary of counterintelligence in 2022.

The SKR has had an unbroken history since the dissolution of the Soviet Union, with the Russian state security service carrying the name Federal Counterintelligence Service from 1993 to 1995. Since the founding of the FSB, foreign counterintelligence was initially within the Department for Counterintelligence, with the name changing to SKR in 2004. SKR contains the following subelements:

- Department for Counterintelligence Operations (DKRO)
- Directorate for Coordination of Analysis and Counterintelligence Activities (UKAKD)
- Directorate of Information Support for Operational-Investigative Activities (UIOORD)
- Center for Information Security (TsIB)
- Directorate for Facility Security
- Directorate of Special Measures (USM)

The Department for Counterintelligence Operations

The Department for Counterintelligence Operations (DKRO) runs the SKR's primary mission: combating foreign intelligence services. Its highest priorities are the American and British services, although the services of other NATO countries and China are also important targets. It monitors foreign diplomats and provides the primary counterintelligence support for the Russian Ministry of Foreign Affairs, which interacts routinely with foreign representatives. DKRO also monitors foreign journalists, especially those who write about controversial subjects that cast a negative light on the Russian government, and it provides support to large-scale events where foreigners are present, such as international sporting events.

As of 2022, the chief of DKRO was Aleksey Komkov, who had previously led the FSB Internal Security Directorate (USB) from August 2016. Komkov was assigned to the DKRO in June 2019, replacing Sergey Korolev, who was promoted to first deputy FSB director. Komkov had been a USB directorate chief under Korolev and is reportedly Korolev's protégé.[1] Komkov made a name for himself with high-profile investigations of corruption within the Economic Counterintelligence Service (SEK), including during the May 2019 arrest of FSB colonel Kirill Cherkalin, who worked for SEK's Directorate K, and during the arrests of two officers from the FSB Investigative Directorate who had demanded bribes from the target of their investigation (see chapter 6).

The assignment of Komkov as DKRO chief was a departure from historical norms. The DKRO chief had typically been promoted from within the directorate, often coming from the DKRO section that runs anti-US operations.[2] Up to 2019, the DKRO was led by Aleksandr Zhomov, a Soviet-era counterintelligence officer who earned a reputation for aggressively operating against the US Central Intelligence Agency (CIA) since the late 1980s. In 1987, he was a rare example of the KGB dangling a genuine staff officer as a double agent against the CIA. The operation was designed to distract the CIA from a more valuable asset: Aldrich Ames. In 1990, when Zhomov, who was known to the CIA as GT/PROLOGUE, was about to defect, he cut off the double agent operation after he had received an exfiltration plan and false documents.[3] He reappeared again in the early 1990s as a liaison officer to the CIA and again in 2010, when the United States and Russia exchanged prisoners after SVR illegals were arrested in the United States.[4] A few years later, he was promoted to be the chief of DKRO in charge of FSB counterintelligence operations.

The Directorate for Coordination of Analysis and Counterintelligence Activities

The Directorate for Coordination of Analysis and Counterintelligence Activities (UKAKD) often appears alongside DKRO. It conducts the missions identified in its name: analysis and coordination. It is unclear in what year UKAKD was established, although a ten-year commemorative badge was issued in about 2008–10, placing the founding of UKAKD likely in the late 1990s. Its director is Aleksandr Roshchupkin, who also serves as a deputy chief of the SKR. The UKAKD's role includes coordinating counterintelligence and covert operations among FSB services. In that role, it appears to be a clearing house for operations. In 2009, the director of UKAKD was included in a list of FSB officials who had the authority to request counterintelligence measures that restrict the constitutional rights of citizens, meaning that the UKAKD director could order communications intercepts and physical surveillance, or even kidnappings or assassinations. That list identified the DKRO and UKAKD chiefs and the chief of the Center for Information Security (TsIB) Operational Directorate within the SKR alongside leaders from other FSB services.[5]

The Directorate of Information Support for Operational-Investigative Activities

The Directorate of Information Support for Operational-Investigative Activities (UIOORD) maintains databases of suspect foreigners and foreigners barred from entering Russia, including those who have served in foreign prisons. When a border guard officer observes a suspicious person trying to enter the country, the officer removes the person from the passenger flow and forwards copies of the suspicious person's travel documents to UIOORD.[6] A team of UIOORD personnel reportedly deployed to Ukraine in 2022. Ukrainian press claimed that Ukrainian military forces struck an FSB unit responsible for analytics and database maintenance in occupied Melitopol in December 2022.[7] This team's mission would likely be to support the deportation of Ukrainian citizens to Russia.

The chief of UIOORD, Viktor Krivoshlyapov, may have held that position for as many as twenty years. He was appointed in 2002 as the FSB's representative to the interdepartmental commission on regulating the entry and stay of foreign citizens and stateless persons on the territory of the Russian Federation.[8] In 2005, he was listed as the FSB's representative in an interagency committee for creating and implementing the "central data bank for the registration of foreign citizens."[9] This central data bank was created in 2006 and is administered jointly by the FSB, Federal Immigration Service, and ministries of Internal Affairs, Foreign Affairs, Economic Development and Trade, and Information Technology and Communication. It is populated by various law enforcement organizations, with the FSB's input likely focused on counterintelligence- and counterterrorism-related data related to barred foreigners.

The Center for Information Security

The Center for Information Security (TsIB), also known as Center 18 (Military Unit 64829), has become one of the more prominent subelements of the SKR. TsIB's publicly acknowledged mission is to protect Russia's Internet. It also conducts internal Internet monitoring directed at Russian citizens and foreign intelligence collection. TsIB is the direct heir to the KGB's mission to monitor the Soviet population, and it is headquartered in a building that formerly housed a KGB computer center. The FSB inherited TsIB from the former FAPSI. It was first discussed in public as an FSB element in relation to requests to Internet service providers for information about Internet users. For example, the owner of the website Roem.ru received a request from a TsIB officer in 2011, originating from the email address "cybercrime@fsb.ru," asking for information about a subscriber.[10]

Sergey Skorokhodov became the TsIB chief in June 2017, having previously served as the deputy TsIB chief. Before that, he was involved in immigration policy. In 2012, he participated in an international roundtable on human trafficking,[11] and in 2013, he was the FSB's representative on an Interdepartmental Commission for implementing the state program to assist Russian compatriots living abroad to voluntarily resettlement to Russia.[12] How those previous assignments prepared him to lead the FSB's computer security, communications, and computer-based intelligence collection is unclear.

The Other Two SKR Subelements

Less information is available about two other SKR subelements. The first, the Directorate for Facility Security, may provide counterintelligence support for sensitive facilities, such as nuclear plants. Such a directorate existed during the Soviet era beginning as early as 1945, eventually falling under the KGB SCD.[13] That mission has likely continued in the post-Soviet era, now subordinate to the SCD's successor, the SKR. The second subelement, the Directorate of Special Measures (USM), may interact with DKRO in handling security measures for major events, especially those attended by foreigners.

The Service for Defense of the Constitutional Order and Combating Terrorism

The Service for Defense of the Constitutional Order and Combating Terrorism (SZKSiBT), or Second Service, houses an amalgam of functions that have existed since the Soviet era. It is responsible for combating terrorism, extremism, and separatist ethnic groups. It conducts counterintelligence activities in the ministries of Health, Culture, and Education, in the religious sphere, and in nongovernmental organizations, analogous to the Department of Military Counterintelligence Service (DVKR) mission in the military (see below). It is also responsible for investigating and neutralizing dissident and oppositionist individuals and groups. Thus, the same people who investigate terrorism also investigate internal instability created by dissent or protests. Consequently, oppositionists are often charged with violating extremism laws linked to terrorism laws. According to the journalist Andrei Soldatov, "When the concept emerged that terrorists were dangerous not primarily because they, for example, kill a lot of people, but because they strike against political stability in the country, then it was decided to create a subelement to defend the constitutional order—or in its Russian translation, to protect the political regime—and include those subelements in the antiterrorist structure of the FSB."[14]

Some of those missions reflect the Soviet-era concept of "ideological counterintelligence," or countering "ideological sabotage," which was the responsibility of the KGB Fifth Directorate. The Fifth Directorate was created in 1967, soon after Andropov was appointed KGB director, when several units that monitored internal political dissent split from the SCD. According to the KGB specialist John Barron, the KGB's Fifth Directorate initially consisted of subelements responsible for investigating the intelligentsia, ethnic groups, religious groups, and Jewish activist groups that were demanding the right to emigrate.[15] The Fifth Directorate came to be the most feared KGB element for Soviet citizens. It was the KGB organization that pursued anyone who spoke or wrote against the Soviet Communist Party or who participated in religious activities. By the late Soviet era, according to Yevgenia Albats, the Fifth Directorate consisted of eleven departments:

- First: anti-Soviet organizations abroad
- Second: ethnic groups and nationalism
- Third: informal associations and organizations
- Fourth: religious organizations
- Fifth: organized crime and mass disorders
- Sixth: terrorism
- Seventh: anonymous letters
- Eighth: Israel and Zionism
- Ninth: youth groups and universities
- Tenth: analysis
- Eleventh: sports groups[16]

In 1989, during Mikhail Gorbachev's glasnost effort, the Fifth Directorate was renamed Directorate Z, or the Directorate for the Defense of the Constitutional Order. According to Albats, the KGB chose the letter "Z" to represent the Russian word "защитить," which means to protect.[17] In 1989, when Directorate Z was created, KGB director Vladimir Kryuchkov used chekist language to explain the KGB's reasons for turning the Fifth Directorate into a directorate to protect the constitution:

> In the conditions of revolutionary renewal of Soviet society and the expansion of democracy and openness, the special services of capitalist countries, anti-Soviet centers associated with them, and other organizations are conducting their underground activities against the USSR on a new strategic and tactical platform. Based on their goals and forms, they assume the character of a struggle against the constitutional bases of the

USSR. By invigorating nationalism, chauvinism, and clericalism, Western special services and anti-Soviet organizations are actively trying to inspire hotbeds of societal tension, antisocialist manifestations, and mass unrest and to instigate adversarial elements and actions directed at a violent overturn of Soviet power.[18]

The name change did not significantly alter the directorate's operations, although the KGB was less open about pursuing dissent in the last several years of the Soviet Union. The number of personnel assigned to Directorate Z did not change, and the director of the Fifth Directorate remained.[19] Directorate Z was eliminated in 1991, when the Soviet government disestablished the KGB, becoming the only KGB element that did not make the transition to the post-Soviet environment. Over the following decade, however, many missions and methods identified with the Fifth Directorate / Directorate Z have returned under the Second Service, whose name is even eerily reminiscent of the Soviet-era Directorate "Z."

Soon after Directorate Z disappeared, the new Directorate for Combating Terrorism emerged as Russia found itself in a war against extremists in the Caucasus. After the 1995 Budennovsk hostage crisis, the directorate expanded into the Antiterrorist Center, which was further reorganized into the Department for Combating Terrorism in 1997. Separately, in 1998, during Vladimir Putin's tenure as FSB director, a new element responsible for political investigations called the Directorate for Constitutional Security emerged within the FSB. The two organizations—combating terrorism and constitutional security—merged in 1999 to become the Department for Defense of the Constitutional Order and Combating Terrorism. In 2004, the department became a service.

Within the Second Service are these subelements:

- Directorate for Protecting the Constitutional Order (UZKS)
- Directorate for Combating Terrorism and Political Extremism (UBTPE)
- Directorate for Combating International Terrorism (UBMT)
- Organizational-Operational Directorate (OOU)
- Special Purpose Center (TsSN)
- Operational Investigative Directorate (ORU)

The Directorate for Protecting the Constitutional Order

The Directorate for Protecting the Constitutional Order (UZKS) is engaged in domestic political investigations and resembles the KGB's Fifth Directorate more than any other FSB subelement. It monitors groups across the political spectrum, including left-wing and right-wing groups and other groups that the FSB interprets as potentially threatening to the Russian regime. UZKS's activities are often directed against civil society organizations, which the FSB counters with a mix of human and technical operations. It monitors public opinion leaders and influential party activists and actively works to influence and neutralize protest movements, isolating them from financial and media resources that might allow them to spread. The primary predicate for UZKS involvement is that a group opposes the Putin regime, regardless of the group's political orientation.

The chief of UKZS, General Lieutenant Aleksey Zhalo, was born in 1957, making it likely that he joined state security during the Soviet era. He is probably originally from Rostov-na-Donu and worked in that city's FSB office. In February 2005, he was appointed chief of the FSB office in the Republic of Ingushetia while a colonel.[20] Before 2010, he was promoted to chief of UZKS. Rumors surrounding Zhalo provide an indication of the type of cases that UZKS pursues. Zhalo was reportedly involved in investigations of neo-Nazi groups, including the Militant Organization of Russian Nationalists (BORN), which was behind several murders of judges and lawyers who fought against fascism, and the Movement Against Illegal Immigration (DPNI), which was labeled an extremist group and banned in 2011.[21]

The Directorate for Combating Terrorism and Political Extremism

The Directorate for Combating Terrorism and Political Extremism (UBTPE) goes further than UKZS by physically surveilling and confronting groups that the FSB sees as dangerous. UBTPE was created in 1999 within the Department for Combating Terrorism.

In addition to elements that operate against dissidents, several subelements within the Second Service operate against what most other countries would traditionally define as terrorism—violence, especially against civilian targets, in pursuit of political goals.

The Operational Investigative Directorate

The Operational Investigative Directorate (ORU) conducts counterterrorism operations predominantly in the North Caucasus region. According to the Dossier Center, those operations often result in the extrajudicial deaths of suspected terrorists. The ORU actively recruits Islamists, even at times cooperating with Wahhabists to penetrate terrorist groups. A Dossier Center source claims, however, that ORU is more concerned about flashy statistics than about actually preventing terrorist attacks.[22]

The Special Purpose Center

The Special Purpose Center (TsSN) (Military Unit 35690) is officially subordinate to the Second Service but often operates independently. It is the FSB's Spetsnaz, or special purpose forces, organization responsible for direct action focused primarily on counterterrorism. It consists of at least five operational directorates and one administrative directorate:

- Directorate A, Alfa
- Directorate V, Vympel
- Directorate S, Smerch
- Directorate K, Kavkaz
- Directorate T, Taurida
- Organizational-Operational Directorate

Directorates K and T both share designations with directorates under the Economic Counterintelligence Service but are separate and unrelated.

Alfa, formally known as Directorate A, has been in existence longer than any other FSB Spetsnaz unit. KGB director Yuriy Andropov created Alfa in 1974 to counter terrorist and other violent actions, such as hostage situations or hijackings, both inside the USSR and abroad. It continues those missions today. Alfa, sometimes called "Andropov's Group," was organized within the KGB Seventh Directorate, which conducted surveillance of KGB targets within the USSR.[23] When the USSR dissolved, Alfa shifted to the newly created Main Directorate for Protection (GUO), which was responsible for presidential security. Yeltsin ordered Alfa to storm the White House, where the Russian parliament convened, during the Russian political crisis of October 1993; however, Alfa members reportedly refused and negotiated the safe exit of Yeltsin's political rivals from the building instead.[24]

Vympel, formally known as Directorate V, was established in 1981 within the Eighth Department of KGB Directorate S, which was responsible for covert sabotage and assassination operations abroad. According to former Directorate S officer Alexander Kouzminov, the Eighth Department planned sabotage and diversionary operations in the event of full-scale war.[25] Vympel was involved in covert operations in Afghanistan, as well as in an operation to free four Soviet diplomats taken hostage in Beirut in 1985.[26] Ironically, one of the four diplomats released in that operation, Oleg Spirin, defected to the United States five years later.[27]

Vympel was subordinate to the MB in the early post-Soviet years. Like Alfa, Vympel members were also ordered to storm the White House in 1993 but refused. Yeltsin retaliated against Vympel by transferring it from the MB to the MVD, which according to the author Mark Galeotti, was more than just a transfer: Vympel personnel were assigned to police work and their salaries were cut. Most Vympel personnel simply refused to make the transfer.[28] Under the MVD, the unit was renamed "Vega," and from 1994 to 1995, former Vympel personnel trained MVD special operations personnel.

Both Alfa and Vympel returned to the FSB in 1995 under newly appointed FSB director Mikhail Barsukov, and in 1998 the name Vympel returned under FSB director Putin. They received the formal designations "A" and "V" within the FSB Antiterrorist Center and then came under the TsSN.[29]

The Directorate of Special Operations (USO), also known as Directorate S, is another TsSN special operations element separate from both Alfa and Vympel, about which less is known publicly. The "S" designation is associated with the Russian word *смерч* (*smerch*; English translation, *tornado*).[30] USO traces its history to December 1991, when a new group was created within the short-lived Interrepublic Security Service, which transitioned into the MB. It was initially a section within the Main Directorate for Combating Organized Crime but was subordinated to the Moscow FSB office's Service for Combating Illegal Armed Formations and Banditry in 1999. Its first director was Valentin Grigoryevich Andreyev, who subsequently commanded Alfa. It later fell under the TsSN.

The specific missions assigned to Directorate S are not publicly known beyond a generic description of providing "operational-combat support to FSB organs' operational-investigative activities" to counter terrorism and dangerous criminal organizations. In an address commemorating the twentieth anniversary of Directorate S in 2011, Sergey Goncharov, a retired Alfa colonel who was later elected to the Russian State Duma, said, "You [Directorate S], along with Directorates A and V, are the backbone of the Center for Special Operations of the FSB of Russia."[31]

Two additional specialized TsSN units operate in the Caucasus region and on the Crimean Peninsula.[32] Directorate K (Kavkaz) is specifically responsible for special operations in the Caucasus, the FSB's most active Spetsnaz region. TsSN created another unit in Crimea in 2015, reportedly called Directorate T, which stands for Taurida.[33] Taurida is a historical name originating from the time of a Greek settlement in Crimea, which the Russian Empire gave to a province in the eighteenth century that included Crimea and southern Ukraine. Russian nationalists picked up the name after Russia's annexation of Crimea in 2014 and have proposed renaming Crimea since then.[34] Thus, the directorate's name is an indicator of the FSB's intentions in Crimea.

One remaining subelement of the Second Service is the Organizational-Operational Directorate (OOU). This unit is seldom discussed publicly, but from its name, it can be assumed that it is involved in administrative tasks. Its director was also listed among the FSB officials who were authorized to request counterintelligence measures that restrict the constitutional rights of citizens.[35] Its mission may be similar to the Directorate for Coordination of Analysis and Counterintelligence Activities within the SKR, providing support to other Second Service elements.

The Department of Military Counterintelligence

The Department of Military Counterintelligence (DVKR) is sometimes called the Third Service, Third Department, or Third Directorate. During the KGB era, the military counterintelligence organization was called the Third Chief Directorate, and the number "3" continues to be used with it today. The FSB's public materials list DVKR as subordinate to SKR rather than a separate service. However, its mission is historically distinct from the SKR and it operates independently, even if it does have an organizational relationship.

DVKR is heir to one of the oldest state security missions in the Soviet Union / Russia. The mission of DVKR is to conduct counterintelligence operations within military units both to prevent the loss of critical military information and to ward off disloyalty within the military ranks. Military counterintelligence units appeared in 1918 because Bolshevik military forces initially consisted primarily of non–Communist Party members who fought either for mercenary motives or by coercion. Most officers in the Bolshevik Workers and Peasants Red Army were trained during the tsarist era and agreed to serve the new Russian regime, although the Bolsheviks did not trust them fully. In December 1918, the VChK formed the Special Section (OO), unifying military counterintelligence units that had sprung up in individual military units into a single, centrally managed entity. Over the years, OO officers gained a reputation for interfering in military affairs, especially during the Yezhovshchina, when respected military officers like Marshal Mikhail Tukhachevskiy were arrested, accused of espionage, and executed.

In 1943, OOs transferred to military control under a department that was renamed the Counterintelligence Directorate (UKR) Smersh, a portmanteau of the Russian words *смерть шпионам* (death to spies). Smersh was subordinate to the People's Commissariat for Defense, which Stalin himself supervised. The MGB subsumed Smersh in 1946, retaining only the acronym UKR. The Smersh name was retired at that time, but its menace lived on in popular literature as Ian Fleming gave the name to a fictitious Soviet organization where several of James Bonds's antagonists worked.[36] DVKR is the descendant of OOs, UKR Smersh, the MGB's UKR, and KGB's Third Chief Directorate. In 2004, the Directorate of Military Counterintelligence, as the element was called after the dissolution of the Soviet Union, was reorganized as a department.

According to Agentura.ru, DVKR answers directly to first deputy FSB director Sergey Korolev, who, before returning to the FSB in 2011, served four years as a special assistant to then–minister of defense Anatoliy Serdyukov. DVKR consists of subelements responsible for different military organizations, including MoD headquarters; the headquarters of the airborne forces, military space forces, transportation aviation forces, military academies, and scientific research institutes; each military district and fleet headquarters; and some specific units. DVKR also posts officers to units of the Russian National Guard (Rosgvardiya) and is responsible for external monitoring of the SVR and GRU. This distribution of FSB personnel and the recruited agents that they acquire gives the FSB broad visibility over the sentiments, morale, and loyalty of military personnel.

The Economic Counterintelligence Service

The Economic Counterintelligence Service (SEB), or Fourth Service, is the FSB unit tasked with preventing economic damage to the ruling regime. The objectives and methods to accomplish that have remained similar across the hundred-plus years since the Bolshevik Revolution. Economic counterintelligence uses various clandestine means to fulfill its missions, which operate in several primary directions: to prevent the leakage of Russian technology or economic information abroad, even information that most countries publish openly; using economic levers to punish antiregime activists at home; and investigating financial corruption, such as fraud, embezzlement, and extortion.

What is today the Fourth Service was created in 1998 as the Department of Economic Security (DEB). It was the successor to the Economic Security Directorate that was created within the MB and continued into the FSK, the heir to the KGB's Sixth Directorate. Also within the FSK was the Directorate for Counterintelligence Support to Strategic Facilities, which monitored the defense industry and critical infrastructure. The DEB combined these previous organizations and expanded them in 1998 at a crisis time in the Soviet economic system when the ruble collapsed and the Russian government defaulted on foreign loans. The first director of the DEB was Nikolay Patrushev, who replaced Putin as FSB director in 1999. In 2004, the DEB became the SEB (Fourth Service), and its director became Aleksandr Bortnikov, who was promoted to the rank of army general in 2006 and replaced Patrushev as FSB director in 2008.

Fourth Service headquarters consists of leadership staff, a secretariat, a personnel section, and a finance section. The service's operational directorates are organized to provide counterintelligence support for different sectors of the Russian economy: industry (Directorate P), transportation (Directorate T), and credit and banking (Directorate K). The Fourth Service also has an Organizational-Analytical Directorate, about which little is known publicly, although it is possibly similar to the analytic organizations of other FSB services.

Directorate P reportedly has nine sections that conduct counterintelligence and criminal investigations in Russian state-owned corporations, such as Rostec, Rosnano, Roskosmos, gas and oil companies, large defense factories, atomic electricity generation stations, and gold mining companies, among others. The exact subdivision of these organizations into sections is not clear. Directorate P investigates crimes at these facilities, both economic crimes and espionage.

Directorate T is responsible for investigations in the transportation and communications infrastructures. The responsibilities of Directorate T have a long history in Soviet state security. Transportation security was one of the earliest areas where Soviet state security focused its efforts; the VChK created a railroad section soon after its founding. Felix Dzerzhinskiy was the first people's commissar for the means of communication while also serving as VChK chief.

The number of sections within Department T is unclear, but they are likely divided by transportation modalities, such as air, rail, and roads. In 2020, Directorate T received a new chief, Viktor Gavrilov, who came from the board of directors of Aeroflot. Gavrilov is reportedly close to the Fourth Service chief Alpatov and previously worked in the FSB's Center for Protecting Information and Special Communications.[37] He is an example of a state security officer who moved from state security to industry and back to state security. Dmitriy Vorontsov, a career Directorate T officer, who previously led the aviation section, became Gavrilov's deputy and is rumored to be the real chief behind the scenes.

Directorate K is the most visible Fourth Service directorate. It is responsible for providing counterintelligence support to the banking and credit industry. That places the FSB in a controlling position over billions of rubles of the country's finances. Directorate K's sections align with various financial sectors:

- First: countering money counterfeiting
- Second: responsible for banks and insurance companies
- Third: not publicly available
- Fourth: not publicly available
- Fifth: responsible for gold and precious metals

- Sixth: countering counterfeiting of money and immigration documents
- Seventh: responsible for customs agencies and countering contraband
- Eighth: countering organized crime and the illegal trade in explosives and chemical and toxic substances
- Ninth: Countering narcobusiness

It is unclear why two different sections (First and Sixth) have responsibility for countering money counterfeiting. The Ninth Section, which is responsible for investigating illegal narcotics trafficking, was formerly a directorate of its own within the Fourth Service, Directorate N, but in about 2015, it was subsumed as a section under Directorate K.[38]

The Service for Operational Information and International Relations

The Service for Operational Information and International Relations (SOIiMS), or the Fifth Service, is the FSB's strategic analysis organization. Although other FSB operational services have their own operational analytic organization that directly serves the individual service, the FSB also has an analytical element that provides the president with strategic analytic assessments on which to make national security decisions. This function came to light in relation to Russia's invasion of Ukraine in 2022, with the Fifth Service reportedly providing optimistic forecasts about the prospects for Russia's success. However, analysis is not the only mission that falls under the Fifth Service. The service is also one of the FSB's primary foreign intelligence organizations, operating predominantly in the former Soviet space.

The Fifth Service consists of at least four directorates that are responsible for these two missions:

- Information-Analysis Directorate (IAU)
- Operational Information Department (DOI)
- International Cooperation Directorate (UMS)
- Open Information Section (OOI) (no further information available)[39]

The Information-Analysis Directorate

The KGB did not have an analytic culture, and analysis was not a respected career path. The KGB and its predecessor organizations had an Information and Statistics Section, which provided some analytic support but also monitored internal KGB performance. The KGB's First Chief Directorate (now SVR) had an analytical unit that packaged foreign intelligence reports and forwarded them to the KGB leadership. The first structure that could be called analytic was a small group created in the early 1960s to synthesize data about the adversary. In 1966, it was renamed the Group of Referents under the chairman of the KGB. When Andropov became the KGB chief, he repurposed that analytic group to become an inspectorate that monitored internal KGB functions, and it lost its foreign intelligence analytic functions. However, Andropov also ordered the creation of a team of ten analytic consultants that provided strategic analysis, and another small analytical unit was created within the new KGB Fifth Directorate in 1967 that was responsible for "synthesis and analysis of data on the adversary's activities in conducting ideological sabotage."[40]

No central KGB analysis organization existed until the Analysis Directorate in 1989. According to Agentura.ru, what is now the Fifth Service dates its official beginnings to 1991, when the Information-Analysis Directorate was formed from an expansion of the KGB's Analysis Directorate. That Information-Analysis Directorate's mission was "analysis and synthesis of information related to the identification of threats to the country's security and the preparation of proposals for public authorities." That entity later became the FSB's Department of Analysis, Forecasting, and Strategic Planning. In 2004, that department was reorganized into the Fifth Service. Since then, it has been the FSB's analytic voice to the Russian leadership.

Unlike during the Soviet era, leading the Information-Analysis Directorate in the 1990s was career-enhancing. The directorate's chief from 1996 to 1998 was Aleksandr Mikhailov, who left the position to become chief of analysis for the MVD. He reportedly returned to operational work at the beginning of the second Chechen war, and in 2003 he became the deputy chief of the State Drug Control Service. He retired as a general lieutenant and went on to write books on the theme of state security.[41]

Mikhailov was replaced by Sergey Ivanov, who led the directorate during Putin's tenure as FSB director in 1998 and 1999. Ivanov was the directorate chief when Putin ordered its expansion to include an FSB foreign intelligence capability. Ivanov's previous KGB foreign intelligence and post-Soviet SVR experience was suitable for that task, and his close personal relationship with Putin gave him Putin's trust.[42] Ivanov became a member of the Security Council when Putin became the prime minister in 1999, and then went on to become Russia's minister of defense from 2001 to 2007.[43] The current Fifth Service chief, Sergey Beseda, rose through the analysis organization to eventually lead it.

The Operational Information Department

The Operational Information Department (DOI) is the organization responsible for conducting intelligence operations in former Soviet states. During the Soviet era, the KGB maintained regional offices in all Soviet republics. Those offices were essentially smaller versions of KGB headquarters, with most functions present in them, including foreign intelligence. Correspondingly, each regional office had a "first section" that monitored and tried to recruit foreigners. The FSB inherited "first sections," even those that were outside the Russian Federation, giving the FSB a foreign intelligence infrastructure.

In April 1992, soon after the dissolution of the Soviet Union, the newly created SVR signed an agreement among the twelve non-Baltic former Soviet states by which those states agreed not to conduct intelligence activities against each other. However, the SVR represented only a portion of the former KGB, the bulk of which was then in the MB and eventually in the FSB. That portion of the Russian intelligence and security establishment did not sign the same agreement.[44] As the FSB is primarily an internal security service, its presence in former Soviet states ignores their sovereignty and is an indicator of Moscow's perception that they are still part of Russia's internal threat environment.

The International Cooperation Directorate

The International Cooperation Directorate (UMS) has a foreign liaison role, managing FSB officers assigned to international organizations and

Russian embassies abroad and serving as the FSB's interlocutor with other countries' security services (see chapter 5 for details of the FSB's foreign liaison functions).

The Science and Technology Service

Much of what is today the FSB's Science and Technology Service (NTS) was founded in the 1970s as a resource for supplying the KGB with advanced technology to use in intelligence and state security operations. It is sometimes called the Third Service, which has no relation to the DPRK, which also sometimes carries that title.

When the KGB replaced the MVD in 1954, it had multiple special sections that developed intelligence technology, such as producing secret writing systems, counterfeiting documents and signatures, developing signal intercept equipment and hidden microphone technologies, and producing poisons used in assassination operations. In 1959, those separate sections merged into a new KGB directorate, the Operational Technology Directorate, referred to as Directorate OT. The structure of this directorate evolved over the rest of the Soviet era; by the late 1960s, it began to include automated information systems. The separate Scientific Research Institute of Intelligence Problems also emerged within the KGB First Chief Directorate; it employed over 1,200 people, and in 1977 the Central Scientific Research Institute for Special Research was formed.[45] The latter included a section that studied explosives and supported the prevention and investigation of terrorism.[46]

The KGB's scientific and technology capabilities were divided after the dissolution of the Soviet Union, with some espionage-related capabilities going to the SVR, computer and communications capabilities going to FAPSI, and security and investigative resources going to the MB/FSK/FSB. The resubordination of much of FAPSI to the FSB in 2003 brought these capabilities back into state security.

The Science and Technology Service consists of centers and a directorate:

- Eighth Center, Center for Information Defense and Special Communications

- Tenth Center, Central Scientific Research Institute of Special Technology
- Eleventh Center, Special Technology Center
- Organizational Analysis Directorate

The Eighth Center, or Center for Information Defense and Special Communications, carries the number "eight" because it is the heir to the KGB's Eighth Chief Directorate, which was responsible for communication security and encryption during the Soviet era. It was the Main Directorate for Communications Security under FAPSI until 2004, and the Center for Communications Security (TsBS) from 2004 until about 2017. Its main responsibility is to secure Russian communication systems.

In 2018, FSB director Bortnikov announced the creation of the National Coordination Center for Computer Incidents (NKTsKI) within the Eighth Center. NKTsKI was created to coordinate the detection and prevention of computer attacks and the response and neutralization of their consequences. The center is authorized to send requests to critical information infrastructure sites and coordinates the work of combating computer attacks. NKTsKI shares information about computer attacks within Russia and abroad.[47] Its website is htpps://gov-cert.ru, indicating its connection to computer emergency response teams elsewhere. It is similar to the US Critical Infrastructure and Security Agency under the Department of Homeland Security, although a larger portion of Russia's critical infrastructure is government-owned, giving NKTsKI greater authority to control responses. In early 2021, after the US government threatened to respond in kind to cyberattacks on US infrastructure targets originating from Russia, NKTsKI issued a warning to Russian information infrastructure sites and recommended that they raise their defense level.[48]

The Tenth Center (Military Unit 35533) was called the Central Scientific Research Institute of Special Technology under the KGB's Directorate OT. The center specializes in hardware and software research and development for state security agencies.

The Eleventh Center develops investigative and intelligence technologies, such as those that the FSB uses for screening individuals, baggage, cargo, and vehicles. The center also certifies items such as a portable radio jammer designed to protect against radio-controlled explosive devices. The center has also developed unmanned photoreconnaissance drones, special encrypted telephones, nonlethal firearms, and explosives robots.

The Eleventh Center also contains two science and research institutes (NII) specializing in various scientific fields that directly support FSB missions. NII-1, Special Technology (Military Unit 68240), nicknamed "Progress," is involved in researching and developing a wide variety of investigative and security technologies. During the 1990s, it was called the Scientific-Technical Support Directorate. Aleksey Reznev, the previous director of NII-1, was reportedly known for developing devices to defeat foreign intelligence services.[49] Reznev was listed as the chief of NII-1 as early as 1995, when he was among FSB representatives on an interagency committee for weapons and special equipment.[50] In 2013, he was an FSB representative to an interagency working group on developing the supercomputer industry in Russia. He died in 2021.

NII-2, the Criminal Forensics Institute (Military Unit 34435), was created in 1977 as the KGB Central Scientific Research Institute, reportedly after three bombs exploded in Moscow. It subsequently developed bomb detection systems and other antiterrorism technologies and became one of the leading research institutes in Russia on that topic. NII-2's personnel are scientifically trained experts and publish scientific papers in various fields applicable to forensic research, such as narcotics and explosives detection and automated voice recognition.[51] It merged in 1994 with the former KGB's polygraph laboratory, which had existed since 1975 and offers courses for polygraphers. NII-2 scientists even studied the Shroud of Turin and determined it was not a modern fake.[52]

Other NTS Subelements

Like other FSB services, NTC has a dedicated analytical directorate, the Organizational Analysis Directorate. Little specific information is available about the workings of this directorate. Some sources list two other elements within NTS: the Directorate for Operational-Technical Measures (UOTM) and the Directorate for Orders and Deliveries of Weapons, Military, and Special Equipment. It is unclear where or whether they fit within the service. UOTM is described in more detail under FSB Headquarters below. The other is also listed under NTS; however, its mission and actual organizational subordination are unclear.

The Border Guard Service

The Border Guard Service (PS) is responsible for protecting Russia's borders on land and sea and at airports. It protects internal seas, territorial seas, and Russia's exclusive economic zone and continental shelf and their natural resources. It is the largest organization of the FSB based on number of personnel. The service's exact manpower numbers are unknown, but in 1998, retired chief of the Federal Border Guard Service, Andrey Nikolayev, numbered the border guard staff at 212,500. He stated that was down from 250,000 at the end of the Soviet era.[53]

What is today the Border Guard Service is one of the oldest security structures in Russia. Russia has had some form of border protection service since the sixteenth century. A formalized border guard service emerged in the late nineteenth century under the tsarist Ministry of Finance, responsible for collecting import duties. It transitioned almost intact into the Soviet regime after the Bolshevik Revolution, initially in the People's Commissariat of Finance, following the tsarist pattern. In 1920, border guards moved into the state security service and remained there throughout the various reorganizations of state security. Border guards became a KGB chief directorate in 1978.

Just before the dissolution of the Soviet Union, the Committee for the Defense of USSR State Borders was one of the three separate entities into which the former KGB was divided. Less than a year later, in October 1992, the briefly independent border guard service was subsumed into the MB, but that lasted just over a year. In December 1993, when the FSK replaced the MB, border guards were removed and again became an independent agency answerable directly to the president, called the Federal Border Service—Main Command of Border Guard Forces of the Russian Federation. A year later, the name was simplified to the Federal Border Service (FPS) of the Russian Federation. It was further simplified to the Border Service of the Russian Federation in 2000. The service existed independently until June 2003, when Putin ordered that it be subsumed under the FSB.

The Border Guard Service consists of departments and directorates. The two main operational units are the Border Protection Department and the Coast Guard Department, which command border troops positioned around Russia's land borders of over 22,000 kilometers and patrol over 36,000 kilometers of coastline. Border guard troops on both land and sea are responsible for protecting Russia from illegal border crossings of people and goods; protecting Russia's natural resources, including preventing poaching and illegal fishing; and preventing foreign military or terrorist infiltration. Both departments have their own headquarters element with the Operational-Organizational Department and the Analysis and Coordination Department. The Border Protection Department also has the Operational-Investigative Directorate to investigate suspicious activity around Russia's borders. The Coast Guard Department has the State Maritime Inspectorate with affiliates located along the country's maritime boundary responsibility for certifying seagoing vessels.

Because the PS was a KGB main directorate and then a post-Soviet independent agency for ten years with a mission quite different from the rest of the FSB, it established a headquarters and infrastructure of its own. The PS's headquarters has directorates that mirror many functions handed at the FSB headquarters level:

- Operational coordination
- Strategic planning
- Technology development
- Personnel
- Training
- Finance and economics
- Supply
- Inspection
- Financial services

The PS also runs its own training institutions across the country separate from other FSB educational institutions, including the cadet corps, four border officer academies, the Golitsyn Border Institute, and five training centers. It also runs its own scientific research center, archives, museum, and publishing house—"Granitsa"—all located in Moscow.

The PS even has a dog training center in Smolensk. The Border Guard

Service has used dogs for much of its history. Grigoriy Burlutskiy, a Border Guard lieutenant colonel who defected across the Turkmenistan border into Afghanistan in 1954, provided a detailed description of the types of dogs that the KGB used at the time and the training they received. The KGB used dogs for tracking, border duty, and as watchdogs.[54] John Barron described a border guard exercise in 1972 in which dogs demonstrated their ability to prevent an unauthorized person from crossing the border in either direction.[55] The PS today adds explosive and drug detection to that list of canine missions.

The Border Control Department (DPK) runs passport control services at Russian border crossings. One of its largest detachments is at Moscow Sheremetyevo International Airport.

FSB Headquarters Elements

FSB Headquarters also has a range of elements that directly answer to it, including the National Antiterrorist Center, internal affairs elements, administrative services, educational institutions, and several special operational entities.

The National Antiterrorist Committee (NAK) is an interagency body that coordinates counterterrorism operations, policy, and training. It proposes antiterrorism measures to protect Russian society and assist the victims of terrorism. The NAK also represents Russia in international counterterrorism forums. The FSB director leads the NAK, and NAK members include the FSB director; ministers of internal affairs, emergency situations, foreign affairs, defense, justice, health, industry and trade, computer development and communications, transportation, and energy; first assistant director of the Presidential Administration; directors of the SVR, National Guard, Federal Protective Service, and Financial Monitoring Service; chief of the Russian General Staff; chairman of the Investigative Committee; deputy secretary of the Security Council; and the first deputy chairs of the Federation Council and the State Duma. An FSB deputy director leads the NAK secretariat. Unlike most FSB elements, the NAK has its own website, http://nac.gov.ru/, where it publicizes terrorism arrests and operations, the public contents of NAK meetings and press conferences, and counterterrorism exercises.

Internal Affairs Elements

The FSB has two internal affairs elements that conduct inspections of FSB operations and investigations of crimes by FSB personnel, and a third element that conducts investigations within the MVD and other Russian law enforcement organizations.

The Control Service is responsible for internal inspections and financial audits that can have a significant impact on promotions and appointments of employees. The Control Service was created in 1999 as the Inspection Directorate, and in the reorganization of 2004 was expanded to the Control Service, consisting of the Directorate of Inspections, the Controller-Audit Directorate, and the Personnel Inspectorate.

The Internal Security Directorate (Ninth Directorate; USB) is responsible for conducting criminal investigations of FSB employees, especially counterespionage. It is reportedly divided into six subelements, called "services":

- First: investigations within central FSB headquarters
- Second: investigations within the subelements subordinate to FSB headquarters
- Third: investigations within regional FSB offices
- Fourth: investigations among FSB officers assigned outside the FSB
- Fifth: unknown
- Sixth: security for witnesses and operational support to the FSB's criminal activities

The Sixth Service was created in 2004–5 and carries the nickname "Sechin's Spetsnaz." The name comes from Putin's close associate from Saint Petersburg, Igor Ivanovich Sechin, the CEO of the Russian megaoil company Rosneft who, according to Stratfor, represents the FSB in the Russian oil industry.[56] Sechin uses his FSB connections to protect his and Putin's personal fortunes, resulting in several high-profile FSB arrests (see chapter 3 for further information).

Directorate M is the equivalent of DVKR but operates inside other Russian law enforcement organizations rather than the military. Directorate M is the FSB's eyes and ears within the subject agencies and is effectively those agencies' internal affairs arm. It has three subelements called services: the first covers the MVD, the second covers the Ministry of Emergency Situations, and the third covers the Federal Penitentiary Service and the Ministry of Justice. Directorate M is the operational element where the FSB's rivalry with the MVD plays out.

Directorate M is the resurrection of an element created in 1983 that had the same function; it was created after a series of missteps by MVD internal troops in the early 1980s. After the dissolution of the Soviet Union, law enforcement agencies removed state security influence from within their ranks and created their own internal security elements instead. However, KGB-era influence returned in 1999, soon after Putin moved from FSB director to prime minister. At that time, the new Department M was created under the then–Directorate for Economic Security, responsible for counterintelligence investigations within the MVD and other law enforcement agencies.[57] In 2002, Putin assigned a group of FSB counterintelligence officers to senior positions in the MVD, including Rashid Nurgaliyev, a close associate of FSB director Nikolay Patrushev, as minister, further solidifying the chekist control over Russian law enforcement agencies. The FSB officers were sent to the MVD under active reserve status, meaning they retained their FSB affiliation while working inside the MVD (see the Seconded Personnel Section below). By 2002, Roustam Kaliyev of EurasiaNet described the relationship between the FSB and MVD as "constant competition and interagency 'war.'"[58]

The MVD also views itself as the agency to monitor the FSB in that "war." In the early 2000s, the MVD, in collaboration with the General Procurator's Office, initiated a series of corruption investigations against corrupt FSB officers, particularly related to illegally importing consumer goods and customs fraud (see chapter 6). However, the FSB took control of those investigations and forced the MVD out, protecting its people from prosecution. In the FSB reorganization of 2004, Department M was elevated to directorate level within the Economic Counterintelligence Service, whose chief was Aleksandr Bortnikov. When Bortnikov was appointed FSB director in 2008, he brought Directorate M with him into the FSB front office.[59]

Directorate M is a particularly influential unit, and several senior ranking officers passed through as director, made their name for cracking down on corruption within the MVD and Federal Drug Control Service, and then continued to more senior positions. Vladimir Kryuchkov was the first Directorate M chief from 2004 to 2010. He was replaced by Aleksey Dorofeyev, who led it from 2010 to 2012, and was later named the chief of the FSB Directorate for Moscow and the Moscow Oblast. Anatoliy Tyukov was directorate chief from 2012 until about 2014, when he moved to the Presidential Administration, where he leads the Transportation Directorate. Sergey Alpatov led Directorate M from about 2014 until 2018, when he was moved to be the deputy chief of the Fourth Service and subsequently as chief. And Aleksey Vertyazhkin led the directorate from 2018 until he was named the chief of the FSB Internal Security Directorate in 2019.[60]

Administrative Services

The FSB has administrative services that provide personnel, educational, acquisition, construction, and morale and welfare support for the organization. Most have a Moscow headquarters as well as regional offices around Russia that manage the vast FSB network of facilities and personnel.

The Organizational and Personnel Service (SOKR) (Sixth Service) deals with hiring, firing, promotions, and awards. It connects with the Russian military benefits system since most FSB personnel have military ranks and FSB service counts as military service. Because many FSB employees are undercover, the SOKR's operates in a secure environment. The SOKR is also reportedly responsible for hiring, equipping, and managing mercenaries who were fighting in the Donbas region of Ukraine beginning in 2014. According to Ukrainian reporting, FSB offices across Russia were assigned in 2014 to recruit volunteers, yielding over 3,300 mercenaries from twenty-five Russian regions between August and December 2014.[61]

Connected to the SOKR is the Seconded Personnel Section (APS), which manages "former" FSB officers hired by large Russian firms or seconded to other agencies. These temporarily reassigned officers, colloquially known as *апээсники* (APSniks), leave the FSB on paper, while in reality remaining on the FSB salary posted in the status of active reserve, to represent FSB interests inside their new employers and report their observations to FSB handlers.[62] According to a Dossier Center source, there are two categories of FSB officers managed by the APS. Infiltrated officers publicly leave the FSB and gain employment elsewhere, and their affiliation with the FSB is classified. Seconded officers are openly sent on temporary assignment to another government or corporate organization, often in the role of chief of security. Both categories are different from recruited sources within the organizations, which number many more than APSniks.[63]

The Activity Support Service (SOD)—the Seventh Service—handles various administrative functions for the FSB. Its directorates include:

- Material-Technical Supply Directorate (UMTO; Military Unit 54729)
- Capital Construction Directorate (UKS)
- Military Construction Directorate (VSU)
- Finance-Economic Directorate (FEU)
- FSB's fire monitoring section

The Seventh Service is the primary purchasing organization for day-to-day goods used by the FSB, such as office supplies. It has eighteen regional offices responsible for construction and acquisition requirements across the country.[64] The FEU works with the SOKR to pay employees, administer housing subsidies, and manage pensions for retirees. It works with the UKS to provide funding for building acquisition and construction. It develops the FSB's budget and monitors other FSB elements' budget expenditures.[65]

According to Dossier Center, the Social Welfare Service (SSBO) is also subordinate to the Seventh Service. The SSBO provides the food services in FSB cafeterias and administers the FSB's nearly twenty morale and welfare sites, sanitoriums, and resorts. The SSBO also has at least forty-seven affiliated offices across the country that manage the food supply and morale, recreation, and welfare requirements.

Related to the SSBO is the Military Medical Directorate (VMU), which has provided medical care exclusively for state security personnel since the early KGB years and sends personnel to SSBO-managed sanatoriums for rest and treatment. However, even with a dedicated medical staff, some have questioned whether FSB personnel, especially those who have served in special operations units and suffer from posttraumatic stress, receive sufficient psychological support.[66]

Other administrative offices are the Contract and Legal Directorate

(DPU), responsible for providing legal counsel to FSB leadership; the Correspondence Directorate; the Registry and Archives Directorate; and the Commandant Directorate, which commands FSB headquarters security forces. Only forces subordinate to the Commandant Directorate are authorized to carry firearms inside FSB facilities.

Educational Institutions

The FSB has a range of educational institutions, including the FSB Academy, which is both a tradecraft training and a degree-granting institution. Many FSB officers receive their entry training and initial degree at the FSB academy. The FSB also has training centers in Saint Petersburg, Novosibirsk, Yekaterinburg, and Nizhniy Novgorod, as well as two specialized centers for information systems education, both in Moscow: the Institute of Cryptography, Communications, and Informatics (IKSiI); and the Moscow Institute of New Information Technologies (MINIT). The FSB runs the Institute of Coastal Defense in Anapa on the Black Sea coast, as well as a range of educational institutions dedicated to training border guards (see above). The FSB also has a dedicated Central Physical Fitness Center (TsSFP) (Fourteenth Center) to train FSB employees.

Headquarters Operational Elements

The Public Relations Center (TsOS) publicly communicates the FSB message through the FSB's website, the FSB's journal *FSB: For and Against*, and press releases that give the FSB's side of public stories. The TsOS is the element that interacts with journalists to publicize operations and successes and arranges journalist interviews with FSB personnel. Although a public relations office is not typically considered an operational element, since in the late 1990s, another element that spun off from the TsOS has had an operational mission. According to Agentura.ru, the Directorate for Support Programs (UPS) works with and against journalists to conduct disinformation operations, known in the post-Soviet era as "measures of support" or "programs of support," and to counter anti-Russian media reporting. In 2009, the UPS chief was added to the list of FSB officers authorized to "restrict the civil rights" of Russian citizens if they pose a threat to Russia's interests.[67] This reportedly gives UPS officers authorization to order the interception of journalists' communications for purposes of suppressing or controlling their activities. Few specific such operations are publicly known, although many examples of the FSB pursuing Russian journalists have been reported, including the Agentura.ru authors Andrei Soldatov and Irina Borogan.[68]

The Investigative Directorate (SU) is the FSB's element that prepares criminal indictments. It is separate from the Investigative Committee of the Russian Federation and works specifically for the FSB. The SU has small investigative teams that reflect the FSB's missions: counterintelligence (espionage), counterterrorism, military counterintelligence, computer crimes, and so on. The SU develops prosecutorial evidence when an investigation in another FSB area reaches the point of being referred to the judiciary for trial. Consequently, it is often the public face of the FSB in major terrorism and espionage cases.

Soviet state security organizations had an investigative directorate for especially important cases as early as the 1940s, and it continued through the rest of the Soviet era.[69] The SU continued into the post-Soviet MB. However, Yeltsin ordered that the SU be disbanded in 1993, when the FSK replaced the MB—the FSK did not have criminal investigative authorities. Some SU investigators transferred to the Main Military Procurator, while others left altogether. The SU was reestablished in 1995 when the FSB replaced the FSK and regained a law enforcement mission. Its first chief after the directorate, who was transferred back to the FSB, was Nikolay Oleshko, who, before the dissolution of the Soviet Union, had led the Anti-Soviet Section of the SU, which reflected the KGB Fifth Directorate's mission.[70]

Connected to the SU is the Lefortovo Investigative Detention Center (CIZO). Lefortovo is where suspects are held while awaiting the SU's preparation for their prosecution. Suspects can wait in Lefortovo for months before their case goes to trial. Lefortovo was built as a prison during tsarist times and was transferred to the new Soviet state security structure after the Bolshevik Revolution. It gained an ominous reputation as an interrogation and execution facility during Stalin's reign and remained subordinate to state security throughout the rest of the Soviet era. The Lefortovo facility transferred to the MVD in 1993, when the SU was disbanded, but returned to state security in 1995. It again changed subordination in 2005 when it moved to the Ministry of Justice, and it officially remains there as of 2023. However, the SU's offices continue to be located inside the Lefortovo CIZO, and FSB officers are temporarily reassigned to Lefortovo in management positions, making it practically an FSB element.[71]

The FSB maintains its own Aviation Directorate (UA), which supports its investigative, border security, and special operations missions, and transportation needs. The UA operates a variety of aircraft, including fixed-wing aircraft and helicopters specially designed for low noise, along with unmanned vehicles and dirigibles equipped with video and communications geolocational capabilities. Today's UA is the continuation of Soviet state security aviation that began in 1923. After the dissolution of the Soviet Union, much of that aviation capability was assigned to the Federal Border Guard Service (FPS). However, the FSB's Spetsnaz elements required their own aviation assets, especially in Chechnya. The FPS supported the FSB Spetsnaz during the late 1990s; but in 2000, the FSB reacquired a separate aviation capability separate from the FPS, not anticipating the future merger back into the FSB. When that occurred in 2003, the FSB and FPS aviation units merged into the single Aviation Directorate.

Special Headquarters Operational Elements

Several FSB Headquarters operational elements are involved in offensive and defensive operations in the Russian information environment. Their targeting is primarily internal, although they also offer access to international communications.

The Center for Operational Technical Measures (TsOTM), known as Center 12, runs the System of Operational-Investigative Measures (SORM). SORM is Russia's system that facilitates law enforcement agencies' monitoring of Russia's communications network. TsOTM is the heir to a long history of Soviet organizations that intercepted telephone and postal communications, dating back to the 1930s. In the 1950s and 1960s, telephone intercept operations inside the Soviet Union fell under the Operational-Technical Directorate (OTU), but the element responsible for those operations became an independent section soon after Andropov became the KGB chief in 1967. That entity was called the 12th

Section, and the number "12" continues to be associated with domestic communications interception today.

The Electronic Intelligence and Communications Center (TsRRSS; Center 16) (Military Unit 71330) is the FSB's signals intelligence organization. It is the heir of the KGB's Sixteenth Directorate, Radio-Electronic Intelligence, which had a foreign SIGINT mission that separated from the Eighth Chief Directorate in 1973. According to a 1989 assessment, the Sixteenth Directorate had about 2,000 personnel and was growing in importance within the KGB when the Soviet Union dissolved.[72] The designator "16" continues today. During the Soviet era, the KGB's collection of foreign embassy communications was handled jointly by the Sixteenth Directorate for intelligence purposes and the Second Chief Directorate for counterintelligence purposes. That cooperation continues today, with Center 18, subordinate to the FSB's Counterintelligence Service, cooperating with Center 16 to penetrate communication systems for different missions. In May 2023, the US Department of Justice announced the dismantling of a Center 16 computer intrusion capability that had been operating globally for over twenty years, using sophisticated malware labeled "Snake," which was run from an FSB facility in Ryazan, Russia.[73]

Several other FSB headquarters elements are also engaged in communications systems operations, although less information is available about them.

The Special Service (Cryptography) may be involved in the security and encryption of the FSB's communications.

The Radio Counterintelligence Directorate (Directorate R) (Military Unit 48852) is a collection and analysis unit. It probably operates a series of radio direction-finding stations spread around the Moscow area that pinpoint signals emitted by foreign intelligence services. Agentura.ru lists these sites as being affiliated with Center 12, although they may be operated by Directorate R.[74]

The Center for Licensing, Certification, and Defending State Secrets (TsLSZ) is responsible for registering companies that import and export cryptographic hardware and software, certifying information assurance systems, and accrediting laboratories that produce them. It is a part of Russia's system to protect state secrets, which encompass a wide swath of Russian information.[75]

Regional FSB Offices

The FSB has ninety-nine regional offices called directorates spread across the country. These offices are miniaturized versions of FSB Headquarters, with subelements similar to the services at the federal level. They are the local execution arms of many of the FSB's law enforcement, counterintelligence, and counterterrorism functions. In addition to these directorates, some FSB services have their own subordinate offices across the country, such as the Border Guard Service and DVKR, where their functions are most needed. Other FSB services, such as the Activity Support Service and Aviation Directorate, have separate subordinate offices that handle construction management and aircraft basing. There are also over twenty FSB resorts and sanitariums across the country.

Some regional offices are particularly large, corresponding to the amount of work they manage. The Moscow and Saint Petersburg directorates are the most powerful, as they are the locations where most foreign diplomats reside, multiple terrorist attacks have occurred, and the bulk of Russian government corruption occurs. Regional offices in and near the North Caucasus—such as in the Stavropol and Krasnodar Krays, Chechnya, and Dagestan—carry heavy counterterrorist responsibilities. FSB directorates in the Far East—such as in the Amur Oblast, Jewish Autonomous Oblast, and Zabaikalskiy and Primorskiy Krays—have the legacy of countering Chinese threats. Directorates in the west of Russia, such as the Pskov and Smolensk Oblasts, border NATO countries and particularly focus on counterintelligence.

Service in a regional directorate can be a stepping stone for further advancement, and many senior leaders have served a tour as the chief of a regional directorate. However, many rank-and-file employees remain in regional directorates for much of their careers.

FSB Personnel

Not surprisingly, the names and personal information of FSB personnel are not easy to obtain—the FSB is, after all, a security service. However, in March 2022, the Ukrainian government released a list of 620 FSB personnel whose passports were registered using FSB Headquarters as their address, birth dates, telephone numbers, SIM card numbers, and other

Table 2.1
FSB Personnel from the List Released by the Ukrainian Government

Age (years)	Women		Men	
24–34	18	15.1%	49	9.8%
35–44	50	42.0%	230	45.9%
45–54	45	37.8%	161	32.1%
55–64	6	5.0%	55	11.0%
65+	0		5	1.0%
No birth date			1	
	119		501	

personal data.[76] Some of the names have been previously noted publicly, but many are otherwise unknown. Some have also moved on from the FSB but are still active in Russian government service.

An analysis of the list allows a preliminary characterization of FSB employees, although it is unclear how representative the list is of the entirety of the FSB's staff. The average age of people on the list is forty-four years. The list shows 482 employees born in 1972 or later, making them twenty years old or younger when the Soviet Union dissolved. Thus, over three-fourths of people on the list would have known the Soviet Union either as students or children and likely joined a Russian state security service in the post-Soviet era. Sixteen were born after January 1, 1992, meaning they never lived during the Soviet era at all. That relative youth contrasts with most senior FSB officers, who joined the KGB in the 1980s and earlier (see chapter 4).

Of the 620 entries, 501 are men and 119 are women (80.8 percent vs. 19.2 percent). Although the average age of both men and women is 44, the age distribution among men and women is quite different. More men are at the older end of the spectrum, and more women are at the younger end. Of the 119 women, 18 are younger than 35 years as of May 2022 (15.1 percent), compared with 49 men who are younger than 35 years (9.8 percent). Many more men than women are over 55; 60 men (12 percent) and only 6 women (5 percent). The lower number of older women is partly a function of different retirement ages for men and women in Russia: 56.5 years for women and 61.5 years for men. However, it may also represent fewer female employees hired during the Soviet era.

The fewer older women and greater number of younger women also indicates lower average service seniority based on assigned tasks, with women generally holding lower ranks than men. That seniority difference is likely the result of women typically performing secretarial, medical, linguist duties, and occasionally border guard assignments, while men are more often assigned to operational duties that lead to higher ranks. One woman on the published list is Lyudmila Nazarenko, a soloist in the FSB Orchestra.[77] A Russian website that provides information about FSB salaries confirms that women predominantly work in lower-ranking nonoperational duties.[78] Only one woman in FSB history has held the rank of general: Natalya Klimova, former first deputy chief of the FSB's Military Medical Directorate, who retired in 2009.[79]

The FSB's website provides instructions for individuals wishing to apply for employment. All candidates for employment in the FSB are expected to meet high standards. They must be a Russian Federation citizen. They must be physically fit, in good health, and free from dependence on alcohol or narcotics, and they must undergo a preemployment psychological evaluation. They must be trustworthy in keeping state secrets, and their trustworthiness is investigated thoroughly before employment. Background investigations do not differ for men or women, and the FSB site even includes both husbands and wives among the people who are scrutinized during a prospective employee's background investigation.[80] However, the education requirement for women is lower than for men: men must hold a university degree, and women must have graduated from an institute. That likely indicates the lower level of responsibilities assigned to women.

Women occasionally work in operational assignments, although it is the exception. In 2008, Colonel Olga Spiridonova retired as the commander of an all-female FSB Alfa special operations subunit. She had joined the KGB in the 1980s as one of few females working in senior leader and facility security. Her FSB Alfa unit, which was created in 1998, consisted of five women who performed various special operations tasks, such as testing antiterrorism measures at critical infrastructure facilities, conducting surveillance, and improving facility security. The unit was also involved in the FSB's response to the 2002 Dubrovka Theater hostage crisis in Moscow, in which many hostages were women. During the unit's ten-year existence, it received multiple medals. Nevertheless, Spiridonova stated in interviews in 2019 and 2020 that the female unit constantly had to prove that it was just as good as the men. The unit was disbanded in 2008, after Spiridonova's retirement, and had not been reestablished as of 2020, to Spiridonova's disappointment.[81]

This author witnessed firsthand some senior FSB officers' views toward women serving in positions of responsibility. In 2003, this author participated in a US delegation that hosted DVKR officers who visited the United States. The visit included a tour of a US naval vessel, including the operations department. The officer-of-the-deck was a female US Navy lieutenant who briefly described the department's duties. After the tour, the FSB officers discussed among themselves their shock that the US Navy would place a woman in such a position, saying the FSB would never allow that. These officers all had Soviet-era service, and their views represented an older generation; however, they were among the FSB's leaders at that time, and many leaders in the 2020s are still from the same era. The Soviet-era generation will soon age out of the service, however, and a younger generation hired since the dissolution of the Soviet Union will begin to take the lead. It is unclear whether views will change as older KGB-era officers retire from the service.

Summary and Comparison with the United States

The FSB is sometimes compared with the US Federal Bureau of Investigation. In reality, there is no single US department or agency that equates to the FSB. The FSB contains the equivalents of numerous US intelligence, national security, and criminal investigative organizations far beyond the FBI:

- Office of the Director of National Intelligence—National Counterintelligence and Security Center and National Counterterrorism Center, Intelligence Advanced Research Projects Agency
- Department of Justice—FBI, portions of the Department of Justice's National Security Division and Criminal Division, and portions of the Drug Enforcement Administration
- National Security Agency—SIGINT mission and Information Assurance Directorate
- Central Intelligence Agency—National Resources Division, In-Q-Tel

- Department of Homeland Security—Office of Intelligence and Analysis, Cybersecurity and Infrastructure Security Agency, Coast Guard, Transportation Security Administration, and portions of Customs and Border Protection and the Secret Service
- Department of Defense—military counterintelligence organizations (Naval Criminal Investigative Service, Air Force Office of Special Investigations, and Army Counterintelligence), US Cyber Command, and portions of the US Special Operations Command
- Environmental Protection Agency—Office of Enforcement and Compliance Assurance
- Portions of the Securities and Exchange Commission

These responsibilities overlap considerably with those of other Russian agencies, often causing duplication and rivalry, such as with the Federal Customs Service, Investigative Committee, Federal Drug Control Service, and the FSB's most bitter rival, the MVD.

This accumulation of authorities into one agency is similar to the reach of the KGB during the Soviet era, with two significant differences. First, the FSB omits KGB elements that now form separate Russian agencies: Russia's HUMINT agency, the SVR, is not part of the FSB, although the FSB does have its own HUMINT capability, operating mainly within the former Soviet states; and the senior leadership protection element of the KGB is now in the Federal Protective Service. Second, and more important, the political nature of the FSB is different from the KGB's ideological foundation. Unlike the KGB, in which membership in the Communist Party of the Soviet Union was a requirement, an FSB employee can be dismissed for being a member of a political party or another public association pursuing political aims or participating in its activities. According to Russian Federation law, organizing political party structures within the Federal Security Service is prohibited.[82] That does not mean FSB officers eschew all political involvement; the FSB is a highly politicized organization. It only means that, unlike during the Soviet era, no organized political structure drives the FSB's activities besides loyalty to the president. In practice, this means the FSB is freed from ideological restraints and operates for the benefit of the president, the power of the Russian regime, and FSB officers themselves. This lack of ideological inhibition is part of the reason why the FSB is often caught in corruption scandals (see chapter 6).

Notes

1. "Staff Changes in the FSB"; Sukhotin, "Gray Beards Begin."
2. "FSB Department of Counterintelligence Operations."
3. Russo and Dezenhall, *Best of Enemies*, 159–66.
4. Corera, *Russians Among Us*, 51–59, 287, 297–98.
5. Russian Federation, Order 465.
6. "Directorate of Information Support."
7. "'Russians Are Panicking.'"
8. "Personnel."
9. Russian Federation, Interdepartmental Order, December 2, 2005.
10. Soldatov and Borogan, *Red Web*, 125–27; see also Sinodov, "Dirty Hands."
11. "Internet Got a New Guardian."
12. Russian Federation, Order 621.
13. Kokurin and Petrov, *Lubyanka*, 127–28.
14. Baryshnikov, "Second Service."
15. Barron, *KGB*, 84–85.
16. Albats, *State Within a State*, 40–43.
17. Albats, 39.
18. Kryuchkov, "Working Note," 730–32.
19. "Service for Defense."
20. "Director of the UFSB for Ingushetia Koryakov Removed."
21. "Nationalist in Russia"; Chernukhin, "Stinger Stuck into Alexander Potkin." The title of this blog entry is a play on words on Zhalo's name, which translates as "stinger." Aleksandr Potkin was the leader of the Movement Against Illegal Immigration, DPNI.
22. "Service for Defense of the Constitutional Order."
23. Sotnikov, "Ambassador."
24. Knight, *Spies*, 76.
25. Kouzminov, *Biological Espionage*, 35–36.
26. "USSR's Intellectual Spetsnaz."
27. Soldatov, "How a Renegade 'Middle Eastern Mafia' Invented Modern Russian Espionage."
28. Galeotti, *Russian Security*, 41.
29. Lezina, "Dismantling the State Security Apparatus," 13.
30. "Unit 'Smerch.'"
31. Barmin, "Spetsnaz Opera."
32. "Center of Special Operations."
33. "New Directorate of the FSB TsSN."
34. Balmforth, "You Say Crimea."
35. Russian Federation, Order 465.
36. Fleming, *From Russia with Love*, 6.
37. "Man from 'Aeroflot.'"
38. Sergeyev and Syun, "FSB Economic Security."

39. "Service for Operational Information and International Relations."
40. Soldatov, "Analysis"; "How Was the KGB-FSB Analysis Service Created."
41. "Biography of Aleksandr Mikhailov."
42. Sinelschikova, "Sergei Ivanov."
43. Shchegolev, *Who Is Who*, 167–69.
44. Soldatov, "Untold Story."
45. Mzareupov, "Operational Technology Directorate."
46. Khlobustov, *August 1991*.
47. "FSB Created a National Center."
48. "FSB Structure Warned."
49. "FSB Will Apply the Developments."
50. Russian Federation, Interdepartmental Order, December 10, 1996.
51. See, e.g., Popov et al., *Method*; Gorokhova et al., "Drug Simulator"; and Fesenko and Milovsorov, "Determination," 81–87.
52. "FSB Forensics Institute."
53. Yegorov and Bulavinov, "Andrey Nikolayev."
54. US Central Intelligence Agency, "Use of Dogs."
55. Barron, *KGB*, 85.
56. "Russia: FSB Branches Out."
57. "FSB Directorate 'M.'"
58. Kaliyev, "Can 'Power Ministries' Be Reformed?"
59. "FSB Directorate 'M.'"
60. "Directorate 'M.'"
61. "Russian Mercenaries."
62. Anin, "Who Arranged the Hunt?"
63. "Seconded Personnel Section."
64. "FSB."
65. "Financial Economic Directorate."
66. "Military Medical Directorate"; "FSB, GRU, FSO, . . ."
67. Russian Federation, Order 465.
68. "Center for Support Programs."
69. "Investigative Section."
70. "Espionage Section."
71. "FSB Investigative Directorate."
72. Ball, *Soviet Signals Intelligence*, 3–4.
73. US Department of Justice, "Justice Department Announces Court-Authorized Disruption."
74. "FSB Center 12."
75. "FSB's Licensing Center."
76. Ministry of Defense of Ukraine, Main Intelligence Directorate, "Russia FSB Employees."
77. Mendyukov, Shilova, and Shmatov, *Who Is Who*, 335.
78. "Salaries in the FSB."
79. "Woman Generals"; Andreyev, "There Are 44 Women."
80. FSB, "Process for Admission."
81. Litvinova, "Olga"; Orlov, "Unweak Sex."
82. Russian Federation, Federal Law 15-FZ.

3

Activities—Including Operations, Analysis, and Technology Development

The FSB's activities span the spectrum of operational, analytic, and science and technology areas. These general fields of activity are identified in the FSB's founding law, although the law does not describe them to their full extent. The FSB's activities fall into these broad categories:

- Counterintelligence
- Counterterrorism
- Combating crime
- Intelligence
- Information security
- Analysis
- Science and technology development

Counterintelligence

The Russian definition of counterintelligence includes countering foreign intelligence services but goes beyond that. It encompasses countering any activity that threatens the ruling regime, whether committed by a foreign state or a Russian citizen, and whether it poses a threat to classified information or just the regime's chosen narratives. As already noted, the FSB's "chekist mind-set" invariably sees domestic and foreign threats as converging. Thus, for the FSB, counterintelligence is a broad activity that touches on all aspects of Russian government and society.

The FSB's counterintelligence activities mostly divide along service boundaries into the areas of counterespionage (First Service), military counterintelligence (DVKR), economic counterintelligence (Fourth Service), and ideological counterintelligence (Second Service and Fifth Service).

Counterespionage

The First Service is the FSB's counterespionage organization, and DKRO is the core subelement for this responsibility. DKRO's central mission is to monitor foreign diplomatic representations and prevent espionage. It does this through various means, including recruiting foreign service nationals working for foreign embassies, surveilling foreign diplomats within Russia, and monitoring foreigners' communications and the communications of Russians who interact with them. This activity has led to arrests of foreign diplomats in Moscow, whom the FSB claims to have caught "red-handed" receiving classified Russian information or participating in unsanctioned demonstrations. The governments these diplomats represent unsurprisingly claim that the diplomats were doing nothing wrong and were set up for arrest. DKRO was heavily involved in these cases regardless of the genuineness of the crimes.[1]

One method DKRO uses to inhibit foreign embassy operations is to harass foreign diplomats in Russia. Arbitrary police stops, physical assaults, and break-ins into diplomats' homes increased dramatically after 2014, along with the occasional publication of diplomats' personal details on state TV channels, placing them at risk of harassment.[2] The FSB employs diplomatic harassment for several reasons: as a tool to retaliate for counterintelligence or law enforcement operations against Russian diplomats abroad, to identify diplomatically covered intelligence officers, to provoke a response that can be used in Russian propaganda messaging, or simply to create stress among the diplomatic staff. In general, DKRO's harassment of foreign diplomats is a counterintelligence method that the FSB uses to reduce the overall effectiveness of foreign intelligence operations in Russia.

DKRO's mission also includes monitoring foreign journalists in Russia, especially those who write articles that cast Russia in a negative light. This mission dates to the Soviet era, when the SCD Tenth Department was tasked with monitoring and recruiting foreign journalists inside the Soviet Union.[3] KGB operations included assigning co-opted interpreters to foreign journalists, reminiscent of Olga Farmakovskaya, who was tasked with monitoring and reporting on the activities of the Canadian journalist Peter Worthington in the 1960s.[4] The KGB also used technical surveillance to intercept journalists' communications and human provocations to catch journalists and coerce them into cooperation.[5]

DKRO inherited those KGB missions. Today, the SKR may cooperate with the FSB's Center for Support Programs, which targets foreign journalists for disinformation purposes. In 2006, the FSB initiated an operation targeting a US television news team that was investigating the fallout from the 2002 Dubrovka Theater hostage crisis in Moscow. Journalists contacted over 100 surviving hostages and asked about their health, with nearly all indicating health challenges probably resulting from the incapacitating gas that FSB special forces used during the crisis. The FSB monitored the journalists' investigation and compiled a report based partially on a human source the FSB had recruited inside the US company's Moscow bureau. The FSB assessed that the company planned to release the article just as Putin was to host the Group of Eight's Summit for the first time in Russia, intending to embarrass Putin internationally. An American journalist involved in the investigation claimed no such intent. The initial title of the FSB report, possibly compiled by analysts in the FSB Fifth Service, was a bland statement about the plans of foreign correspondents. After FSB director Patrushev reviewed the report, the title changed to "Anti-Russian Activities," and the FSB then provided the report to Putin, who reacted by asking what counteractions the FSB planned to take.[6]

This incident provides several insights into FSB counterintelligence operations. First, the FSB reportedly recruits sources inside the offices of foreign journalists' organizations. Second, the FSB interprets any activity by a foreign organization in the most nefarious way possible, even when no such intent exists. Both characteristics are direct holdovers from the Soviet era, when, according to the retired FSB officer Valentin Klimenko, the KGB regularly overestimated the size, capabilities, and intent of the CIA in the Soviet Union. The KGB identified any diplomat, cultural center employee, or journalist working in the USSR who contacted a dissident, a refusenik, or anyone who might provide a negative report about the Soviet Union as a CIA officer. The KGB eventually learned that real CIA officers avoided such contacts to avert unwanted attention, but the FSB has forgotten that lesson and has resurrected tactics based on chekist interpretations.[7]

DKRO also conducts intelligence monitoring of migrants living in the Russian Federation, claiming that spies, saboteurs, and terrorists are among them. In 2013, the chief of the First Service's UKAKD, Aleksandr Roshchupkin, told a State Duma hearing that foreign intelligence services had embedded officers among illegal immigrants. Roshchupkin stated further that foreign nongovernmental organizations and other "destructive forces" like them facilitate this threat by pressing the Russian government on immigration policies.[8]

Hyperbole about the espionage threat is integral to the Russian security state. Since at least 2012, Putin has given an annual address at the FSB's Lubyanka headquarters, where he has praised the service for its success in catching spies. He usually cites implausible statistics about foreign intelligence–affiliated persons whom the FSB neutralized in the previous year, including foreign intelligence service staff personnel and their agents. The numbers rose each year from 2012, reaching nearly 600 in 2018, and only fell in 2020, according to Putin, because of the "demands of the current epidemiological situation."[9]

DKRO is likely responsible for many of these alleged arrests, as they supposedly involve foreign intelligence officers operating inside Russia. Putin makes such outlandish assertions to substantiate Russian claims that Russia is increasingly under siege by adversarial foreign powers. The numbers send a message to the Russian people to be on constant alert for foreign spies and justify the implementation of strict internal security measures, including those that restrict the rights of Russians.

The Kremlin did not publish an equivalent speech in 2022, likely because it typically falls in late February or early March, and in 2022 that coincided with Russia's invasion of Ukraine. Putin's reported dissatisfaction with the FSB Fifth Service's forecasts about prospects for a quick victory in Ukraine, and the press of wartime demands may have overshadowed the annual event.[10] Alternatively, Putin may have proceeded with the speech but did not publish it because it contained criticism of the FSB. Either way, no statistics are available for 2021.

DKRO's mission of providing counterintelligence support for the

Ministry of Foreign Affairs (MID) represents another return of a Soviet-era mission. DKRO's predecessor organization in the KGB managed the MID's security department from the 1970s to the end of the Soviet era. The MID, which never approved of the KGB presence within its walls, succeeded in removing state security in the early 1990s under Andrey Kozyrev. Nevertheless, when Yevgeniy Primakov became the minister of foreign affairs in 1996, the FSB and SVR returned as a combined security presence. DKRO subsequently took the mission, resembling a Soviet-era construct.

When Russia invaded Ukraine in early 2022, the FSB's presence inside the MID rose in priority. Thirty countries, mostly in Europe, plus the European Union, expelled over 470 Russian personnel from Russian diplomatic missions between February and April 2022 in response to the invasion and revelations of Russian troops' brutality. Even though most of the expelled personnel were intelligence officers, not diplomats, their expulsion left a hostile operating environment for the remaining personnel across Europe and negatively affected morale within the Russian MID. According to Agentura.ru, DKRO closely monitors the moods and morale of MID personnel, looking for signs of anti-Russian sentiment.[11] The FSB's emphasis on MID personnel likely rose even further in May 2022, when Boris Bondarev, a Russian diplomat serving in the Russian Mission to the United Nations in Geneva, resigned in protest over Russia's invasion of Ukraine.[12] Such an act would be the very reason why DKRO monitors MID personnel.

The First Service, particularly DKRO, also plays a role in organizing security for major sporting events, such as the 2014 Olympic games, the 2017 FIFA Confederations Cup, and the 2018 World Cup. DKRO deputy chief Aleksey Lavrishchev has built a long résumé representing the FSB in planning for such events. He was the senior FSB representative on the 2015 interagency working group that oversaw the preliminary draw for the 2018 World Cup, and he then served on the coordinating committee for the World Cup.[13] Lavrishchev was included in a list of Russian officials who received commendations for supporting the security of energy supplies during the Sochi Olympics, which also included three other DKRO officers: Sergey Bondarev, Yevgeniy Gromkov, and Aleksandr Gurtopov, along with the then–First Service chief, Oleg Syromolotov and his deputy, Konstantin Sevastyanov.[14] Sevastyanov also served as a member of the construction coordinating committee for the Sochi Olympics.[15]

Lavrishchev was the FSB's public spokesman for explaining the security posture for several major sporting events, including the Olympics and the Confederations Cup.[16] His public statements addressed physical security measures. However, DKRO was likely involved in these events because they attracted large foreign audiences to Russia.

Counterespionage resources also cover the FSB itself. In December 2016, TsIB was thrust into the Russian press when several of its officers were arrested for state treason in a complex case involving an internal settling of scores and perceptions of foreign intelligence threats. According to the Russian press, Colonel Sergey Mikhailov, a directorate chief in TsIB, was arrested for receiving money from a US intelligence service to supply information about Russian computer criminals. A month later, a manager from the Russian computer security company Kaspersky Laboratories, Ruslan Stoyanov, was also arrested, along with Mikhailov's FSB subordinate, Dmitriy Dokuchayev, and the Internet entrepreneur Georgiy Fomchenkov.

The case involves an allegation from 2011 that Mikhailov allegedly used a series of cut-outs to pass operational information about a young Russian entrepreneur, Pavel Vrublevskiy, the founder of a Russian online credit card payment processing company, Chronopay, to the US Federal Bureau of Investigation (FBI). US law enforcement was investigating Vrublevskiy for possible criminal violations involving mass spamming. Vrublevskiy had been at odds with TsIB for several years, partially because of his connection with mass spamming and partially because the FSB maintained a liaison relationship with the FBI that eventually led to Vrublevskiy's 2013 arrest in Russia. Mikhailov, according to one hyperbolic description, "controlled all Internet-business in the country" and "in many ways informally determines the policies in the fields of cybersecurity and Internet commerce."[17] Those powers put him in conflict with Vrublevskiy, who was pushing to increase market control of online commerce in Russia.

Mikhailov's liaison with the FBI also allegedly included reports that Vrublevskiy had organized a distributed denial-of-service attack on the computers of the Russian airline Aeroflot after the company had refused to adopt an online booking system connected to Chronopay. He also reportedly passed information about Roman Seleznev, a Russian criminal arrested in 2014 for trafficking stolen credit cards. Seleznev received a fourteen-year prison sentence in the United States in 2017.[18] Mikhailov and the other FSB officers arrested in 2016 and 2017 were also allegedly suspected of providing the FBI information about Russian hackers who penetrated US Democratic National Committee computer servers in 2016.[19] That case brought the FSB into conflict with the GRU (the Main Directorate of the General Staff of the Armed Forces of the Russian Federation, formerly the Main Intelligence Directorate) because the 2016 information Mikhailov allegedly passed to the FBI may have included information about GRU hacking activity.

TsIB, which is responsible for investigating criminal hacking activity, allegedly employed hackers for its own intelligence collection. The conflict with the GRU reportedly went even deeper. According to the Dossier Center, the FSB used the services of a hacking group called "Shaltay Boltay" (Russian for "Humpty Dumpty"), also known as Anonymous International, to break into servers around the world. Shaltay Boltay was notorious for hacking the email accounts of prominent Russian business and political figures and publishing embarrassing information. One of Shaltay Boltay's victims in 2015 was Kseniya Bolshakova, the secretary to Roman Filimonov, who led the Russian Ministry of Defense (MOD) Construction Department. TsIB allegedly ordered the hack and inadvertently discovered that Bolshakova's email contained classified information. Upon finding that information, the hackers were instructed to publicize the breach to embarrass MOD officials as well as the chief of the FSB's own DVKR, General Colonel Aleksandr Bezverkhniy, who retired soon after the incident. MOD officials, up to the minister, Sergey Shoigu himself, demanded an investigation, leading to the GRU's examination of FSB interference in MOD activities. Sergey Mikhailov, who was arrested for state treason in December 2016, was reportedly one FSB official who was knowledgeable of Shaltay Boltay's FSB-sponsored activities.[20] After the arrests of Mikhailov and Dokuchayev, then chief of TsIB, Andrey Gerasimov, was dismissed under a cloud and sent into retirement. Sergey Skorokhodov, his deputy, replaced him later in 2017. Mikhailov was sentenced in 2019 to twenty-two years in prison for high treason, and Stoyanov from Kaspersky Laboratories received a fourteen-year sentence.

Military Counterintelligence

DVKR is the FSB's entity tasked with preventing foreign penetrations of the Russian military and ensuring the loyalty of Russian forces. To accomplish those tasks, DVKR places officers in military units to recruit agents who report on their fellow service members and keep the FSB informed of activities that fall in any of DVKR's mission areas. The KGB Third Chief Directorate was renowned for using provocation agents to stimulate anti-Soviet statements from soldiers or to dispatch double agents into foreign counterintelligence services. Those long-tested methods continue today.

In 2000, soon after Putin's was elected president, Putin signed a directive "On FSB Directorates in Military Forces" that gave FSB military counterintelligence officers authority over counterintelligence, information security, and counterterrorism within the military, along with fighting organized crime connected to the military, extending the historical role that state security plays in providing security for the armed forces. As Putin was returning to the presidency in 2012 after having served a term as prime minister, he emphasized his view of corruption within the military in an op-ed published under his name in the journal *Foreign Policy*: "Be resolute in eliminating corruption from the defense industry and the armed forces, ensuring that punishment for those who fall foul of the law is inevitable. Corruption in the national security sector is essentially treason."[21] DVKR's counterintelligence mission includes eliminating that "treasonous" corruption. The 2000 directive gave DVKR authority to investigate illegal narcotics trade; organized crime and corruption; illicit trade in arms, ammunition, explosives, and flammable substances; illegal military formations, criminal groups, and individuals that threaten to change the constitutional order of the Russian Federation by force; and countering threats to seize power in the country. These missions have clear overlaps with other FSB elements as well as with the MVD and Rosgvardiya.[22]

Since 2015, the chief of DVKR has been Nikolay Yuryev. He replaced Aleksandr Bezverkhniy, who had served in that position since 2002, the longest-serving military counterintelligence chief in Soviet/Russian history. In 2010, an interview with Bezverkhniy appeared in the FSB's journal, *FSB: For and Against*, titled, "An Army Without Intelligence Is

Blind and Without Counterintelligence is Defenseless." In the interview, Bezverkhniy stated that DVKR pays special attention to Russian forces' military readiness and morale/psychological condition. In Russian terms, this means loyalty to the Russian state. In his 2010 interview, Bezverkhniy claimed that the CIA and other NATO countries' intelligence services were the primary threats to Russia's military. He said, "Russian-American cooperation developed successfully at the highest levels had not so far led to a reduction in the activities of American special services toward damaging Russia's security. Despite the openness of Russia's leadership and the Military Forces on questions of military doctrine, reforms, and the rearming of our military, American intelligence tries to obtain information that Russian law classifies as state secrets."[23] Ironically, Bezverkhniy made his statement at a time when other topics, such as transnational terrorism and wars in Iraq and Afghanistan, absorbed a much greater portion of US intelligence resources than Russia did, and US political leaders were trying in vain to persuade Russian leaders that the US actions did not threaten Russia.[24]

It also came at a time when publicly announced espionage convictions in Russia did not show a predominance of US-related cases. In 2010, the Russian government press service RIA Novosti published a list of espionage cases between 1993 and 2009 involving thirty-seven people. DVKR likely predominated in eighteen cases in which either the accused was a military member or the alleged topic involved a military organization or technology. No single foreign country—even the United States—stood out as dominating the cases; the foreign intelligence services allegedly involved were from China, Georgia, Germany, Lithuania, Poland, Sweden, the United Kingdom, and the United States.[25]

In 2020, the Russian news site *Novaya Gazeta* published another similar list inventorying espionage and state treason convictions of 129 people from 1997 to 2020. The list mostly overlapped the 2010 article, with the two combined totaling 135 people convicted of espionage between 1993 and 2020. The country with the greatest number of people convicted was Georgia, with 24, many of whom were private citizens accused of providing low-level observations of Russian troop movements immediately before or during the 2008 Russian invasion of Georgia. Those included 6 civilian women who received four-to-twelve-year sentences for allegedly texting public observations about Russian forces to a friend. Second in number of cases was Russia's military ally China, with 23 convicted spies, most of whom were accused of targeting military technologies. The United States was third, with 21 people convicted, including FSB officers like Colonel Sergey Mikhailov and his colleagues, who had a declared liaison relation with US counterparts. Other NATO countries made up another 27 of the alleged spies, reportedly involving Belgium, Estonia, Germany, Latvia, Lithuania, Norway, Poland, and the United Kingdom. Ukraine also began to appear on the list in 2015.[26]

Over 70 percent of 135 espionage convictions between 1993 and 2020 were military-related cases, of which only 30 percent allegedly involved a NATO country. Nevertheless, for Bezverkhniy and other FSB leaders, the United States and NATO were still the "main enemy," as they had been during the Cold War. Bezverkhniy added Georgia to his list of enemies in his 2010 interview, less than two years after Russian forces invaded Georgia. FSB leaders seldom openly mention China as a threat, despite the frequency of China-related espionage cases.

Economic Counterintelligence

The Fourth Service is responsible for counterintelligence activities in economic sectors, such as banking and finance, transportation, and industry. Although the FSB calls this counterintelligence, it is more akin to fighting financial crime. That mission is the heir to a long Soviet history of fighting corruption within the Russian system.

A KGB defector, Petr Deryabin, cited a KGB aphorism in his 1959 book *The Secret World* that described the evolving priorities of Soviet intelligence using the image of a god: "In the Yezhovshchina, the god of state security sat in the political section. During the period of collectivization, god sat in the economic section. During the war, god was in intelligence and, after the war, in counterintelligence."[27] During the period of collectivization in the early 1930s, the Stalinist government centralized all economic activity in the country under the government and reformed the Soviet economy from agrarian to industrial. Economic counterintelligence focused at that time on pursuing anyone who opposed harsh collectivization policies.

In 2005 and 2006, the Fourth Service sponsored the publication of a two-volume set of books titled *Lubyanka: Providing the State's Economic*

Security that tells a history of economic counterintelligence, beginning with the VChK, whose expanded name in 1918 represented the economic aspect of state security: the All-Russian Extraordinary Commission for Combating Counter-Revolution, Profiteering, and Corruption. The Economic Directorate in the early Soviet era posted its personnel across Soviet government agencies to monitor fraud, embezzlement, and other economic crimes. As early as 1923, a Soviet government resolution defined the Economic Department's mission as "fighting against economic counterrevolution, economic espionage, and other official and economic crimes." Apart from counterrevolution, this description continues to define the Fourth Service's activities today.[28] The books offer a detailed description of Soviet state security investigations into organized crime, industrial espionage, government corruption, narcotics trafficking, contraband, financial crimes, and crimes involving precious metals and minerals, both by domestic actors and foreigners.

During the Soviet era, people viewed as traitors were often accused of economic crimes. When a Soviet embassy learned of a defection, for example, it reflexively claimed that the defector had stolen or embezzled money and thus should be returned to face Soviet criminal charges. Vladislav Krasnov, in his 1985 book on Soviet defectors, noted that stealing money or property was the most common accusation Soviet authorities made when demanding the return of a defector. However, official Soviet court indictments against defectors included theft in only a small percentage of cases, indicating that the claim of an economic crime was usually only a superficial attempt to besmirch the defector's name and demand extradition.[29]

The FSB's task today is even more complex than the KGB's. During the Soviet era, most international financial transfers went through the Soviet central government bank, Vnesheconombank. With the dissolution of the Soviet Union, private businesses and a private banking system emerged, bringing a significant increase in Russia's integration into the global market. That created both economic opportunities and risks. The financial crisis of the 1990s, which was partially caused by the unregulated privatization of state-owned enterprises leading to the emergence of oligarchs in Russia, led to a more complex economic environment ripe for corruption.

The FSB occasionally cites foreign threats to Russia's economy, but most subjects of Fourth Service counterintelligence investigations are Russians. For example, the FSB has several times weighed in on the proposed privatization of government-owned corporations, not just by foreigners but by Russians as well. These actions likely had input from the Fourth Service. In 2002, the FSB publicly opposed the privatization of the national railroad network, claiming that such a move would put a strategically important sector at the mercy of shareholders. Press at the time called it an unprecedented interference of the state security organs in the national economic reform process.[30] The FSB also halted the privatization of the state-owned company Rosnano in 2018. The CEO of Rosnano, Anatoliy Chubais, had proposed publicly selling shares in the company in 2016. However, with influence from the FSB, a judge declared that proactive work by law enforcement agencies had prevented multiple cases of corruption that saved the country millions of rubles, and that the proposed share price would be significantly less than the company's market value.[31] In 2014, the Russian State Duma proposed legislation that would give the FSB the responsibility to check evaluation data for shares offered in the privatization of state-owned companies and to use operational measures to investigate prospective buyers.[32] The draft legislation would place the FSB in a position of determining who can and cannot buy shares in privatized companies, similar to what it did in the Rosnano privatization.

Ideological Counterintelligence

Suppressing dissent and domestic antiregime activities has been an essential element of Soviet internal security since the foundation of Soviet rule. Today, the FSB has a range of intelligence and law enforcement tools available to suppress internal dissent among Russian citizens, including:

- Tax laws
- Terrorism laws
- Laws against extremism/terrorism, organized crime, money laundering, and narcotics trafficking
- Laws that forbid inciting hatred or publicly insulting an authorized representative in connection with fulfilling his responsibilities

From the beginning of Putin's tenure as president, he has steadily increased internal security services' power to monitor dissent and prevent it from gaining strength inside Russia. Soldatov and Borogan cite an interview with UZKS's first director, Gennadiy Zotov, when the Second Service was established: "'Internal sedition' has always been more terrible for Russia than any military invasion."[33] Zotov joined the KGB in 1969 and spent part of his career in the Fifth Directorate. At the same time, UZKS often assumes nefarious foreign connections in the people it investigates.

Internal sedition can take many forms, from both left-wing and right-wing extremist groups, which the UZKS targeted early in the Putin regime, to any broader definition of political opposition. The Fifth Service's UBTPE became publicly visible in 2001 with the arrest of Eduard Limonov, a shock writer and founder of the National Bolshevik Party (NBP), an extreme political party that espoused elements of Bolshevism and National Socialism. He was arrested for weapons charges and attempting to overthrow the Russian government. Although the court dropped the latter more egregious charge, he still spent four years in prison. In the process, the UBTPE reportedly physically beat Limonov's supporters.[34] The UBTPE also operated against the Marxist movement, the "Vanguard of Red Youth," and other fringe right-wing and left-wing groups.

Not all FSB officers were so enthusiastic about pursuing extreme political groups, and some even sympathized with them. According to the Dossier Center, an FSB officer in Barnaul in the Altai Kray coerced an NBP member to cooperate with the FSB. But at the same time, the FSB officer admitted that he was a secret NBP supporter and offered to protect the party member. The party member reported the contact to the local prosecutor's office, and the FSB officer was demoted. In another case, the FSB deliberately provoked violence between right-wing skinheads and members of the NBP in the early 2000s, with FSB-hired thugs posing as NBP members attacking skinheads, leading to skinhead retaliation against the NBP, even though the attackers were not actual NBP members.[35]

The Russian investigative journalist Roman Anin asserted that the UBTPE's reputation is ambiguous: On one side, UBTPE officers risk their lives combating terrorist groups and hunting down neo-Nazis. But the same officers also engage in physical harm of dissidents.[36] The FSB's ten-year investigation of the political oppositionist Aleksey Navalny serves as an example of the type of operation in which UBTPE engages.

Navalny's case fell under Directorate K of the Economic Security Service for several years. However, when Directorate K lost interest in the case—because it did not offer opportunities to extort any money—the case was transferred to the UBTPE, which pursued it as an extremism investigation. According to Anin, more FSB effort has been expended on Navalny than is usually expended on the most dangerous terrorist. UBTPE likely handled the case in 2020, when Navalny was poisoned with the highly toxic chemical weapon Novichok but survived.

Protecting the Russian constitution, the mission of the Second Service's UZKS, predominantly means neutralizing opposition to the Putin regime. In 2010, UZKS chief Aleksey Zhalo reportedly initiated an investigation against Aleksandr Belov, a political activist in Russia who opposes Putin, accusing Belov of "organizing unrest against authority."[37] However, much of today's effort dates from Putin's 2012 reelection and the public opposition to his running again for president. The year 2012 was a watershed for Russia's response to internal dissent. The previous year, Putin announced he would run for president after one term as prime minister, in what some called a "castling" move.[38] Many Russians saw this as an unconstitutional usurpation of power since Putin had already served two terms as president from 2000 to 2008. Thousands demonstrated against his return to the presidency, chanting "For honest elections," although his reelection was a foregone conclusion.[39]

From December 2011 to May 2012, Russian police arrested hundreds of anti-Putin protesters. Putin's new term as president emboldened him to crack down on dissent, and the Russian security services have followed that political imperative since then. In June 2012, the Russian State Duma passed amendments allowing judges to treat a single-person protest as an unsanctioned assembly if they detect a "common intent and organization."[40] The 2012 protests were led by two prominent oppositionists, Boris Nemtsov and Aleksey Navalny, both of whom were subsequently targeted for assassination, Nemtsov successfully in 2015, and Navalny unsuccessfully in 2020. The assassination operations were likely organized by the UBTPE, with support from the Science and Technology Service.[41]

An example of the tactics that the Second Service uses to root out dissent was revealed in the case of the online chat group called the Club of Plant Lovers. The group was set up in 2017 by friends to discuss hobbies, university studies, and occasionally politics. After a few weeks, another member, Ruslan Danilov, joined the group and began to insert anti-Putin dialogue into the chat group. However, Danilov's rhetoric was not sincere; he was an FSB agent provocateur inserted to draw out antiregime sentiments from the other members. The operation transformed what began as a group of friends into what the FSB called an "extremist society." Seven members of the chat group were arrested, convicted, and sentenced to six or seven years in prison.[42]

Adjunct to pursuing dissidents is the mission to monitor nontraditional religious groups. UKZS appears to have resurrected the Soviet-era mission of monitoring religious groups in Russia that fell under the KGB's Fifth Directorate. However, unlike during the Soviet era, the Russian government distinguishes between approved, government-sponsored religious organizations and those it considers "extremist." Several categories of activity can earn a religious group the label "extremist": religious-based terrorism, especially emanating from the North Caucasus region; foreign, especially Western, connections; and religious competition with the state-sponsored Russian Orthodox Church. Religions that fall into any of those categories are subject to FSB scrutiny.

The FSB operates aggressively against certain religions that are considered "extremist." The journalist Kseniya Kirillova writes that the FSB actively works with and infiltrates agents into groups that have connections abroad, such as the Jehovah's Witnesses and Scientologists, both of which the Russian government has banned.[43] In July 2019, FSB officers raided a Jehovah's Witness service in Sevastopol, seizing so-called extremist literature. At the same time, the FSB identified a Jehovah's Witness congregation in northwest Moscow, which led to a massive, country-wide operation to capture Jehovah's Witnesses, arresting group leaders and congregants and charging them with belonging to an "extremist" organization.[44] The FSB also often announces arrests of Islamist extremists, usually claiming that the arrestees have ties to Central Asian and Middle Eastern states.[45] The FSB finds religious connections in unexpected places; some in the Russian government with FSB ties even blame religious sects in Ukraine for being behind the Euromaidan movement and threatening the Donbas region.[46] Conversely, the FSB pursues those who allegedly show disrespect for representatives of religions and their beliefs, likely focusing on opposition to the Russian Orthodox Church.[47]

Although the FSB's religious operations look different today than they did during the Soviet era, they continue in various forms.

Combating Terrorism

Several FSB services play a role in antiterrorism planning and counterterrorism operations inside the Russian Federation and extending beyond its borders. Since 2016, the FSB has shared this mission with the Rosgvardiya, which inherited quick reaction units from the MVD in 2016. Additionally, both the SVR and GRU have responsibilities for collecting intelligence about terrorism that threatens Russia, and GRU Spetsnaz forces conduct counterterrorism operations, creating overlap and competition between Russia's intelligence and security agencies.

Countering terrorism is the primary mission of Second Service. The Special Purpose Center (TsSN) is the core FSB counterterrorism element. TsSN's Alfa and Vympel groups are often on the front line of that battle, although their tactics have occasionally come into question. Alfa teams have handled multiple hostage incidents in the post-Soviet era. Alfa reportedly freed 347 passengers from a hijacked flight traveling from the city of Mineralnye Vody in southern Russia to Moscow in 1992, and in 1995 freed South Korean tourists whom a terrorist had taken captive in Moscow.

The unit was especially active in the North Caucasus during the Chechen wars, including storming a hospital in Budennovsk, Stavropol Kray, in 1995, where Chechen terrorists had taken over 1,000 hostages.[48] The Alfa response to the Budennovsk hostage crisis led to the deaths of over 200 people, including 130 hostages. Alfa later became famous for its participation in the Dubrovka Theater hostage crisis in Moscow in 2002 and the Beslan, North Ossetia, hostage crisis in 2004, both of which also resulted in the deaths of hostages. More recently, Alfa has participated in Russian military operations in Ukraine, particularly in clearing and detention operations. At least four Alfa officers were reported killed in Ukraine between February and August 2022.[49] From 1998 to 2008, Alfa also contained the FSB's only female special operations unit, which conducted antiterrorism inspections and tested the security of critical infrastructure facilities.[50]

Vympel's post-Soviet public missions have included conducting counterterrorist operations at strategic facilities and locations with a high risk of ecological damage, interdicting terrorist operations against Russian citizens abroad, and actions to defend the constitutional order of Russia. Like, Alfa, Vympel was also involved in the Dubrovka and Beslan hostage crises, for which Vympel personnel received military decorations, including the Hero of the Russian Federation Medal (see chapter 6).

Many of Vympel's counterterrorism missions have occurred in the North Caucasus, where it has targeted and "liquidated" numerous terrorists and separatist militants. Vympel has also renewed the KGB's mission of conducting assassinations outside Russia, particularly targeting Chechens. Putin reemphasized this FSB mission publicly in reaction to a June 2006 incident in which five Russian diplomats were killed or kidnapped in Baghdad. That event precipitated a Russian law on countering terrorism that gives the FSB authorization to conduct assassinations: "It is lawful to deprive the life of a person who commits a terrorist act and to cause harm to the health or property of such a person or other legally protected interests of the individual, society, or the state in suppression of a terrorist act or the implementation of other measures to combat terrorism by actions prescribed or permitted by Russian Federation legislation."[51]

FSB director Patrushev responded to Putin's emphasis: "We should work so that not a single terrorist who commits a crime will avoid responsibility," and that such missions "fit into the logic of what we do."[52] This represents a return to the historical purpose of Vympel—to conduct covert operations abroad.

A joint *Bellingcat–Der Spiegel* investigation determined that the assassins who organized the killing of the Chechen-Georgian militant Zelimkhan ("Tornike") Khangoshvili on August 23, 2019, in Berlin were trained and received direct support, including cover documentation, from former and current Vympel officers.[53] The German court that convicted Vadim Krasikov, Khangoshvili's alleged assassin, who was carrying a French passport in the name Vadim Sokolov, ruled in December 2021 that "state organs of the government of the Russian Federation took the decision to liquidate Tornike Khangoshvili in Berlin" and labeled the act "state terrorism."[54] Khangoshvili was just one in a series of Chechen-affiliated individuals targeted for assassination, numbering as many as twenty-one since 2004.[55] Another Chechen political activist and blogger, Mamikhan Umarov, was killed in Austria in 2020. In June 2022, a Russian went on trial in Germany for attempting to kill a Chechen oppositionist, Mokhmad Abdurakhmanov, in 2020, on orders from pro-Putin Chechen president Ramzan Kadyrov.[56] Several FSB-sponsored external assassinations of Chechens were reportedly done with support from Kadyrov's allies.

The Fourth Service also participates in antiterrorism activities. Occasionally, the Fourth Service's Directorate T, which covers the transportation sector, conducts exercises to test the thoroughness of police activities around transportation nodes, such as airports and train stations. The test might include leaving a package or a backpack unattended and then measuring how long it takes for police to notice it. If the police do not detect the fake bomb, the test may even lead to calls to fire and medical response teams and the evacuation of passengers.[57]

Combating Crime

The FSB's countercrime mission is often an offshoot from economic counterintelligence. The Russian government, particularly the FSB, uses the enforcement of financial crime laws as a lever to inhibit the activities of foreign powers and domestic opposition groups inside Russia. Russian national security leaders have expressed a suspicion similar to Soviet-era leaders that foreign powers are intent on destroying the Russian economy. The definition of counterintelligence as not just catching spies but also preventing anyone, foreign or domestic, from countering the regime's power extends into the economic realm.

These operations often fall to Fourth Service directorates. Directorate P's officers have been involved in several high-profile corruption investigations. For example, an investigation of employees in a Rostec-affiliated plant that manufactured MiG-29 aircraft discovered that from 2017 to 2019, the employees stole turbine blades, fuel lines, and other parts and sold them to undisclosed buyers. The thefts reportedly resulted in nearly 18 million rubles in damages.[58] Directorate P's officers may have also been involved in the arrest in 2020 of Ivan Safronov, a military journalist whom the director of Roskosmos, Dmitriy Rogozin, had hired as a special assistant. Safronov was charged with treason for passing what the FSB deemed to be state secrets to foreign associates, including a Czech journalist, Martin Latyš, and possibly to a political researcher in Germany, Demuri Voronin.[59] While there are many questions surrounding

Safronov's case, the involvement of the FSB is certain. Directorate P's officers also arrested another Rostec employee in April 2022 for threatening to derail a valuable contract for medical equipment unless the company paid him a bribe. The arrested individual, Aleksey Repkin, had previously worked for the FSB.[60]

Other cases demonstrate likely Directorate P tactics and targets. In December 2021, the Russian press reported that the FSB had warned a former employee of a defense firm in the Russian Udmurtia region against committing treason. According to FSB revelations, the employee planned to offer his services to an unspecified US government agency. The FSB approached the person and issued a warning but did not otherwise punish him. Although it is unclear what the person was planning to do or whether any US government agency was actually involved, it does indicate that the FSB detected something that officers perceived as threatening while monitoring his communications, part of what during the Soviet era were called "prophylactic" measures.[61] Directorate P may have also participated in a 2019 investigation into fraud by employees of a defense facility in the Lipetsk region who bought old, Soviet-era military equipment using money received from federal contracts, cleaned up the equipment, and resold it as new. A fellow employee called the case "sabotage and wrecking," language reminiscent of the Soviet era.[62]

The Fourth Service's Department K is the FSB's element for regulating the banking and finance sector, fulfilling a role similar to the US Securities and Exchange Commission. As such, it conducts economic counterintelligence investigations that frequently lead to criminal prosecutions. According to the Dossier Center, under Bortnikov's leadership since 2008, the Fourth Service also became one of the key players in hiding corrupt money, laundering it, and exfiltrating it out of the country.

Directorate K has gained a reputation for being the place to work if an FSB officer desires to get rich. Regulating the banking industry provides many opportunities to skim or extort money from the subjects of investigations. Because money laundering is common in Russian banks, Russian bank regulators can readily claim grounds for pressing their corrupt demands. Directorate K is where Kirill Cherkalin and two former Fourth Service colleagues worked when they were arrested in 2019. According to a source of the investigative journalist site *The Bell*, commercially minded FSB officers like Cherkalin rose to power in the early 2000s at the same time as Russia's money laundering business was booming. The source explained, "If you realize it's useless to fight something, you have to lead it." Department K came to lead the very criminal enterprises it was supposed to be investigating.[63]

Directorate K reportedly competes with Directorate M for that lucrative business.[64] Directorate K provides what in Russian is called "*крыша*" (top cover) to some corrupt bankers to protect them from prosecution while demanding a cut of the money they handle. A former FSB officer, Janosh Neumann (real name Aleksey Artamonov), was serving in Department K when he chose to defect from Russia. He describes Directorate K as the hub of money laundering in the Russian government.[65]

The Sixth Service of the FSB Internal Security Directorate (USB)—colloquially known as "Sechin's spetsnaz"—has also become prominent for using economic crime laws in interagency rivalries. The Sixth Service provides significant economic opportunities by protecting approved illicit activities and sharing the proceeds. According to the Dossier Center, the leaders of the Sixth Service enjoy personal access to Putin and Sechin, bypassing their FSB chain of command. In 2016, the FSB arrested Russian minister of the economy Alexei Ulyukayev and accused him of trying to extort $2 million from Sechin's Rosneft to approve its purchase of the state-owned oil company Bashneft. When Ulyukayev was arrested, the director of security for Rosneft was FSB general Oleg Feoktistov, a close confidant of Sechin's, who had recently transferred from a job as first deputy director of the USB. The case likely resulted from infighting between Sechin, an economic hard-liner, and Ulyukayev, an economic liberal. Sechin won the battle—Ulyukayev received an eight-year prison sentence in 2017.

The Sixth Service was connected to the arrests of several other high-ranking Russian government officials, including the governor of the Kirov Oblast, Nikita Beliy, and Vladivostok mayor Igor Pushkarev.[66] The Sixth Service's fingerprints were also on the 2014 arrest of General Denis Sugrubov, the chief of the MVD Anticorruption and Economic Crimes Directorate. According to the Dossier Center, Sugrubov's arrest resulted from an FSB operation led by Feoktistov to provoke MVD employees. A Dossier Center source who claimed direct involvement in the events stated that the operation against Sugrobov began because the general possessed compromising evidence about corruption by Sixth Service employees. The source claimed that the provocation was intended to recast the shadow onto the MVD rather than the FSB.[67] Sugrubov received a twenty-two-year prison sentence for abuse of office and creating a criminal group.[68]

Intelligence

The FSB has both human and technical intelligence and covert influence missions. These activities occur in three tiers: inside Russia, in former Soviet states, and further abroad.

HUMINT and Covert Operations

In 2002, Andrei Soldatov revealed that the FSB had a clandestine foreign intelligence capability in the former Soviet states, where the FSB maintains primacy among Russian intelligence and security services. The capability initially fell under the Directorate for Coordination of Operational Information, now called the Fifth Service's Operational Information Department (ORU).[69] The FSB initially established a foreign intelligence function during Putin's tenure as FSB director in 1998, and it was institutionalized in law in 2003.[70] Putin's urgency to strengthen FSB intelligence capabilities within the former Soviet states grew in the early 2000s, when pro-Moscow governments fell in three former Soviet states, in what came to be called "color revolutions": the 2003 Rose Revolution in Georgia, 2004 Orange Revolution in Ukraine, and 2005 Tulip Revolution in Kyrgyzstan. The Russian leadership viewed those events not as spontaneous manifestations of popular dissatisfaction with autocratic leaders but as foreign (American in particular) covert regime-change operations. That interpretation gave Russian leaders, Putin especially, the impression that the United States was out to get them. The creation of a foreign intelligence capability within the former Soviet states provides both a warning mechanism for threats to Russia and a platform from which to manipulate the governments in states surrounding Russia.

ORU is directly involved in source handling, and one of its most famous officers was lauded for collecting clear and accurate information about the political situation in the North Caucasus. In 2007, Alikhan Kalimatov, a native of Ingushetia, was awarded the Hero of the Russian

Federation Medal, albeit posthumously. He joined the FSB in 2000 after working in Ingush Republic politics during the 1990s. He ran sources within political circles in Ingushetia; however, he was killed in 2007 in an ambush while sitting in his car.[71]

The First Service's DKRO also reportedly conducts FSB-sponsored clandestine operations in the former Soviet space. According to Yuriy Shulipa, a Russian-Ukrainian legal analyst, DKRO employs specially trained action agents for what Shulipa calls "sharp chekist measures" (*"острые чекистские мероприятия"*; OChM), which include assassinations and kidnappings. DKRO conducts the planning and agent handling and works through the *rezident* from the FSB Fifth Service in the target country. The First Service's Directorate for Coordination of Analysis and Counterintelligence Activities (UKAKD) coordinates OChM missions across FSB directorates.[72]

Several incidents in Ukraine support Shulipa's analysis. On April 14, 2020, Ukrainian major general Valeriy Shaytanov was arrested for maintaining contact with the FSB. He was reportedly recruited by a DKRO officer and was a source of information for the FSB to support the assassinations of two Ukrainian intelligence officers, Maksim Shapoval and Aleksandr Kharaberyush. Kharaberyush was killed in March 2017, when a car bomb exploded in the Ukrainian city of Mariupol, and Shapoval died in a car bomb attack in Kyiv in June 2017. Shaytanov's reporting also supported an FSB-sponsored attempt on the life of Chechen militants Adam Osmayev and his wife Amina Akuyeva in 2017 in Ukraine; the Russian government accused Osmayev of planning to assassinate Putin.[73]

Other countries have also accused FSB officers of interfering in their internal affairs. In 2017, Moldovan officials accused the FSB of laundering $22.3 billion through the Moldovan financial system between 2011 and 2014.[74] The Estonian government connected the FSB to eleven individuals convicted of espionage in Estonia between 2012 and 2018.[75] Lithuanian police arrested an FSB-connected person in May 2015, claiming that the individual's tasking was to penetrate the ruling circles of the Lithuanian government and manipulate policy decisions.[76]

Historically, Soviet Border Guards also had missions that extended beyond border protection to collecting intelligence up to 12 kilometers across the border. Former Border Guard Service chief Andrey Nikolayev discussed the Border Guards' intelligence and counterintelligence mission in the 1990s, saying, "the border cannot be protected otherwise."[77] The mission of running agents and conducting other clandestine activities in the close-border region to identify smugglers—or, at times, to facilitate smuggling operations—and to obtain warning of potential terrorist actions likely continues. According to the Latvian State Security Service, Latvian nationals are useful to Russian intelligence services such as the FSB because they are relatively easy to recruit based on threats of criminal charges, and their arrest does not cause significant damage to Russia's intelligence interests in Latvia.[78]

Russian border guards have been involved in several controversial cross-border situations in the past decade. The Estonia-Russia border has been particularly tense.[79] On September 5, 2014, Russian officers crossed into Estonian territory and captured an Estonian officer, Eston Kohver, who was investigating Russian smugglers. The capture occurred just two days after US president Barack Obama visited Estonia. A Russian court convicted Kohver of espionage the next year, a charge the Estonian government vehemently denied. A few weeks after Kohver's capture, FSB maritime border guard vessels seized a Lithuanian fishing boat sailing in what Lithuania asserts were international waters off Russia's northern coast.[80] Then, in November 2018, Russian Border Guard forces fired upon and captured three Ukrainian naval ships, claiming they had entered Russian territorial waters in the Azov Sea. Ukraine denied that its vessels entered Russian territory and swapped them the following year for two individuals, including a Russian suspected of involvement in the 2014 shootdown of Malaysian Airlines Flight MH17 over Ukraine.[81]

Technical Operations

The FSB has nearly unfettered access to Russia's domestic communications environment through the System of Operational-Investigative Measures (SORM). According to Agentura.ru, the originator of SORM was FSB general colonel Andrey Bykov, who served as the chief of KGB's OTU and then deputy director of the FSB and its predecessors from 1992 to 1996.[82] SORM was initially implemented in 1995 and has been updated several times. SORM requires Russian voice and Internet communication providers to install devices on their networks that allow the FSB to track all electronic traffic. According to the 1995 law governing the

FSB, "Conducting counterintelligence measures restricting the rights of citizens to the secrecy of correspondence, telephone conversations, postal, telegraphic and other communications transmitted on electrical and telecommunications networks shall be permitted only on the grounds of a ruling by a judge and under the procedure provided for in Russian Federation legislation."[83] The laws available to the FSB to justify such "restrictions of civil rights" are numerous, and the close relationship between the FSB and the Russian judiciary removes obstacles from the FSB's path for obtaining such authorizations. Intercepting Russian citizens' communications is one of the areas for which FSB officials were granted expanded authority in 2007.[84]

Multiple investigative organizations inside Russia have access to SORM data: the FSB, including the Border Guard Service; Russia's Tax Police within the MVD; the Federal Protective Service and its sub-elements; the Kremlin Regiment and the Presidential Security Service; and parliamentary security services. The FSB also offers communications-monitoring capabilities to former Soviet states, which often use Russia-based communications lines.

As Internet technology has advanced, SORM's rules have adapted. A 2016 law, called the Yarovaya law, named for State Duma sponsor Irina Yarovaya, requires Internet providers, social media, and messaging services to store user data for three years and to grant authorities access to encrypted communications. Rights activists call it Russia's "big brother law."[85] Data storage requirements needed to satisfy the law are immense, and companies are required to cover the cost themselves. The volume of storage required to maintain the resulting data has forced the delay of the law's implementation.[86] Storage requirements increased further during the COVID-19 pandemic in 2020, when all smartphones sold in Russia were required to preinstall Russian-made, government-approved applications that include search, the Global Positioning System, social networking, personal digital assistants, and public service and payment apps.

The FSB's foreign collection operations extend beyond the Russian Federation in the form of computer-network threat actors, including one known in the West as Venomous Bear, aka Turla, which is affiliated with the FSB's Center 16.[87] Turla has been traced to numerous foreign computer intrusion operations, often directed against government and military targets. The first recorded operation involved the malware Agent.btz, which infected US Department of Defense computers in 2008.[88] Turla-related malware was also connected to intrusions into the Swiss defense firm RUAG between 2014 and 2016 and targeted a Swiss defense company again in 2017.[89] Other attacks have targeted foreign ministries and ministries of defense in various other countries. The US Department of Justice's (DOJ) announcement regarding the disabling of "Snake" malware attributed the long-running operation to Turla.[90]

In the 2000s, Center 16 has engaged heavily in computer-based collection. In August 2021, a US federal grand jury indicted three Center 16 officers for computer fraud and abuse, wire fraud, aggravated identity theft, and causing damage to the property of an energy facility. The indictment alleges that, between 2012 and 2017, the officers, working in a hacking group known variously in the West as "Dragonfly," "Berzerk Bear," "Energetic Bear," and "Crouching Yeti," broke into computer networks of companies and organizations in the global oil and gas firms, utility and electrical grid companies, nuclear power plants, renewable energy companies, consulting and engineering groups, and advanced technology firms, specifically targeting supervisory control and data acquisition (SCADA) systems.[91] According to the US and UK governments, Center 16 has conducted similar operations against critical information technology systems and infrastructure in Europe, the Americas, and Asia (figure 3.1).[92]

In 2017, the US DOJ indicted two FSB TsIB officers and two Russian hackers for stealing information about at least 500 million Yahoo email accounts in 2014, giving them access to the accounts of Russian journalists, US and Russian government officials, and private-sector employees of financial, transportation, and other companies. One of the indicted TsIB officers was Dmitriy Dokuchayev, who was later arrested in connection with the Sergey Mikhailov case (see above). According to the DOJ indictment, the FSB officers "protected, directed, facilitated and paid criminal hackers."[93] One of the hackers, Aleksey Belan, had been the subject of US criminal indictments since 2012 and was named one of the FBI's Cyber Most Wanted criminals in November 2013. Nevertheless, TsIB officers continued to use him for operational purposes after that designation. TsIB reportedly also targets Ukrainian political, law enforcement, and military entities.[94]

Figure 3.1 FBI "wanted" poster for indicted Center 16 officers

Source: Federal Bureau of Investigation.

Border Protection

The Border Guard Service (PS) is both a military and a law enforcement organization that enforces the Russian Federation's laws regarding border crossing and immigration. Its personnel have military status and conduct military, intelligence, counterintelligence, and operational-investigative missions related to Russia's borders. PS facilities are spread along Russia's 60,000-kilometer border, of which over 20,000 is on land. PS has

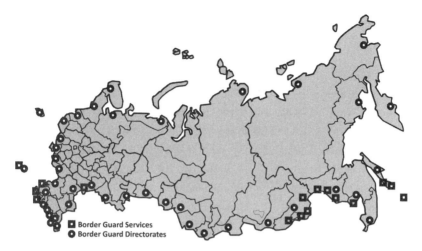

Figure 3.2 FSB Border Guard locations
Source: "FSB," Dossier Center.

forty-two border directorates that cover routine border protection duties, and sixteen Border Services located in areas of particular border scrutiny, particularly in the North Caucasus region, Crimea, and along the border with China. In May 2020, the chief of PS, Vladimir Kulishov, who also is a first deputy FSB director, claimed that 6,000 illegal immigrants attempted to enter Russia each day, most from Southeast Asia, Central Asia, the Middle East, Ukraine, and Moldova.[95] The veracity of this statement cannot be confirmed (figure 3.2).

The PS Border Control Department (DPK) staffs passport control positions at Russia's borders. According to General Lieutenant Rafael Daerbayev, first deputy chief of the DPK, over 77 million people entered through Russian border control points in 2018, most of whom were Russian citizens. Border guard offices detained over 65,000 for insufficient documents and denied about 38,000 people entry into the country. The FSB arrested nearly 1,000 people for illegally entering the country in 2018, a minor increase from the previous year.[96]

Safeguarding Information Security

The FSB's counterintelligence role includes protecting Russia's government and private-sector computer networks from foreign penetration.

That consists of both cryptology missions and computer intrusion detection and mitigation. TsIB's declared mission is to combat computer-based crimes and illegal hacking activity. In January 2013, Putin instructed the FSB to create a system for detecting, preventing, and eliminating the consequences of computer attacks on information technology resources inside Russia and in Russian diplomatic missions and consular offices abroad. TsIB runs that system, which is known by its Russian acronym GosSOPKA (State System for Detecting, Warning, and Liquidating the Consequences of Computer Attacks—*Государственная система обнаружения, предупреждения и ликвидации последствий компьютерных атак*). The Russian government integrated GosSOPKA into the broader Russian policy for protecting the critical information infrastructure in 2017.[97]

TsIB officials are heavily involved in interagency and civil Internet security policymaking bodies. The former TsIB chief, Andrey Gerasimov, reportedly sat on several policy boards, including the supervisory board of the League for a Safe Internet, a Russian body created by Putin-allied businessman Konstantin Malofeyev that claims to prevent the spread of dangerous information over the web. Gerasimov also sat on the executive committee of the Association of Documentary Telecommunications, which bills itself as a catalyst for achieving the needs of citizens, businesses, and state authorities in information communication technologies and information security technologies. Until his arrest, TsIB officer Sergey Mikhailov was a member of the information security group of the Russian Association of Electronic Communications, and TsIB officers serve as adjunct professors in information security academic programs in Russian universities.[98]

The Eighth Center is involved in developing information assurance technologies and cryptographic systems and in proposing information assurance policies. For example, in 2017, the FSB proposed legislation on protecting critical infrastructure elements from information attacks. FSB spokespersons have often given grand statistics about the number of cyberattacks directed against the Russian government's Internet sites, simultaneously proclaiming that the FSB's defenses are successfully protecting against them. In 2004, then–FSB director Nikolay Patrushev claimed that Russian government Internet sites experienced over 730,000 attacks during 2003, 100,000 of which were directed at the Russian president's website. He added, however, that the FSB's defenses successfully neutralized all the attacks.[99] In June 2006, Eighth Service director Viktor Gorbachev declared that hackers, particularly Americans and Chinese, were continually trying to penetrate Russian government websites. He claimed, however, that the security resources that the FSB had participated in creating repulsed every attack.[100] In January 2017, Eighth Center spokesperson Nikolay Murashov announced that Russia's information infrastructure had absorbed about 70 million computer attacks in a year, the majority of which came from abroad. He said critical infrastructure objects like the national rail service and Gazprom are well equipped to defend against the attacks; however, he admitted that many smaller organizations are not prepared.[101]

Analysis and Data Processing

Although the KGB did not embrace analysis, the FSB appears to have done so. The Fifth Service has a strategic analytic mission to provide analytic support directly to Putin, likely via the Security Council, the secretary of which is former FSB director Nikolay Patrushev. Fifth Service analysis is not usually publicly visible, although it gained notoriety in 2022 for supplying Putin with erroneous information about the prospects for a quick victory in a Russian invasion of Ukraine. Fifth Service chief Sergey Beseda and his deputy were reportedly placed on house arrest, although the Russian government denied the report.[102] At the same time, Ukrainian government officials reported that "about eight" Russian generals were fired for providing faulty intelligence.[103] Although not specified in the media reporting, the erroneous assessment probably came from Fifth Service's Information-Analysis Directorate.

In addition to the Fifth Service's strategic analysis, other FSB services have organic analytic elements that support service-specific operations. The First Service, for example, has the Directorate for Coordination of Analysis and Counterintelligence Activities (UKAKD), and the Second Service has the Organizational-Operational Directorate. The PS's Border Protection Department and Coast Guard Department each have an Analysis and Coordination Department. The NTS has the Organizational

Analysis Directorate. These elements likely provide direct investigative, targeting, and operational support.

As noted in its name, UKAKD is also responsible for analyzing foreign intelligence activities. In March 2012, the Russian TV channel NTV ran a documentary titled *The Anatomy of a Protest*, which asserted that unspecified foreign intelligence services sponsored anti-Putin protests in Russia in late 2011. Aleksey Navalny, a prominent organizer of the demonstrations, requested that the Russian government comment directly on the allegations in the documentary. After a ten-month investigation, the FSB responded that there was no evidence that the protests had received foreign funding. The FSB organizations specifically cited as being involved in arriving at that conclusion were DKRO, TsIB, and UKAKD.[104]

UKAKD may also be involved in labeling Russian citizens "foreign agents," according to a BBC report. In June 2021, the FSB published a draft order that identified sixty-one types of military and military-technical information that, if a Russian citizen were to seek to obtain them, would land them on a list of foreign agents.[105] The FSB published the order for public comment. However, according to the BBC's Telegram channel, the public's ability to access and comment on the draft order was severely limited. UKAKD was the point of contact for an independent anticorruption review of the document.[106]

The First Service's UIOORD has a data management role that supports analytic efforts. A court case in 2021 demonstrated an instance of the UIOORD connection to a decision to bar a person from entering Russia. In November 2021, Yelena Vidmanova, a resident of the unrecognized Donetsk People's Republic, was turned away at the border of Russia. When she approached the border, her data were transmitted to UIOORD. She took UIOORD to court, complaining that she had received no information about the reason for being refused. The court hearing concluded that UIOORD does not have the authority to make immigration decisions but is only a record-keeping entity that is consulted when questions arise. Thus, the court denied the plaintiff's complaint.[107]

A job announcement for an analyst working in the Radio Counterintelligence Directorate (Directorate R) posted on a Russian online job site in 2004 provided a partial indication of the unit's analytic responsibilities. The job announcement sought candidates with these skills:

- Collection, processing, and systematization of large volumes of information (including in foreign languages), and work with databases;
- Work with geographic information systems (based on MapInfo);
- Preparation of analytical reports for management and interested departments;
- Making proposals to the management of the department for optimizing work processes and upgrading software;
- English-Russian and Japanese-Russian translation of technical literature and instructions for electronic devices; and
- Performance of operational tasks on business travel within Russia and abroad (two weeks to six months).[108]

Science and Technology Development

Several FSB elements, especially in the NTS, conduct science and technology development to support the FSB's operational missions. The NTS's Tenth Center, for example, has functions that include:

- Development and production of transportation security technologies, including technical systems, detection systems, and intelligent video surveillance;
- Development of radiation control devices and gas analytical and chemical devices; and
- Development of hardware and software detection devices and algorithms for detecting dangerous situations.

The Tenth Center also tests electronic devices and software that enters the supply chain for military and civilian uses in Russia. It is probably the element mentioned in 2018 by the US National Counterintelligence and Security Center that was responsible for an increased demand for source code reviews for foreign technology being sold in Russia.[109]

The Eleventh Center's two scientific research institutes are devoted wholly to developing technologies for the FSB. NII-1 researches technologies related to FSB counterintelligence, counterterrorism, and border control missions. In the early 2000s, NII-1 collaborated on a project for the Border Guard Service to develop an automated reader for passports and visas.[110] In 2012, the federally funded Biysk Institute for Problems of Chemical-Energy Technologies in the Altai Kray, part of the Siberian Branch of the Russian Academy of Sciences, received a two-year, 29-million-ruble contract from NII-1 to develop methods for "remote detection of traces of nitrogen-containing explosives on clothing and human skin, the surface of hand luggage and luggage in conditions of heavy passenger traffic." In 2018, a junior scientist at the Biysk Institute defended her dissertation on the same topic, and an FSB officer affiliated with NII-1 was on her defense committee.[111]

NII-2 began at least as early as 2011 to contract with Russian scientific research organizations to develop chemical substances. In September 2011, the FSB contracted with the Biysk Institute for unspecified "chemical products not included in other groups." In 2013, NII-2 opened another two-year contract for research and experimental developments in the field of chemical sciences. The last contract with the Biysk Institute ended in 2016, and was to produce proprietary medical chemicals under the code name "Tourist-14."[112] NII-2 became prominent in 2020 and 2021, when the investigative journalism publications *The Insider* and *Bellingcat* revealed that the institute had cooperated with the FSB Second Service in supplying poisons used against the Russian oppositionists Aleksey Navalny and Vladimir Kara-Murza, along with several other Russian oppositionists and human rights activists between 2014 and 2020.[113] NII-2 was also suspected of being the source of polonium-210 used to assassinate Aleksandr Litvinenko in 2006.[114] In these cases, NII-2 operated similarly to several Cold War cases of poisonings, such as of Nikolay Khokhlov, who was poisoned using radioactive thallium in 1957.[115]

TsIB also develops new tools for operating in the computer-based domain. A 2020 BBC report claims that the FSB ordered the creation of a malware application called "Fronton" that is capable of exploiting "smart" devices and penetrating the Internet of Things. The BBC cited reporting from a leak by the hacker group Digital Revolution, which claims to have penetrated the company creating it. Digital Revolution reported that TsIB, using its designation "Military Unit 64829," contracted with a Russian company, InformInvestGroup, to develop software that could turn smart devices into "zombies" under the control of a remote actor. These zombies could then be marshaled together to conduct massive denial-of-service attacks. The leaked documents specify that the software should not contain any notations in the Russian language or the Cyrillic alphabet to hide the FSB's sponsorship.[116]

Conclusion

The FSB's wide range of functions makes it self-sufficient in identifying, investigating, and neutralizing threats to the Russian regime, whether from foreign countries, oppositionists inside Russia, or rival Russian government agencies. Its elements perform the whole operational cycle, developing collection tools, applying them, analyzing the results, and executing operations based on them. No other Russian organization compares with the FSB in power and scope of activities.

Notes

1. See, e.g., Hoffman and Pincus, "American Accused"; "US Embassy Diplomat Caught"; Ustinova, "Russia Detains Romanian"; Weir, "Russia Arrests US Diplomat"; Neuman, "American Paul Whelan"; "Russia: FSB Detains Ukrainian Diplomat"; Ostroukh and Sytas, "Estonia Decries Detention."
2. US Department of State, "Department of State Actions"; Mendez and Mendez, *Moscow Rules*.
3. US Department of State, "Moscow"; Richelson, *Sword*, 28.
4. Worthington, "Worthington's Top Secret Story."
5. Kovacevic, "How KGB Spied."
6. "FSB Against CBS News"; Knobel, "Putin's Spies."
7. Klimenko, *Notes*.
8. "FSB Has Uncovered an Underground Network."
9. "Conference of the FSB Collegium." Also see Riehle, *Russian Intelligence*, 86–88.
10. "Putin Began Purges."
11. "MID under the FSB's Hood."
12. Cumming-Bruce and Troianovski, "Russian Diplomat Resigns."
13. Russian Federation, Ministry of Sport, Order 84; "FSB Department of Counterintelligence Operations."
14. Russian Federation, Ministry of Energy, Order 22.
15. "Minister of Regional Development Slyunyaev Leads 'Olympstroy' Supervisory Committee."
16. "Security During the Olympics"; "FSB Reported on the Level of Security."
17. "'Kaspersky Laboratory.'"
18. Eckel, "In Moscow Treason Trial"; US Department of Justice, "Russian Cyber-Criminal Sentenced."
19. "Ex-FSB Officer and 'Kaspersky Laboratory' Manager Convicted."
20. "'Shaltai-Boltai' and Colonel Mikhailov."
21. Putin, "Being Strong."

22. "Military Counterintelligence Department."
23. Arshanskiy, "An Army Without Intelligence," 10.
24. "Idea of US Threat to Russia"; "US Fails to Persuade Russia."
25. "Those Convicted in Russia."
26. "List of Russians Convicted."
27. Deriabin and Gibney, *Secret World*, 63.
28. Stavitskiy, *Lubyanka*, vol. 1, 21.
29. Krasnov, *Soviet Defectors*, 88.
30. "Unprecedented Instance."
31. "Putin Stopped the Privatization."
32. "FSB Will Check Participants."
33. Soldatov and Borogan, *New Nobility*, 56—citing Sokut, "Defense of Identity."
34. Genzlinger, "Eduard Limonov."
35. "Service for Defense of the Constitutional Order."
36. Anin, "Who Arranged the Hunt?"
37. FSB, *Belov List*."
38. Jahn, "Castling of Presidential Functions."
39. Vinogradov, "'For Honest Elections' Movement."
40. Gabowitsch, *Protest*, 11.
41. Barry and Schwirtz, "Arrests."
42. Higgins, "Chat Group."
43. Kirillova, "'For Faith.'"
44. "FSB Officers Revealed"; "FSB Conducted a Massive Special Operation.'"
45. See, e.g., "FSB Rendered Harmless a Group"; "FSB Stopped the Activities of Religious Extremists," *Izvestia*; "FSB Stopped the Activities of Religious Extremists," News.ru.
46. "Political Significance"; Kirillova, "'For Faith.'"
47. Gerts, "FSB Detains a Sevastopol Resident."
48. "Guys from Alfa."
49. Ivshina, "Cargo 200"; Litvrinm, Twitter post; Donetsk DNR News, "Eternal Glory"; "Senior Officer of the FSB Center for Special Operations Liquidated."
50. Afonskiy, "Where a Man Doesn't Go."
51. Russian Federation, Federal Law 35-FZ.
52. "Patrushev: Special Services."
53. "'V' For 'Vympel.'"
54. Escritt, "German Court."
55. Soldatov and Borogan, *New Nobility*, 200–208.
56. "Russian Accused."
57. "Economic Security Service."
58. Balashov, "Criminal Group."
59. "Military Journalist"; "German in the Safronov Case."
60. Trifonov, "Medical Equipment."
61. "'Warned Against State Treason.'"
62. Baranets, "Why Did the FSB Descend Upon Defense Factories?"
63. "Rise and Fall of an FSB-Run Money-Laundering Empire."
64. "Economic Security Service."
65. Hammond, "Becoming a Russian Intelligence Officer."

66. Kudryavtseva and Mikhailov, "Sechin's Spetsnaz"; "Russian Ex-Minister Ulyukayev Gets Eight Years"; Nikolskaya and Korsunskaya, "Russian Ex-Minister Ulyukayev Jailed."
67. "Internal Affairs Directorate."
68. "Russia's Former Anticorruption Police Chief Sentenced."
69. Soldatov, "How Many Intelligence Services Do We Have?"
70. Russian Federation, Federal Law 86-FZ.
71. "Kalimatov Alikhan Maksharipovich."
72. Shulipa, *How Putin Kills*, 172–74.
73. "Ambush Wounds 'Anti-Putin Plotter.'"
74. Williams, "Moldova Sees Russian Plot."
75. Juurvee and Perling, *Russia's Espionage*.
76. "Spy from the Russian FSB Detained."
77. Yegorov and Bulavinov, "Andrey Nikolayev."
78. Latvian State Security Service, *Annual Report*.
79. Chapple and Alliksaar, "Some Shall Pass."
80. Higgins, "Tensions Surge"; Feldschreiber, "Russia Convicts Estonian Border Guard."
81. Osborn and Polityuk, "Russia Fires on and Seizes Ukrainian Ships"; Lapin et al., "Film Director."
82. "FSB Center 12."
83. Russian Federation, Federal Law 86-FZ.
84. Russian Federation, Order 465.
85. "Russia's 'Big Brother' Law."
86. Goode, "Russia and Digital Surveillance."
87. Osborne, "Russian APT Turla."
88. Barnes, "Pentagon Computer Networks Attacked."
89. Chirgwin, "Swiss CERT Publishes Reveals Details"; "Swiss Defence Ministry Foils Cyberattack."
90. US Department of Justice, "Justice Department Announces Court-Authorized Disruption."
91. US Department of Justice, "Four Russian Government Employees Charged."
92. US Cybersecurity and Infrastructure Security Agency, "Russian State-Sponsored and Criminal Cyber Threats."
93. US Department of Justice, "US Charges Russian FSB Officers."
94. Crowdstrike, *2019 Global Threat Report*, 36.
95. Shashkov, "Chief of the Border Guard Service."
96. "FSB Border Guard Service."
97. Russian Federation, Federal Law 187-FZ.
98. "Internet Got a New Guardian."
99. "Chekists Repulsed about 100 Thousand Attacks."
100. "Hackers Try to Break into Ministry's Sites."
101. "FSB Reports of 70 Million Cyberattacks."
102. Soldatov and Borogan, "Putin Began Purges."
103. Pleasance, "Russia Has Fired 'About Eight' Generals."
104. Makutina, "FSB Did Not Find 'State Department Cookies.'"
105. Pushkarskaya, "'Even the Cook.'"

106. BBC News Russian Service Telegram Channel.
107. Meshchanskiy Regional Court.
108. "Analyst with Knowledge."
109. US National Counterintelligence and Security Center, *Foreign Economic Espionage*, 14.
110. Zhukov and Kuteynikov, "Automation.""
111. "'Services to Society as a Whole.'" The dissertation is by Kuzovnikova, "Development."
112. "'Services to Society as a Whole.'"
113. "Laboratory"; "Journalist, Activist, and 'Patriot'"; "Countersanctions"; "Russian Poet Dmitry Bykov Targeted."
114. Barabanov and Voronov, "Who Killed Litvinenko and Why."
115. Reevell, "Before Navalny."
116. Soshnikov, "'Turn Off the Internet.'"

4
Leaders

According to the FSB's establishing statute, "The activity of federal security service organs shall be directed by the President of the Russian Federation." Thus, the president is the primary decision-maker for Russia's state security, with authority delegated to subordinate leaders.[1]

The FSB leadership that receives this delegation consists of a director, two first deputy directors, and two deputy directors. The FSB director answers to the president and is a member of the Security Council, giving the FSB both influence on Vladimir Putin's perceptions and direct guidance from him about how to mitigate threats. One of the first deputies is also the chief of the Border Guard Service, while one of the deputies leads the National Counterterrorism Center.

The current FSB leadership structure has been in place since 2004, when it was changed significantly by a presidential directive that streamlined the FSB and reduced the number of director-level positions.[2] Before 2004, the FSB leadership consisted of a director, three first deputy directors, a state secretary, a deputy director over the Inspection Directorate, and six deputy directors over major departments, totaling eleven director-level officials.

The 2004 presidential directive reduced the number and elevated the FSB director to ministerial status, also granting the first deputy directors and deputy directors status equivalent to first deputy ministers and deputy ministers. This returns the FSB to a position of ministry within the

Russian government. State security has held ministerial status through most of the Soviet and post-Soviet eras. Feliks Dzerzhinskiy, the first Bolshevik state security director, was initially a close adviser to Lenin, and thus held practically ministerial status, although he did not receive the formal title "people's commissar" (the Bolshevik equivalent to a government minister) until 1923. After the dissolution of the VChK in 1922, the State Political Directorate (GPU) that replaced it was reduced bureaucratically and subordinated to the People's Commissariat of Internal Affairs (NKVD). However, in 1923, when the Union of Soviet Socialist Republics was created, the GPU was renamed the Unified State Political Directorate (OGPU) and raised to a status equivalent to a ministry. The OGPU was demoted bureaucratically again in 1934 and made the Main Directorate of State Security (GUGB) within the NKVD. State security was raised to "people's commissariat" status in 1943, and then changed its name from "people's commissariat" to "ministry" in 1946, along with all Soviet ministries. State security briefly merged with the MVD in March 1953 in the wake of Stalin's death. However, in May 1954, state security was split from the MVD and again reduced bureaucratically to a state committee, becoming the KGB, the name by which it was known for the rest of the Soviet era.

Initially, the KGB director was subordinate to the Council of Ministers, without ministerial status; however, KGB director Andropov became a full member of the Politburo of the Soviet Communist Party in 1973 and was promoted to ministerial status in 1978. The KGB director remained a minister up to the disestablishment of the KGB in 1991. Yeltsin ordered in December 1991 that the MVD and state security organs be merged into the Ministry of Security and Internal Affairs, returning to the construct that had existed several times during the Soviet era. However, the early post-Soviet environment had changed, and the Russian Constitutional Court ruled the merger unconstitutional. State security and internal security each became separate ministries in 1992. That lasted until 1994, when former KGB elements split further into border guards, signals intelligence, and counterintelligence, none of which had ministerial status. The 2004 reorganization returned the FSB director to ministerial status once again.

This fluctuation between parity with and subordination to the MVD created a rivalry between the two functions that remains today. State security officers view themselves as superior in education and training to the MVD police, and the MVD views state security officers as placing themselves above the law. Yeltsin's choice of MVD officers Vadim Bakatin and Sergey Stepashin to run state security organs in early post-Soviet Russia aggravated that rivalry. But a state security officer returned to the helm in 1995, and all directors since have had a KGB background.

Despite the passage of over thirty years since the dissolution of the Soviet Union and the disestablishment of the KGB, most senior-level leaders began their careers in the KGB. This means that many were born in the 1950s, placing them now in their sixties or seventies. Their careers often date to the 1970s, as Putin's did, or the early 1980s. For them, the ascension of Andropov to the Politburo while still the sitting KGB director and then to the position of general secretary of the Communist Party of the Soviet Union was a proud moment when a state security officer—a chekist—was ruling the country. Even though Andropov did not begin his career as a chekist, seventeen years at the helm of the KGB granted him the privilege of that label.

The Current FSB Director

At the time of writing, the FSB director is Aleksandr Vasilyevich Bortnikov, who was born in 1951. Putin named Bortnikov FSB director in 2008, and he is the longest-serving officer in that position. Bortnikov is a firm believer in the value of the chekist spirit, and he presented his chekist perspective in an interview to commemorate the 100th anniversary of the VChK in 2017. When asked whether it bothered him that FSB officers in Russia were often called "chekists," Bortnikov answered, "It doesn't bother me at all. . . . The history, experience, and traditions that are reflected in the name are not limited only to the period of the Cheka's existence or, as you said, 'the punishing sword of the revolution.' It is much wider. And denying the word 'chekist' is like consigning generations of our predecessors to oblivion.[3]"

Bortnikov began his career in 1975, assigned as a counterintelligence officer in Leningrad, where he was a direct colleague of Putin. He likely later benefited from Putin's position as deputy mayor of Leningrad / Saint Petersburg, ending his time there as FSB chief of the Leningrad Oblast. He moved to Moscow in 2004 to lead the Fourth Service. Since then,

Bortnikov has gained a reputation for being a Russian hard-liner. After the February 21, 2022, Russian State Duma vote recognizing the independence of the Luhansk and Donetsk "people's republic," Bortnikov stated three days before Russian troops invaded Ukraine:

> For several years now, the Lugansk and Donetsk People's Republics and the citizens of those republics have been watching with hope and asking the Russian Federation to protect them in their hope to work, raise their children, and live in peace. I am absolutely convinced that it is necessary to realize their right and protect them. I am convinced that the adoption of a decision on the recognition of these republics will precisely contribute to this. We will realize this hope unambiguously.[4]

Since Russia's invasion of Ukraine, Bortnikov has claimed that the FSB has caught various groups of so-called Ukrainian neo-Nazi terrorists on Russian territory, claiming that the FSB has captured explosives, weapons, and planners of terrorist acts.[5] Allegations of Ukrainian terrorism ramped up considerably after Russia's invasion began, with FSB leaders calling for "modern forms and methods of prophylactic work," or in other words, giving the FSB greater authorities.[6]

Past Directors

Bortnikov is the seventh and by far the longest-serving FSB director. His predecessors came from various backgrounds, with the earlier directors chosen for their connections to Boris Yeltsin and the later directors for their loyalty to Vladimir Putin.

General Lieutenant Sergei Vadimovich Stepashin was appointed director of the FSK in 1994, just two months after that organization was established. He was serving in that position when the organization was renamed the FSB in April 1995. His career had been in the MVD, not the KGB. Stepashin was an associate of Yeltsin, and he led the State Commission to Investigate the Activities of the Committee for State Security and the State Committee for the State of Emergency, which was responsible for investigating the August 1991 coup. He resigned less than two weeks after the Budenovsk hostage crisis and after less than four months as FSB director.

General of the Army Mikhail Ivanovich Barsukov replaced Stepashin in July 1995. He had spent his career in Kremlin security, reaching the position of deputy commandant of the Kremlin during the Soviet era and then as commandant after the August 1991 coup attempt. In 1992, he was appointed director of the Main Directorate of Security (GUO), the successor to the KGB's Ninth Directorate, which was responsible for senior leader security—the GUO later was subsumed into the Federal Protective Service (FSO). In that position, Barsukov led Yeltsin's personal security service. According to Agentura.ru, Barsukov came to the position of FSB director with a plan, approved by Yeltsin, to resurrect an organization that contained all the powers of the former KGB, although that plan did not materialize under Barsukov. He did, however, make changes to the organization, including bringing the Alfa special operations unit back to the FSB from the MVD. Barsukov was removed under a cloud in June 1996 after less than a year as FSB director in response to the so-called Xerox affair, in which election officials were caught leaving the White House in Moscow carrying a box filled with money that was supposed to support Yeltsin's 1996 presidential campaign.[7]

Barsukov was replaced in June 1996 by General Nikolay Dmitryevich Kovalev, who was born in 1949 and served in the KGB from 1974. He reportedly worked in the Fifth Service of the Moscow regional KGB office, which was the regional affiliate of the Fifth Directorate responsible for ideological counterintelligence. He deployed to Afghanistan for counterintelligence and security duties from 1987 to 1989, when he also conducted negotiations with Afghan mujaheddin. He worked in the Moscow region until 1994, finishing there as the deputy director of the regional FSK office. He was named deputy director of the FSK in 1994. He is famous for his claim that the FSB uncovered and surveilled nearly four hundred foreign intelligence officers in Russia in 1995 and 1996 and that Soviet/Russian state security organizations had not arrested so many spies since the time of World War II, when Germany sent agents into the Soviet Union.[8]

Kovalev was the FSB director during several key moments in Russian security history. The Russia-Chechnya Peace Treaty was signed during his tenure in May 1997, temporarily ending hostilities in Chechnya and leading to the removal of federal forces, including most FSB personnel, from the republic.[9] Kovalev participated in resolving a hostage situation in Moscow in December 1997, in which a Swedish diplomat and his wife were taken captive and held for ransom. One FSB officer, Anatoliy Savelev, was posthumously awarded the Hero of the Russian Federation Medal for his service during the crisis by allowing himself to be exchanged for the Swedish diplomat. He then reportedly died of a heart attack, although rumors circulated in the Russian press that sniper bullets intended for the kidnappers hit Savalev and killed him.[10] The case raised more controversy when the mother of the claimed terrorist wrote an open letter to a Russian newspaper describing FSB investigators' mishandling of the case.[11]

Kovalev was replaced by an unusual choice of an FSB director: former KGB lieutenant colonel Vladimir Vladimirovich Putin. Putin was born in 1952 and joined the KGB in 1975, serving his first decade in the Second Chief Directorate in Leningrad and then moving to the First Chief Directorate and to an assignment in Dresden, East Germany, where he was working when the Berlin Wall fell in October 1989. He left the KGB in 1990 to join Anatoliy Sobchak in the office of the mayor of Leningrad, later Saint Petersburg, eventually becoming Sobchak's deputy.

Hill and Gaddy assess that the chaotic 1990s in Russia, and in particular the government crisis of October 1993, during which Yeltsin ordered tanks to fire on the parliament building, profoundly affected Putin.[12] Russia's defeat at the hands of Chechen forces in 1996 also left a mark on Putin, as did bilateral treaties that the Yeltsin administration signed with individual regions of the Russian Federation intending to prevent Russia from splitting into multiple pieces as the Soviet Union had.[13] Before his appointment as FSB director, Putin had served as Yeltsin's point man for relations with Russia's regions, giving him a front-row seat on the deteriorating center–periphery relationship with the regions. In that position, Putin came to Yeltsin's attention for his political abilities and loyalty to Yeltsin. While previous FSB directors had become enmeshed in politics, none before Putin was more involved in the president's inner planning. That was to remain after Putin became president himself and vaulted the FSB into political prominence.

Yeltsin made a surprise announcement in July 1998 that he was removing Kovalev and replacing him with Putin, who was forty-five years old. Putin immediately announced that he planned to strengthen the FSB. Prime Minister Sergey Kiriyenko stated that Putin's primary task would be to concentrate on domestic economic espionage and illegal capital flight.[14] Putin tried to downplay his relative lack of rank by saying that he and Kovalev had both entered the KGB as junior operational officers at about the same time, Kovalev in Moscow and Putin in Leningrad.[15] He did not mention that he was the first—and still the only—FSB director to have never reached the rank of general. In November 1998, Yeltsin appointed Putin as a permanent member of the Security Council of Russia, elevating the FSB into the center of national security decision-making.[16]

On November 20, 1998, Russian State Duma member Galina Starovoytova was shot and killed in the entryway to her apartment. As FSB director, Putin had a direct role in leading the investigation into her murder. A month after the incident, Putin publicly blamed Starovoytova's friends and relatives for impeding the investigation; her supporters held the FSB responsible.[17] Although the two hitmen responsible for shooting her were prosecuted, the parties that ordered her murder have never been identified. Starovoytova's strong opposition to restoring KGB-like power to the Russian security services likely played a role in the FSB's lack of urgency to solve the murder.

Putin distinguished himself by protecting the Yeltsin "family," which included his daughter and several other close political operatives, from being investigated for corruption. In April 1999, Putin removed FSB officers who were pursuing corruption investigations, including the chief of the Economic Security Directorate, Aleksey Pushkarenko, and the chief of the Directorate for Counterintelligence Support to Strategic Sites (later called Directorate T), Igor Dedyukhin.[18] Putin's loyalty to Yeltsin and his sheltering of Yeltsin's supporters from corruption allegations contrasted with the actions of Viktor Barannikov, Yeltsin's minister of security from 1992 to 1993. Barannikov, who had sided with Yeltsin during the events of 1991, refused to throw his unmitigated support behind Yeltsin during the 1993 political crisis in Moscow. Barannikov reportedly passed information about corruption among Yeltsin's political faction to rivals in the Supreme Soviet, leading to Barannikov's dismissal in July 1993.[19] Putin used his insider skills six years later to protect Yeltsin's faction, leading to political promotion.

Putin's tenure as FSB director lasted just over a year. Yeltsin rewarded his loyalty in August 1999 by appointing him prime minister after Sergey Stepashin had served in that position for only three months. In Putin's place as FSB director, Yeltsin chose Nikolay Platonovich Patrushev.

Patrushev was the FSB's fifth director in its five years, which had followed four years of state security instability before the creation of the FSB. Patrushev's appointment as director, and equally importantly, Putin's appointment as prime minister and subsequent election as president, introduced a period of stability in the FSB that had not existed in Russian state security since the dissolution of the Soviet Union.

Patrushev is a year older than Putin. They joined the KGB at nearly the same time and worked together in Leningrad in the 1970s and 1980s, where they reportedly became close friends. Unlike Putin, Patrushev did not leave state security at the end of the Soviet era but remained throughout the 1990s. He came to Moscow in 1994 as chief of the FSK Directorate of Internal Security. In October 1998, Patrushev was appointed chief of the Directorate for Economic Security and deputy director of the FSB. In April 1999, he became FSB first deputy director under Putin, then director in July 1999.

Patrushev's time as FSB director began with a series of bombings that destroyed apartment buildings in Moscow and Volgodonsk in Russia and Buynaksk in Dagestan in September 1999, killing over three hundred people. The FSB quickly blamed the explosions on Chechen terrorists; however, circumstances surrounding the explosions, as well as the conspiratorial nature of the Yeltsin regime overall, gave birth to other explanations, some focusing on the FSB as the possible culprit.

The Russian government's treatment of the September 1999 attacks did little to ease suspicion and conspiracy theories. Investigators detained and interrogated hundreds of Chechen nationals living in Moscow; however, the individuals arrested or sought for the attacks were Karachais, Uzbeks, and Dagestanis, not Chechens.[20] The Russian government has never allowed a complete, independent investigation into the bombings. When a State Duma member, Sergey Kovalev, attempted to conduct an investigation, the FSB refused to cooperate.[21] Patrushev's handling of the incident raised further questions. The day after the second bombing in Moscow and the third bombing in three weeks, local police caught a group of FSB officers in Ryazan carrying suspicious sacks that the police identified as explosives. The police arrested the officers, but Patrushev's response was to claim that the sacks contained nothing but sugar, and that the event was a security training exercise; there was no actual threat of an explosion. The next day, Russian forces invaded Chechnya. That event added to conspiracy theories that the bombings were the work of the FSB designed as a pretext to launch an invasion of Chechnya.

Multiple authors have attempted to untangle the truth regarding the September 1999 bombings.[22] When Yuriy Felshtinskiy and Aleksandr Litvinenko published a book that blamed the FSB for launching the attacks as a false flag operation, Moscow banned the book and included it on a federal list of extremist literature. An August 2001 *Novaya Gazeta* article by Felshtinskiy and Litvinenko previewing the book began with the sentence, "The era of the 'honest chekist,' whom even academic Sakharov mentioned as the least corrupt representatives of the special services, has ended."[23] The American journalist David Satter, whose book *Darkness at Dawn* chronicles Russia's descent into a criminal state, wrote, "I'm absolutely sure that the FSB is responsible for the explosions of buildings in Moscow, Buynaksk, Volgodonsk, and an attempt to blow up a building in Ryazan. I think that those terrorist attacks were planned by people around Yeltsin—most likely Berezovsky, and Putin became the prime minister because he was ready to take part in it."[24] The American political scientist John Dunlop also concluded, based on an investigation of the circumstances surrounding the incidents, that the FSB was responsible.[25] Others, however, including the US diplomat Strobe Talbott and the journalists Andrey Soldatov and Irina Borogan, dismiss conspiracy theories placing responsibility on the FSB. Soldatov and Borogan blame the FSB's repeated refusals to cooperate with investigations of the incident on paranoia and a "crisis of confidence" in the FSB rather than complicity.[26] Talbott called the reigniting of conflict in and emerging from Chechnya a "gruesome bit of luck" for Putin, but that there is no evidence to support a conspiracy theory.[27] Aimen Dean, a British MI6 agent who penetrated al-Qaeda, also claimed to have learned from Chechen jihadists that the bombings were perpetrated by the Islamic Emirate as revenge for Russian military excesses in the Caucasus.[28]

Whether the September 1999 bombings were the work of the FSB to create conditions needed to attack Chechnya and restart a war, the FSB's handling of the investigation gave the impression that it was. As Dunlop stated, "The modus operandi of Yeltsin and his entourage led more or less ineluctably to the growth of various conspiracies."[29] Patrushev's evasive public treatment of the incidents did not help. The attacks were a direct factor in launching Putin's popularity. Putin responded to the attacks using a crude Russian phrase, "We will pursue them everywhere. Excuse me for saying so: We'll catch them in the toilet. We'll wipe them out in the outhouse."[30] This phrase gave Putin a down-to-earth, plain-speaking reputation that Russians, who were coming to the end of a chaotic, humiliating decade, saw as necessary and reassuring.

The FSB took a more aggressive posture during Patrushev's tenure, expanding its external operations, including foreign intelligence collection and assassinations of traitors and Chechen militant leaders. The FSB returned more closely to its KGB heritage with the dissolution of the Border Guard Service and FAPSI in 2003, their functions folding into the FSB. Between 2004 and 2020, at least twenty-one Chechens were the targets of Russian assassinations, either with direct FSB participation or through FSB support to hitmen associated with Moscow-sponsored Chechen president Ramzan Kadyrov.[31]

A few months after the Russian State Duma adopted a 2006 law authorizing assassinations (see above), Patrushev himself was likely behind the assassination of Aleksandr Litvinenko in London. Litvinenko's unrelenting anti-Putin campaign abroad, including his book accusing the FSB of complicity in the September 1999 terrorist attacks in Russia, had transformed him from a nuisance into a threat. As noted previously in this book, the radioactive polonium used to kill Litvinenko is reported to have come from a research institute affiliated with the FSB Science and Technology Service. Litvinenko began his career in the MVD internal troops and was recruited as a KGB Third Chief Directorate secret collaborator to report on disloyalty within those troops. He joined the KGB formally in 1986 and became a military counterintelligence officer in 1991. By the late 1990s, he began to complain about corruption within the FSB, and he emigrated to the United Kingdom in 2000. During the British investigation into Litvinenko's November 2006 assassination, his wife Marina testified that he was aware of connections between the FSB in Saint Petersburg and the Tambov organized crime group, which was involved with smuggling heroin from Afghanistan into Russia. According to his wife, Litvinenko was convinced that Putin and Patrushev were both colluding with that criminal activity. The British investigation concluded that "the FSB operation to kill Mr Litvinenko was probably approved by Mr Patrushev and also by President Putin."[32]

Patrushev lasted over eight years as FSB director, until May 2008, when he was named the secretary of the Security Council, keeping him in Putin's inner circle. He was replaced by Bortnikov, another close associate of Putin's from the Leningrad KGB days.

Senior FSB Leaders

The current senior leaders of the FSB come from a broad spectrum of state security experience. Senior leaders include those at the director / deputy director level and those who lead major FSB services. Even at the level of senior directors, there are some about which little is known publicly. For example, the birthdate, employment date, and rank of Anatoliy Anatolyevich Sablin, the director of the Social Welfare Service (SSBO), are not publicly available. Nevertheless, trends emerge from the available information.

Eight of the sixteen most senior FSB leaders are confirmed to have begun their state security careers in the Soviet-era KGB, while four others for whom the date of their entry into state security is not publicly known are old enough to have worked in the KGB. Only two are confirmed to have begun their state security career after the dissolution of the Soviet Union, one of which, Sergey Borisovich Korolev, is closely connected to the Leningrad / Saint Petersburg clan. They are a mix of longtime professionals in their field, such as special operations or military counterintelligence, along with Leningrad / Saint Petersburg clan members who have benefited from Putin's patronage; at least six of the sixteen began their careers in Leningrad.

Another noticeable trend is that almost all have Russian ethnic surnames—it is rare for a representative of a non-Russian ethnic group to reach a senior FSB center position. While it is not as unknown for a non-Russian ethnic officer to be appointed a regional FSB directorate chief—surnames such as Ibragimov, a Tatar name, are seen occasionally—it is still uncommon. All senior FSB officials are male—there has never been a female FSB director-level official.

Table 4.1 gives brief biographies of the FSB Headquarters senior leaders. First deputy FSB director Sergey Borisovich Korolev is one of the exceptions to Soviet-era service. He is relatively young among the senior FSB leadership. He was born in 1962 and turned sixty in July 2022. Korolev followed a career unlike most other senior FSB officers. He worked for a private security company beginning in 1993 and remained there during the chaos of the 1990s. He came late to federal service, joining the FSB in 2000 in Directorate M, then an element of the Fourth Service. While in that position, he reportedly became enmeshed with organized criminals, the Makozov Group, while also feuding with local Saint Petersburg police. Based on those controversies, he was removed from the FSB in 2004 and assigned to the Federal Tax Service, where the director was Anatoliy Serdyukov. Serdyukov is reportedly a friend of Korolev's family; he is the son-in-law of Korolev's father's hunting partner, Viktor Zubkov, who served as Putin's prime minister in 2007–8, and then as first deputy prime minister during Putin's brief tenure as prime minister from 2008 to 2012.[33] Serdyukov worked as minister of defense alongside Zubkov beginning in February 2007, and Korolev followed him there to become a special assistant with the portfolio of the GRU. Korolev moved back to the FSB in late 2011 or early 2012 to serve as the director of the FSB's Internal Security Directorate, where he oversaw high-profile corruption cases.[34] In July 2016, he was named as director of the Fourth Service. Then, in February 2021, Putin named Korolev the first deputy FSB director and promoted him to full general. He was fifty-eight years of age at the time.

Vladimir Grigoryevich Kulishov was appointed chief of the Border Guard Service and first deputy FSB director in March 2013 and promoted to full general. Kulishov was born in 1957. He initially studied as a civil aviation engineer in Kyiv and worked in an aircraft factory until he entered the KGB Higher School, from which he graduated in 1982. Little is known of his career from 1982 to 2000; however, he was awarded medals that possibly provide some clues. He wears the medal "For Services in Counterintelligence" and the badge "Honored Counterintelligence Officer," as well as the badge "For Polar Service." He moved to FSB Headquarters in 2000. For a brief period in 2003 and 2004, he was the chief of the FSB directorate for the Saratov Oblast, and then he returned to FSB Headquarters to be the first deputy chief of the Directorate for the Fight Against Terrorism in the FSB Second Service. He served for another brief period as the chief of the FSB Directorate for the Chechen Republic, and then in 2008 as deputy director of the FSB and chief of the National Antiterrorist Committee. He was in that position when he was named the chief of the Border Guard Service at the age of fifty-five.

Table 4.1
Senior FSB Leadership as of May 2022

Name	Position	Birth Year	State Security	Background
Aleksandr Vasilyevich Bortnikov	FSB director	1951	1975	Began in Leningrad
Sergey Borisovich Korolev	First deputy FSB director	1962	2000	Background in Leningrad; private security company before joining FSB
Vladimir Grigoryevich Kulishov	First deputy FSB director and chief of Border Guard Service	1957	1982	
Aleksandr Nikolayevich Kupryazhkin	State secretary	1957	1983	
Igor Gennadyevich Sirotkin	Deputy FSB director, chief of the National Antiterrorism Committee apparatus	1960	1983	Began in Leningrad
Vladislav Vladimirovich Menshchikov	Director, First Service, Counterintelligence (SKR)	1959	1983	Began in Leningrad; left state security to go into banking in 1997; returned in 2014
Aleksey Semenovich Sedov	Director, Second Service, Service for Defense of the Constitution and Fight against Terrorism (SZKSiBT)	1954	1980	Began in Leningrad
Nikolay Petrovich Yuryev	Director, Military Counterintelligence (DVKR)	Early 1960s?	??	Background in strategic rocket forces
Sergey Sergeyevich Alpatov	Director, Fourth Service, Economic Security Service (SEB)	1959	??	
Sergey Orestovich Beseda	Director, Fifth Service, Service for Operational Information and International Relations Service (SOIiMS)	1954	??	
Yevgeniy Nikolayevich Lovyrev	Director, Sixth Service, Organizational Personnel Service (SOKR)	1953	1992	
Mikhail Vasilyevich Shekin	Director, Seventh Service, Support Service (SOD)	1958	??	
Eduard Vladimirovich Chernovoltsev	Director, Science and Technology Service (NTS)	1970?	??	
Vladimir Vladimirovich Kryuchkov	Director, Control Service (KS)	1955	1977	Began in Leningrad
Anatoliy Anatolyevich Sablin	Director, Social Welfare Service (SSBO)	??	??	
Aleksandr Yevgenyevich Tikhonov	Director, Special Operations Center (TsSN)	1952	1974	Background in special operations

Colonel General Aleksandr Nikolayevich Kupryazhkin serves as the FSB state secretary. He was born in 1957 and joined the KGB in 1983. As a state secretary, Kupryazhkin is a special assistant to the director and a point of contact with other federal agencies. Kupryazhkin formerly led the FSB Internal Security Directorate, from which it was rumored that he was fired in 2006 because of his alleged participation in a case involving a large shipment of Chinese contraband that was shipped into Russia (see chapter 6). The rumor was never confirmed, and rather than being fired, he was promoted. He was named an assistant director of the FSB in July 2011. His replacement as chief of the Internal Security Directorate was Sergey Korolev, now first deputy FSB director.[35] Kupryazhkin was appointed to his current position in July 2018.

Colonel General Igor Gennadyevich Sirotkin was appointed deputy FSB director and chief of the National Antiterrorism Committee secretariat in 2015. He was born in 1960 in Leningrad, joined the KGB in 1983, and spent his career in Leningrad / Saint Petersburg. Few specifics are available about Sirotkin's career, except that before his promotion to an FSB headquarters position, he was the assistant chief of the FSB directorate for Saint Petersburg and the Leningrad Oblast.[36] In his current position, he represents Russia at international forums related to countering terrorism.[37]

Colonel General Vladislav Vladimirovich Menshchikov has run the FSB First Service since 2015. He was born in 1959 and trained as a mechanical engineer. He joined the KGB in 1983, serving in Leningrad / Saint Petersburg until 1995. Like many KGB officers, Menshchikov left the state security service in the 1990s. In 1995, he took a job in the Russian Central Bank in Saint Petersburg, and from 1997 to 2000, he worked in the Saint Petersburg regional office of the Federal Commission on the Securities Market. He then served as the general director of the Russian Agency for the State Reserves from 2000 to 2003. He left the government banking field in 2003 and entered a private business, working from 2003 until 2014 as the general director of the Russian defense contracting company Almaz-Antey, which manufactures antiaircraft weapons, including the highly touted S-400 antiaircraft system. During his time at Antaz-Antey, he had time to complete a dissertation to become a candidate of technical sciences, the Western equivalent of a PhD, in 2006. His dissertation was directly related to his work. It was titled "Development of Organizational and Economic Methods for Managing a Military-Industrial Company in a Market Economy: Based on the Experience of Joint Stock Company Air Defense Corporation Almaz-Antey." He went on to earn a doctorate in economic sciences in 2009, completing the dissertation titled "Formation and Development of Backbone Integrated Structures of the Defense Industry: Based on the Experience of the Radio-Electronic Complex." He subsequently published both his dissertations as books.[38] Menshchikov's ties to the Saint Petersburg KGB clan eventually brought him back into state security. In 2014, Putin brought Menshchikov into the presidential administration to lead the Directorate for Special Programs (GUSP), where he worked with another Saint Petersburg KGB officer, Sergey Borisovich Ivanov. The GUSP is the heir of the KGB Fifteenth Directorate and administers senior leader emergency shelter sites around Russia. Then, in 2015, Putin appointed Menshchikov to be the chief of the FSB First Service.[39]

Colonel General Aleksey Semenovich Sedov has led the FSB Second Service since 2006. He was born in 1954 and graduated from the Saint Petersburg State University of Aerospace Instrumentation. He joined the KGB in 1980, working in Leningrad as an operational-technical officer. He later worked in the antismuggling unit of the Saint Petersburg KGB office. He worked in state security until 1992, when he left to join the Federal Tax Police Service, where he worked in various capacities in Saint Petersburg and Moscow until 2003, when the Tax Service was disestablished and most of its functions were transferred to the newly formed State Drug Control Service. Sedov was appointed assistant director of the Main Directorate of the State Drug Control Service in the Northwest Federal District, which includes Saint Petersburg. He was promoted to be the agency's assistant director in 2004. He joined the FSB in 2006, when he was appointed to his current position.[40] Sedov's name was in the Moscow news in 2009, when he and his family were injured in a car crash while riding in an FSB-owned Mercedes Benz. Sedov's vehicle attempted to skirt around a traffic jam by turning on its flashing lights and swerving into oncoming traffic when it collided with another car. When his vehicle encountered the traffic jam, Sedov reportedly told the driver that he had to urgently get to the Olympic Sports Complex; the urgency was apparently related to an Elton John concert that evening at that venue. Sedov's accident was one of a series of similar incidents involving FSB drivers around the same time.[41]

Colonel General Nikolay Petrovich Yuryev has led the FSB Military Counterintelligence Department (DVKR) since 2015. Few details are available about Yuryev's life and career. He reportedly graduated in 1982 from the Radio Technical Department of the Rostov Higher Command-Engineering Military Academy for Missile Forces (RVVKIU RV), likely placing his birthdate in the early 1960s.[42] His daughter, Aleksandra Nikolayevna Yuryeva, was born in 1983 in Mirniy, Archangelsk Oblast. Mirniy is a closed town associated with the nearby Plesetsk Cosmodrome, which served as an intercontinental ballistic missile launch site during the Soviet era. Yuryev's stationing there the year after graduation is consistent with his education at a missile forces academy. At what point in his career he joined state security is not publicly available. His public statements are mostly limited to extolling the greatness of military counterintelligence. In 2018, he claimed publicly that, over a five-year period, DVKR had prevented four terrorist attacks against Russian forces and had neutralized the activities of twenty-five terrorist and extremist groups.[43] Most public mentions of him report his attendance at the openings of memorials to Soviet-era state security personnel.[44] The topic for which he is best known, however, is an investigative report published in 2020 describing the lavish lifestyle of Yuryev's daughter Aleksandra, her plush apartment, her multiple luxury cars, and her expensive vacations. The report, published on the Russian investigative journalist site *The Insider*, claims that her lifestyle well exceeds her and her father's combined salaries.[45]

Colonel General Sergey Sergeyevich Alpatov is the interim director of the FSB Fourth Service. Before filling this position, he had a career in anticorruption. He was born in 1959, but information about his initial state security employment is unavailable. He had previously served in the FSB Internal Security Directorate until 2013. From then until 2018, he was the director of Directorate M. He made a public name for himself as a corruption fighter in Directorate M in 2016 when he was associated with the arrests of officials from the MVD and the Federal Drug Control Service. In 2018, he was appointed as a first deputy director of the Fourth Service.[46] Then, in March 2021, he was named interim chief, after Sergey Korolev was promoted to the position of first deputy FSB director.[47] It is unclear how long Alpatov will remain in an interim position; however, *Kommersant* speculated at the time of his appointment that his promotion to Fourth Service director was only a matter of time.[48] Dossier Center identified what it claims is a luxurious 150-million-ruble (over $2 million) mansion located in an elite neighborhood on the outer Moscow ring road, registered with Alpatov's wife in a shallow cover name. The couple have reportedly owned the mansion since 2001.[49]

Colonel General Sergey Orestovich Beseda is the chief of the FSB Fifth Service. He was born in 1954. The date that he entered into state security duty is not publicly available; however, a report on a Russian nationalist website cited Beseda as saying that he had worked in Cuba in the late 1990s.[50] At some point, according to Soldatov and Borogan, he worked in a section that supervised the Russian Presidential Administration.[51] He joined the directorate where he now works in 2003, when he was assigned as the deputy department chief, then chief of the Operational Information Coordination Directorate of the FSB Analysis Forecasting and Strategic Planning Department (DAPSP). In 2004, he was named the first deputy chief of the Fifth Service and the chief of DAPSP. In 2009, he was promoted to service chief. In that position, he traveled throughout the former Soviet space developing intelligence relationships and undermining those of other countries to prevent what Russia perceived as "color revolutions."

Beseda traveled to Kyiv in February 2014 during the Maidan Revolution and requested a meeting with Viktor Yanukovich, although he was reportedly not received. The Ukrainian government subsequently sent a diplomatic note to the Russian government asking to question Beseda about his activities during the event, which resulted in 130 dead and over 1,100 injured. The Russian government claimed that he was there to oversee the security of the Russian Embassy and refused the request to question him.[52] Beseda was placed on a US and European Union sanctions list in 2014.[53] Ukrainian reporting subsequently claimed that Beseda commanded the security services of the self-proclaimed "Luhansk People's Republic" and "Donetsk People's Republic." Beseda became even more prominent in March 2022, when Soldatov and Borogan claimed that he had been arrested for incompetence in his directorate's forecasts regarding an armed invasion of Ukraine and also for embezzling money from the funds set aside for supporting the invasion of Ukraine.[54] They report that he was initially placed under house arrest, and then he was remanded to the Lefortovo CIZO in Moscow.[55] However, the Russian Investigative Committee denied reports that Beseda had been arrested, and Beseda reportedly spoke at the funeral of the former KGB chief of analysis, Nikolay Leonov, in late April 2022.[56] Soldatov interpreted that report and public appearance as an indication that the FSB was trying to cover up the public revelations of Beseda's arrest.[57]

Colonel General Yevgeniy Nikolayevich Lovyrev is the chief of the Sixth Service, the Organizational Personnel Service (SOKR). He previously served as an FSB deputy director from 2001 to 2004, when the number of deputy directors was reduced. He was born in 1953 and graduated from the Moscow Aviation Institute in 1976, but he did not begin his state security career until 1992. He was assigned to his current position in 1999, making him one of the longest-serving senior officers in the FSB. He is the chief personnel officer for the FSB, and he travels around the country in that role introducing newly appointed officers to new leadership positions.[58] He led the FSB's management of mercenaries fighting in the Donbas region of Ukraine in 2014, according to Ukrainian reporting.[59] He simultaneously serves as president of the Dinamo women's volleyball club and chairman of the regional public sports organization Dinamo-24. He is also a member of the presidium of the National Civil Committee on Cooperation with Law Enforcement, Legislative, and Judicial Agencies.[60] Soldatov and Borogan reported that Lovyrev was among several senior FSB officers who received a free plot of land in the prestigious Gorkiy-2 neighborhood west of Moscow in 2003–4. The land was valued at about $2.5 million.[61] Lovyrev's son, Dmitriy, is a partner in a high-powered Moscow law firm.[62]

Colonel General Mikhail Vasilyevich Shekin leads the FSB Activity Support Service (SOD), where he is known as the FSB's "*завхоз*" (supply manager). He was born in 1958; the date he entered state security duty is not publicly available. He has been in his current position since 2007.[63] He controls all purchases that the FSB makes across all functions, giving him access to large amounts of money. He is among a group of twelve FSB officers who own a patent on a method for marking and identifying a material object. The patent was registered in 2007 by the FSB Criminal Forensics Institute, indicating that may be where Shekin was before his current position.[64] Shekin is also involved in sponsoring a Russian volleyball club. He is the president of the observer committee of the All-Russian Federation of Volleyball (VFV) and president of the Dinamo volleyball sports club.[65] One of his daughters, Yuliya Tikhomirova, owns a sports resort called VolleyGrad in Anape on the Black Sea coast, which serves as the training location for Russian national volleyball teams. His other daughter, Anastasiya Zadorina, a fashion designer, owns a company that supplies the uniforms for Russia's Olympics team.[66] Zadorina circulates among the rich and powerful of Moscow, including reportedly traveling in March 2022 to Dubai with Kirill Shamalov, the ex-husband of Putin's daughter Katerina Tikhonova, to celebrate his birthday.[67]

Colonel General Eduard Vladimirovich Chernovoltsev, director of the FSB Science and Technology Service (NTS), has been in his position since 2019. He replaced Andrey Fetisov, who was removed partially due to his age—seventy years—and partially in reaction to the arrests of FSB officers for corruption.[68] Chernovoltsev started being named to Russian government commissions in 2019.[69] Little is known about his background; he may have been born in 1970, making him one of the youngest senior officers in the FSB. That age would also indicate that his career in state security likely began after the dissolution of the Soviet Union. He provided an introductory statement for the InfoForum information technology security conference, scheduled for June 2022, which the organizers posted on the conference website. The statement was written sometime after February 24, 2022, as it referenced Western sanctions levied against Russia.[70]

Colonel General Vladimir Vladimirovich Kryuchkov leads the FSB Control Service. He was born in 1955 and became a KGB officer in 1977 after graduating from the KGB Academy. Although his patronymic suggests a possible relationship with Vladimir Aleksandrovich Kryuchkov, the last director of the KGB, there are no publicly available data confirming a family connection. Vladimir Vladimirovich Kryuchkov was reportedly among a group of state security officers from Leningrad / Saint Petersburg who spent their leisure time together. That group, including Kryuchkov's relative Viktor Ivanov, who led the Federal Drug Control Service from 2008 to 2016, reportedly moved to Moscow gradually after Vladimir Putin made his name there.[71] Kryuchkov began working in Leningrad in 1982, rising from a line officer to the director of the Economic Security Service of the Saint Petersburg FSB directorate.[72] In 2002, he was appointed chief of the FSB directorate for the Lipetsk Oblast, south of Moscow. He was in that position less than two years.[73] Kryuchkov moved to Moscow in 2004, when he was appointed the director of Department M, where he was reportedly involved in money laundering; Directorate M became increasingly corrupt under his leadership.[74] That activity included sheltering corrupt officials in the ministries for which Directorate M was responsible and taking a cut of the proceeds, while taking bribes to protect corrupt banks from federal prosecutors.[75] He was appointed to his current position in 2010.

Anatoliy Anatolyevich Sablin is the chief of the FSB Social Welfare Service (SSBO), which is responsible for equipping and running FSB health, recreation, and welfare facilities. Little is known about Sablin's background. He has led the SSBO since about March 2019. In that position, he is listed as the owner of the Federal State Public Enterprise "Social Welfare Service," which is an incorporated entity that provides services for the FSB.[76] In 2010, a person named Anatoliy Anatolyevich Sablin liquidated his ownership of a company called the Interregional Inspection of the Federal Tax Service for the Altai Kray.[77] It is unclear whether this is the same person; if it is, it might indicate that Sablin had formerly worked for the Tax Service.

Colonel General Aleksandr Yevgenyevich Tikhonov is the chief of the FSB Special Purpose Center (TsSN). Tikhonov was born in 1952 and joined the Tajikistan Republic KGB in 1974 after graduating from the KGB Academy. He is a career special operations officer. In Tajikistan, he was involved in responding to various international conflicts, Afghanistan likely being prominent among them. He was transferred to KGB headquarters in Moscow just before the dissolution of the Soviet Union, and he remained at headquarters through the period of the MB/FSK and after the FSB was established in 1995, where he worked in various counterorganized crime organizations. In 1996, he was named first assistant director of the Alfa special forces unit. He was named the first (and so far, only) chief of the combined FSB TsSN when it was created in October 1998. He was the on-scene commander of special troops during the Dubrovka Theater hostage crisis in October 2002, for which he was awarded the Hero of the Russian Federation Medal—then–FSB director Patrushev and FSB deputy director Vladimir Pronichev were also given the same award, despite the disastrous outcome of the hostage crisis.[78] He later also commanded the special operation response to the Beslan hostage crisis in 2004, which also resulted in large numbers of noncombatant fatalities.[79]

As noted in these biographies, rumors of corruption among senior FSB officers are constant. Their access to large amounts of money, whether through their regulation of banks, through the purchases of supplies and equipment for the FSB, or through their affiliation with corporations, has proven to be tempting for senior officers who enjoy significant power in the Russian government system. According to the Dossier Center, the primary motive of many FSB officers is to be promoted into a position that offers financial benefits. Thus, FSB officers constantly strive for promotion and will do whatever is necessary. One subject of an FSB investigation stated that when FSB officers interrogated him, they were trying hard to obtain evidence of espionage. Espionage is a high-profile allegation that can benefit an officer's career if he can make it stick. The FSB subject, Mikhail Savva, stated, referring to his FSB interrogators, "They openly told me that I was necessary for their career."[80] The higher the rank and position in the FSB, the more financial benefits are available (see chapter 6 for more information about FSB corruption).

Future Leaders

As senior FSB leaders with KGB backgrounds reach the ends of their careers, the FSB will need to look for younger officers who never served during the Soviet era to take their places. The next generation of senior leaders will likely come either from among regional FSB directorate chiefs, or from among the protégés of current senior leaders, such as those from Saint Petersburg.

Regional FSB directors include those who lead eighty-one geographically designated FSB directorates, usually at the oblast or republic level, and nine who lead FSB directorates attached to military districts, fleet headquarters, and Strategic Rocket Forces headquarters. Two other FSB regional directorates have special assignments, one for the Main Directorate of the Russian General Staff (Russia's military intelligence service) and one for special government infrastructure facilities, such as senior leader emergency shelters. Two regional directorates, the Kaliningrad

Oblast and Crimea, double as special military facilities and regional offices: Kaliningrad monitors the Baltic Fleet and forces, and the Crimea office is responsible for the port at Sevastopol.

Directors of regional FSB directorates are mostly general majors (one-star) or colonels. They are, on average, younger than senior leaders, having been born in the late 1960s and 1970s. Most began their state security careers in the 1990s, after the dissolution of the Soviet Union. They rotate every three to five years, and it is common for a regional director to rotate from one region directly to another, and sometimes even to a third, never stopping in an FSB headquarters position in between. However, several senior leaders also spent time during their careers in regional directorships. Patrushev was the FSB chief of the Karelia republic in the mid-1990s; Bortnikov was the regional director of the FSB office responsible for Saint Petersburg and the Leningrad Oblast in the 1990s; and Vladimir Kryuchkov, who leads the FSB Control Service, was the regional director of the FSB office in the Lipetsk Oblast in the early 2000s. Other future senior FSB leaders could come from among current regional directors.

Notes

1. Russian Federation, Federal Law 40-FZ.
2. President of Russia, Resolution 870.
3. Fronin, "FSB Highlights."
4. "Bortnikov: The Hope of Citizens."
5. "Bortnikov Announced."
6. "Nine Terrorist Crimes."
7. "Barsukov Mikhail Ivanovich."
8. Belov, "Quarter Century."
9. Stanley, "Yeltsin Signs Peace Treaty."
10. Topol, "'Alpha.'"
11. Kolomytseva, "My Son."
12. Hill and Gaddy, *Mr. Putin*, 25–26.
13. Hill and Gaddy, 31–32.
14. Dolgov, "Appointment."
15. "New Job."
16. "Yeltsin Appoints 'Permanent' Members."
17. "Russian Security Chief Accuses Murdered MP's Family"; Kaluzhskaya, "Ten Years."
18. Dunlop, *Moscow Bombings*, 33–34; "Newsline."
19. Ebon, *KGB*, 105–6; Knight, *Spies*, 65–69.
20. Steele, "Chechens"; Allenova, "Only One Bomber."

21. Eckel, "Two Decades."
22. The most prominent was Dunlop, *Moscow Bombings.*
23. Felshtinskiy and Litvinenko, "FSB," which is a preview of their book, *Blowing Up Moscow.*
24. Satter, *Darkness*; Volchek, "'All of Russia.'"
25. Dunlop, *Moscow Bombings.*
26. Soldatov and Borogan, *New Nobility*, 109–12.
27. Talbott, *Russia Hand*, 356–58.
28. Dean, *Nine Lives*, 200–201.
29. Dunlop, *Moscow Bombings*, 17.
30. Dixon, "Chechen War."
31. Riehle, *Russian Intelligence*, 208–9.
32. UK Government, *Litvinenko Inquiry*, 15, 246.
33. "Top Russian FSB Official."
34. Vyshenkov, "Main Editor."
35. "Major Staff 'Purge'"; "Kupryazhkin Aleksandr Nikolayevich"; "Directorate of Internal Security."
36. "Sirotkin Igor Gennadyevich"; National Antiterrorism Committee, "Staff."
37. "Deputy Director of the FSB."
38. "Menshchikov Vladislav Vladimirovich."
39. Pertsev, "Vladislav Menshchikov."
40. "Sedov Alexei," Putin's List.
41. Kudryavtsev, "General's Family."
42. List of general officers who are alumni of the RVVKIU, http://pomctap.narod.ru/RVVKIU_RV/general.htm.
43. "FSB Report about the Prevention of Terrorist Acts."
44. Republic of Karelia, "New Memorial"; "Memorial to the Defenders of the Fatherland"; "Tribute to the Ancestor's Deeds."
45. Yezhov, "Russian Federation."
46. Sergeyev, "Corruption Fighter"; "'FSB Spetsnaz.'"
47. "Putin Names First Deputy Director."
48. Sergeyev, "From SEB."
49. "Alpatov of the FSB."
50. Ermolov, "Head of the FSB Fifth Service."
51. Sodatov and Borogan, *New Nobility*, 212–14.
52. Gavrilov, "Ukraine Wants to Question FSB General."
53. "EU Targets Russian Officials."
54. Soldatov and Borogan, "Putin Began Purges."
55. Porter, "Senior Russian Official."
56. "SK Denies Information"; Ermolov, "Head of the FSB Fifth Service."
57. Standish, "Interview."
58. See, e.g., "Colonel G. Drachev Appointed"; "Biography of the New Chief"; and "New Chief, Colonel Tataurov."
59. "Russian Mercenaries."
60. "Ловырев Евгений Николаевич" (Lovyrev Yevgeniy Nikolayevich), Moscow Institute of Aviation, https://history.mai.ru/personalities/item.php?id=113822.
61. Soldatov and Borogan, *New Nobility*, 79.

62. Sokolova, "Where Does the Money for Expensive 'Velvet Revolutions' Come From?"
63. "Senior Officers Invited."
64. "Method for Marking."
65. "Birthday of the President"; "Family of the 'FSB Supply Chief.'"
66. "Shekin Mikhail Vasilyevich."
67. Stewart, "Putin's Billionaire."
68. "Bortnikov to Lose His Right Hand."
69. President of Russia, Resolution N1618-r; Russian Federation, Order 628.
70. "Eduard Chernovoltsev."
71. "Economic Security Service."
72. "Kryuchkov Vladimir Vladimirovich."
73. Denisenko, "Native Kursk Leads."
74. "Directorate 'M,'" Dossier Center.
75. "Directorate 'M.'"
76. "Federal State Public Enterprise."
77. "Individual Proprietor."
78. "Tikhonov Aleksandr Yevgenyevich"; Soldatov and Borogan, *New Nobility*, 140, 153.
79. "Tikhonov Aleksandr."
80. "Service for Defense of the Constitutional Order."

5

International Partners

The FSB is represented outside Russia in numerous countries worldwide for two primary purposes: to perform law enforcement and counterterrorism liaison to facilitate Russia's control of its former empire, and to extend the FSB's intelligence collection reach. Some of this foreign presence is declared to foreign partners, and some is clandestine.

Foreign Liaison and Cooperation; Control versus Sharing

Several FSB elements maintain declared relations with foreign partners. But this cooperation has occasionally been met with uneasy reactions from "chekists." When the Soviet Union dissolved, the remnants of the KGB opened their doors to cooperative relations with foreign powers to combat Russia's problems: organized crime, unsecure nuclear components, terrorism, and counterintelligence. The last KGB director, Vadim Bakatin, famously went as far as revealing to US ambassador Robert Strauss the existence and locations of KGB listening devices inside the new US Embassy building in Moscow as a sign that the Soviet Union was putting the past behind it.[1] Strauss reported that Bakatin made this revelation out of a sense of cooperation and goodwill, with "no strings attached." Bakatin's action encountered harsh criticism within the state security apparatus, including allegations of treason.[2]

During the 1990s, the FSB's declared liaison presence grew, with FSB officers responsible for formal counterintelligence and law enforcement liaison reportedly serving at forty-nine Russian embassies worldwide. The first such declared position was in Kazakhstan, and others soon followed in other post-Soviet states.[3] FSB embassy-based representations are the rough equivalent of FBI legal attaché offices. In most countries, they are usually small, often only one or two officers, although in some former Soviet states—like Armenia, Kyrgyzstan, and Tajikistan—they are likely much larger.

The FSB posts officers abroad to certain foreign entities, such as Kyrgyzstan, with which Russia has security treaties, and the unrecognized breakaway regions of Abkhazia and South Ossetia, as specialists to provide "advisory and methodological assistance to their special services and law enforcement agencies during operational-investigative and special activities."[4] Additionally, military counterintelligence officers are posted to locations where Russian military forces are deployed abroad—including Abkhazia, South Ossetia, and Kyrgyzstan, as well as Tajikistan, Armenia, Syria, Vietnam, and the unrecognized breakaway region of Transnistria. Military counterintelligence officers likely also deploy with Russian occupation forces in Ukraine, especially in light of reports of Russian troops in Ukraine refusing to fight.

The FSB runs the Antiterrorist Center of the Commonwealth of Independent States (CIS), which on the surface is a venue for CIS states to coordinate counterterrorism information and operations, but also serves as a mechanism for Moscow to influence the priorities and threat perceptions of CIS states' national security structures. Its director as of early 2022 was FSB general colonel Yevgeniy Sysoyev, whose state security career began in the KGB and continued into the post-Soviet state security structure. From 2013 to 2015, Sysoyev was the FSB deputy director and chief of the National Antiterrorism Committee; and from 2016 to 2018, he led the executive committee of the Shanghai Cooperation Organization (SCO) antiterrorism structure.[5]

The Border Guard Service has the authority to interact directly with the border guard services of other countries, especially with the fourteen countries that share land borders with Russia, and with the United States and Japan, with which Russia's maritime claims intersect.[6] Russian border guards are also posted to borders outside Russia in other post-Soviet states. From the dissolution of the Soviet Union until 2005, Russian border guards protected the border between Tajikistan and Afghanistan. Although Russian border guards left Tajikistan in 2005, a border guard advisory group remained, and Russian officers continue to train and exercise with Tajikistani border guards.[7] Russian border guards also provide security on Armenia's border with Iran and Turkey, based on a 1992 agreement signed between the two countries.[8] After the 2020 Azerbaijan-Armenia War, Armenia proposed that Russia control the border with Azerbaijan as well, although Moscow declined.[9] Russia also serves as the border guard service for the unrecognized breakaway regions of Abkhazia and South Ossetia.[10]

The purpose for declared FSB officers is to share law enforcement and counterterrorism information of mutual interest. At times, that liaison presence has led to cooperation with the United States. For a brief period in the early 2000s, particularly after the terrorist attacks on September 11, 2001, DVKR and the US Department of Defense had an intelligence liaison relationship through which each shared information about threats to the others' naval vessels during ports of call. Each organization invited the other to its capital for threat briefings and cultural activities for several years. During one such event in 2004, Rear Admiral Sergey Korenkov, deputy to then–DVKR director Aleksandr Bezverkhniy, led a delegation to the United States.[11]

Despite Bezverkhniy's 2010 interview, in which he identified the United States and NATO as Russia's primary threats (see chapter 3), the two sides continued to share some threat information. In 2011, the FSB provided the US government with information about Tamerlan Tsarnayev, who in 2013 became known as the Boston Marathon bomber. The FSB's data led to Tsarnayev being added to the US terrorist watch list. However, when Tsarnayev traveled to Dagestan in 2012, US officials did not flag him, reportedly because of a spelling error in his name.[12] In both 2017 and 2019, the US government shared counterterrorism information with the Russian government that, according to the Russian media, resulted in the FSB thwarting planned terrorist attacks in Russia.[13]

Some Americans involved in those efforts echo Bezverkhniy's skepticism about a Russian-US intelligence-sharing relationship. Former Central Intelligence Agency (CIA) officer Steven Hall wrote in 2017 that Russian law enforcement organizations, including the FSB, "do not find the Western approach to intelligence sharing compelling; in fact, they find it quaint and perhaps a bit naive. For the Russians, information truly is raw power, and sharing it—even inside the Russian government—is viewed first and foremost through a political lens."[14] The FSB's liaison relationships with former Soviet states likely fall within that description of using intelligence sharing for power and influence purposes. Hall joined a group of other retired CIA officers in 2020 and put it this way, "Each attempt [to share intelligence with Russia] failed . . . for the same reason: Putin's Kremlin is not interested in a constructive relationship with the United States. Instead, Putin sees himself in a political war with us. And he benefits domestically by blaming the United States for all his ills."[15] In other words, Putin has a "chekist mind-set."

That perspective seemed to be borne out in the 2016 arrest and severe sentencing of TsIB officer Colonel Sergey Mikhailov for sharing intelligence about computer-based crimes with the United States. Although Mikhailov's arrest was at least partially based on interagency rivalries within Russia, it had a dampening effect on intelligence sharing. Amid the turmoil between the United States and Russia, Bortnikov, along with the SVR and GRU directors, traveled to Washington in early 2018 for discussions with their US counterparts; the content of the meetings was not made public.[16] Bortnikov had previously traveled to Washington in 2015 for an international conference on countering violent extremism, but the presence of all three Russian intelligence chiefs in Washington at the same time was highly unusual.[17] Then, in January 2022, after the United States had experienced months of damaging ransomware attacks against critical infrastructure facilities from Russia-based criminal groups, some cooperation reemerged, but only after US president Joe Biden warned Putin that the United States would take action against cybercriminals if Russia did not.[18] Amid tension over Russia's build-up of troops on Ukraine's border, the FSB loudly proclaimed in January 2022 that it had arrested fourteen people associated with a ransomware group in Russia and seized millions of dollars in assets.[19]

FSB officers have also traveled to various former Soviet states as clandestine Russian government representatives. Ukrainian security officials reported that FSB officers arrived in Kyiv in December 2013, at the invitation of the Yanukovich government, in a plane believed to be carrying weapons. As noted above, UKZS chief, General Lieutenant Aleksey Zhalo, traveled to Kyiv in January 2014 to meet with then–Ukrainian president Yanukovich. Ukrainian press also reported that a group of FSB generals—including the Fifth Service chief, Sergey Beseda—traveled to Kyiv in the midst of the Maidan unrest in February and March 2014. Two Fifth Service generals, Oleg Khramov and Operational Information Department chief Anatoly Bolyukh, reportedly lost their positions after Yanukovich was ousted from Ukraine.[20]

Expanding Intelligence Reach

Another reason the FSB develops liaison relations with foreign countries is to expand its global intelligence collection reach. During the Soviet era, the KGB had intelligence liaison relationships with many countries. The KGB Sixteenth Directorate, for example, operated a Soviet SIGINT facility at Lourdes, Cuba, as well as other ground-based SIGINT facilities in Soviet-allied countries, including Vietnam, South Yemen, Burma, Mongolia, and Nicaragua, along with Afghanistan while Soviet troops were stationed there from 1979 to 1989. Those facilities were transferred to FAPSI in 1993, but gradually closed during the 1990s due to Russian funding shortages. When the FSB subsumed FAPSI's SIGINT mission in 2003, the legacy of those external SIGINT missions transferred with it. Since 2014, Russian commentators have made tangential statements that Lourdes should reopen. The Russian government has made no formal announcement of such a plan, although it has offered to return military support to Cuba, as was provided during the Soviet era.[21]

Putin also visited Vietnam in 2013, during which visit the two countries signed agreements that allowed Russian ships to pull into Cam Ran Bay, where the KGB's SIGINT facility had been.[22] The public statements did not mention the reestablishment of a SIGINT base in Vietnam, but the location of Russian ships in Cam Ran Bay provides at least the opportunity for ship-borne SIGINT there. Further, Yevgeniy Lovyrev, chief of the FSB Sixth Service, and Andrey Fetisov, then–chief of the FSB Science and Technology Service, received the Vietnamese Order of Friendship at a ceremony in Moscow in December 2017. The award was for unspecified "active and effective contributions to strengthening the friendship and comprehensive cooperation between the Vietnamese Ministry of Public Security" and the FSB.[23] The public justification for the award was vague, but the two named awardees could indicate FSB training of Vietnamese technical intelligence personnel.

Intelligence sharing with India has also received high-level FSB attention. Nikolay Patrushev visited India in September 2021 to discuss Afghanistan.[24] That followed a March 2017 meeting by Bortnikov, which publicly focused on counterterrorism. However, the Indian home minister, Rajnath Singh, said after the meeting with Bortnikov that cooperation between the two countries should cover bilateral, regional, and international issues in military and technical, energy, and economic security sectors and disaster management.[25] No further details emerged about what technical cooperation in international issues might mean.

Russia's intelligence relationship with India requires a delicate balance with other regional powers, especially China and Pakistan. All three are members of the SCO as of 2017, but they retain high levels of suspicion toward each other. The stated purpose for the SCO is to deepen economic and political cooperation between its members, and it has focused heavily on security and counterterrorism cooperation. But the relationships undoubtedly go beyond counterterrorism issues. Bortnikov was rumored to have taken an unpublicized trip to Pakistan in February 2017, the month before his publicized visit to India. The visit was reportedly to discuss Russia's participation in the China-Pakistan Economic Corridor.[26] Bortnikov also traveled to China in June 2019, also possibly related to economic cooperation.[27]

How deeply Russia's and China's intelligence-sharing relationship goes is unclear. While Russia and China synchronize their diplomatic strategies and conduct combined military exercises, the FSB has regularly accused Russians of espionage on China's behalf. The FSB's historical narratives remind Russians about times when Russia and China were adversaries, such as in 1969, when Soviet border guards fought armed battles with Chinese forces. The FSB Border Guard Service places a robust presence on the Chinese border. Although FSB leaders seldom publicly mention China as a current threat, the FSB may not be entirely in synch with other Russian government organizations on the question of trusting China.

Conclusion

Although the FSB is primarily an internal security service, it conducts a spectrum of activities outside Russia that support its internal missions: counterintelligence, counterterrorism, and criminal investigations. Some of these external operations are declared to the host country for liaison purposes, although for the FSB, intelligence sharing is heavily weighted toward information control rather than mutual interests. Other external operations are clandestine, including assassination operations and intelligence collection. All ultimately support the FSB's primary mission of securing the Putin regime and enriching FSB personnel themselves.

Notes

1. "KGB Passes Secrets."
2. Ebon, *KGB*, 61–62.
3. "International Cooperation Directorate."
4. Russian Federation, Federal Law 97-FZ.
5. "Russian Representative Will Lead SCO Antiterrorism Operations."
6. See, e.g., "US Coast Guard."
7. Kulikov, "Russian Border Guards"; Nurshayeva, "Russian Border Guards' Return"; Manenkov, "Russian, Tajik Troops."
8. "Russian Border Guards' Presence."
9. Kucera, "Pashinyan Proposes Russian Border Guards."
10. Corso, "Georgia."
11. The author participated in several of these events.
12. US government, "Unclassified Summary"; Winter, "Russia Warned US."
13. "Trump Putin Call."
14. Hall, "Intelligence Sharing."
15. Sipher et al., "Trump Wants the CIA."
16. Eckel, "Chiefs."
17. Schmidt, "FBI Chief Not Invited."
18. Matishak, "Biden Says He Told Putin US Will Hack."
19. Balmforth and Tsvetkova, "Russia Takes Down REvil Hacking Group."
20. Leshchenko, "Why Did an FSB General?"
21. Lee, "Satellite Images."
22. "Cam Ran Military Base."
23. "Friendship Order Presented."
24. Haidar, "Afghanistan."
25. "Rajnath Meets Russian Intel Chief."
26. Korybko, "Indian Fears."
27. "China-Russia Energy Cooperation."

6

Cultural Representations of the FSB

The FSB is portrayed in popular media inside Russia in contradictory terms. The FSB claims to be the defender of Russians' rights and security, and FSB officers often appear as heroic soldiers on the front lines against corruption and foreign intrigues. The FSB values this image, and its public-facing priorities can partially be discerned by analyzing the traits of FSB officers who have received the highest Russian government award, the Hero of the Russian Federation Medal. This award—along with publicity events, pro-FSB art and literature, and statements by FSB leaders—reveals the FSB's idealized organizational culture. However, the FSB faces a simultaneous reality of increasingly visible corruption and incompetence that clashes with that ideal.

The FSB tries to control its image through a mix of public affairs programs. Between 1995 and 2020, for example, 59 FSB officers received the Hero of the Russian Federation Medal. Of those, 31 were awarded posthumously, a considerably higher proportion than average. Up to May 2022, 1,141 total individuals had been so awarded, 484 of which were posthumous, including 108 World War II–era awardees. During the same period, 195 officers from the FSB's rival organization, the MVD, received the Hero of the Russian Federation Medal.

Fifty of the FSB awards were for counterterrorist operations in the North Caucasus. The first post-Soviet state security officer recognized as a hero was Captain Sergey Gromov, a military counterintelligence officer serving with the 106th Guards Airborne Division. Gromov joined the KGB in 1990 and was assigned to Chechnya in November 1994, "fulfilling military tasks to restore constitutional law and order in the Chechen Republic." He reportedly requested to remain in Chechnya for a second deployment. He was killed by a sniper in February 1995, not long before the FSK was renamed the FSB.[1]

The first recipients of the Hero of the Russian Federation Medal after the FSB's creation were 4 officers serving in Grozny, Chechnya, 3 of whom were posthumous. They were among 90 FSB personnel billeted in a building in Grozny on August 6, 1996, the first day of the Battle of Grozny, when over 100 Chechen militants surrounded the building and demanded their surrender. The FSB personnel refused, and a three-day battle ensued. The 4 awardees had all been Soviet-era KGB officers and represented the FSB's need to deploy any officers available for duty in Chechnya. The most senior of the awardees was Lieutenant Colonel Aleksandr Alekseyev, who had been in the KGB since 1982. He was a personnel officer in the Komi Republic when he received orders to deploy to Chechnya.[2] Major Vyacheslav Yevskin had been in the KGB since 1987 and as a military counterintelligence officer assigned to the Krasnodar Kray in 1992.[3] Major Sergey Romashin began his career in the army and joined the KGB in 1988 after graduating from the KGB Academy as a border guard officer. In 1992, he reportedly asked his father, KGB general Viktor Romashin, to assist with a transfer to the Vympel special operations group. He was serving in that unit in Chechnya.[4] Major Sergey Shavrin began his career in the Army and transferred to the KGB in 1987, going straight into Vympel. He had completed multiple assignments in Chechnya before he was killed. Of the 4, Shavrin was the only one who survived the event.[5] It is unclear how long these officers had served together when they fought for their lives alongside each other. According to Romashin's father, he had phoned home the day before the battle to tell his family that he would be returning from deployment in the next several days.[6]

Indicative of the way that Russia reveres its heroes, Romashkin's secondary school in Yuzhno-Sakhalinsk in the Russian Far East was renamed in his honor in 1997.[7] A memorial was erected to Yevskin, and a street was named after him in the town of Anapa, Krasnodar Kray, in August 2016.[8] Several monuments were raised to Alekseyev; a memorial bust was erected and a street and school were renamed in his honor in his hometown of Ukhta, Komi Republic, in 1999; and in 2017 he was named an "honored citizen of the Komi Republic."[9]

Senior FSB leaders have also received the Hero of the Russian Federation Medal, likely to showcase the FSB's leadership, especially in combating terrorism in Chechnya. This occurred in particularly the early 2000s, when five general officers received the medal in three years. General Lieutenant Grigoriy Khoperskov, chief of the FSB office for the Republic of Chechnya, in February 2000; FSB director, General Colonel (later Army General) Nikolay Patrushev, in March 2000; and Vice Admiral (later Admiral) German Ugryumov, chief of the FSB Second Department? in December 2000, were all awarded the medal for leading the FSB's counterterrorist war in Chechnya. General Colonel Vladimir Pronichev, deputy FSB director, in December 2002, was awarded for his role in leading the Dubrovka hostage crisis response. General Colonel Aleksandr Tikhonov, TsSN chief, was awarded the medal in January 2003 for leading counterterrorist operations. These awards sent a public message that Russia was winning the war. However, according to Soldatov and Borogan, Ugryumov's award was, in fact, related not to his leadership in countering terrorism but to his performance in his previous position as deputy chief of the Military Counterintelligence Directorate, where he supervised the investigation of the military journalist Grigioriy Pasko, who reported on Russia's dumping of nuclear waste in the ocean.[10] Ugryumov died in 2001, and a memorial was erected to him in 2004 in his hometown, Astrakhan, and another in the city of Stavropol in 2015.

Like Ugryumov, medal winners are often honored with statues, memorials, and even commemorative postage stamps. Since 2012, over fifty recipients of the Hero of the Russian Federation Medal have appeared on Russian commemorative postage stamps. Of these, eleven were FSB officers, all but one of whom received the medal posthumously. The one exception was Ugryumov, who died of natural causes only a year after receiving the medal. In the ever-present FSB–MVD competition, eighteen MVD officers have appeared on postage stamps.

TsSN is the most decorated element of the FSB. It is the element that actively operates against terrorist threats inside Russia and abroad. TsSN's Alfa and Vympel groups have developed legendary status in Russia for their supposed bravery and toughness and have been well rewarded. Ten

Alfa and thirteen Vympel personnel have received the Hero of the Russian Federation Medal, most posthumously. The first commanders of both Alfa and Vympel were KGB officers who had previously received the Hero of the Soviet Union Medal, and five past Alfa group chiefs were medal recipients. Alfa was established by Major Vitaliy Bubenin, who was awarded the medal as a border guard officer for service against Chinese border violations in 1969. Bubenin was honored in the book *Gold Stars of "Alfa,"* which highlights the threat China posed to the Soviet Union.[11] Vympel was founded by Captain Second Rank Evald Kozlov, an officer in the Eighth Department of Directorate S of the KGB First Chief Directorate. He was awarded for leading the operation to assassinate Afghan president Hafizullah Amin in December 1979.

Other FSB officers have been awarded the Hero of the Russian Federation Medal for different types of missions. In 2007, a member of the Aviation Directorate, Vladimir Pismenniy, was awarded the medal, although not for an FSB operational mission. Pismenniy began his career as a flight navigator in KGB Border Guard aviation and clocked over 5,000 flight hours, becoming a navigation instructor when the PS merged with the FSB in 2003. In 2006 and 2007, Pismenniy was the navigator for an experimental helicopter expedition that flew over 9,000 kilometers from South America across Antarctica, testing the FSB's aviation capabilities in extreme weather conditions. The awarding of the medal was for his part in the expedition.[12]

These public accolades are an attempt by the Russian government to exemplify models of bravery, sacrifice, leadership, and patriotism for Russian society. The Russian website *Heroes of the Country* (*Герои Страны*), which lists all known awardees both during and after the Soviet era, is dedicated to publicizing the "example of military feats by defenders of the Fatherland."[13] Many in Russia receive this publicity with enthusiasm.

The FSB has done much to trumpet its glories over the years. In 2003, DVKR published a book regaling its history, which it counts from 1918. The book only briefly mentions the dissolution of the Soviet Union, while connecting today's organization to the heroic exploits of the Soviet era.[14] That same year, the FSB opened an exhibit within the Central Museum of the Armed Forces commemorating the sixtieth anniversary of the creation of Smersh.[15] Both venues omit less-flattering portions of the organization's history, such as the extreme measures Smersh took during the war to punish disloyalty and defeatism.

Both the Border Guard Directorate and TsSN also operate museums. The TsSN museum opened in 2005 and connects current TsSN operations to the tsarist era, beginning in the fifteenth century with Ivan IV, "The Terrible." TsSN has done much to foster the reputation of FSB special operations personnel as the most capable, strongest, patriotic, and fearsome of all Russian forces. Alfa and Vympel have veterans' organizations that are fiercely loyal to the Putin regime and continually heroize FSB special operations. The museum furthers that objective.

Public accolades can also take different forms. Near the end of the Soviet era, in an attempt to show a softer, more human side, the KGB announced the selection of a "Miss KGB," a young administrative employee named Lieutenant Yekaterina (Katya) Mayorova. In a 1990 interview with a Western journalist, Mayorova said, "I guess they think I'll be the new face of the KGB."[16] Mayorova's award came not long before the dissolution of the Soviet Union, and she soon disappeared from public view. Post-Soviet services have not held any similar contests, although local FSB offices occasionally hold beauty contests on May 8, Russian Mother's Day.[17]

More successful than beauty contests, however, has been an art and literature competition that honors artists and writers whose works match the narratives the FSB is trying to publicize. This competition also has its roots in the Soviet era. In 1978, KGB director Andropov established a competition for artistic works that portrayed a positive image of the KGB as the protector of the country and the communist ideology. In 2006, Nikolay Patrushev, who did much as FSB director to return the organization to the form and function of Andropov's KGB, established a similar competition to honor artistic works in the fields of literature (fiction and nonfiction), radio and TV programming, music, cinema, acting, and the visual arts. Since then, over four hundred people have received FSB awards.

The awardees include numerous documentary films that cover intelligence and state security topics. Many are historical, exploring aspects of Soviet-era history like establishing the first Soviet state security service, fighting Nazis during World War II, biographies of prominent Soviet KGB (and predecessor organizations') leaders, and catching American spies. Others address more recent topics, especially the heroism and patriotism of Russian Spetsnaz and Border Guard officers and the dangers of terrorism.

Visual arts awardees frequently include the sculptors of monuments around Russia that commemorate FSB heroes and battles, including forty-two statues, monuments, and stellae. One-fourth of those memorials are dedicated to border guards, a frequent topic for FSB awardees. For example, a third-place prize winner in 2018 was a memorial titled "To the Glory of the Defenders of Territorial Integrity, Sovereignty, and Security of the Fatherland," which commemorates border guards in the city of Novokuznetsk near the border with Mongolia. A second-place winner in 2009 was a memorial in the city of Dalnerechinsk near the Russian border with China that commemorates the border guards who lost their lives during clashes with China in 1969—the same battle for which Vitaliy Bubenin, the founder of the KGB's Alfa group, was awarded the Hero of the Soviet Union Medal.

Cinema and acting awards go to nominees whose works cover a similar group of subjects. World War II and its aftermath are frequent themes in Russian cinema in general, and state security officers typically appear in those movies as the saviors of the country. The 2009 four-part miniseries *Ordered to Destroy: Operation Chinese Casket* portrays a World War II Smersh investigator who uncovers a German plot to use a Soviet soldier detained in a German prisoner-of-war camp to assassinate Stalin. It is set in German-occupied Ukraine after the Soviet Army had recaptured Crimea and was preparing to attack Ukraine. A 2013 FSB award winner was the film *The Cry of the Owl*, set in 1957 in a small Soviet town that the German Army had occupied during World War II. It begins with an MVD officer being injured during a robbery investigation. While the MVD officer was unconscious in the hospital, he cried out in his native German, setting off a KGB counterintelligence investigation that uncovered German infiltration of the MVD using agents left behind in the Soviet Union. The 2017 cinema prize winner, *Three Days Before Spring*, was set during the siege of Leningrad. In it, a young state security officer teams with a doctor to prevent a major catastrophe.

Another theme often central to Russian films that show the FSB in action is terrorism, particularly Chechen terrorism. The 2018 film *Decision to Liquidate* portrays a 1999 counterterrorism operation targeting a Chechen terrorist named Shamil Bazgayev, a thinly veiled cover for the real Chechen warlord Shamil Basayev, who masterminded multiple terrorist attacks in Russia in the 1990s and early 2000s, and whom the FSB killed in 2006. In the film, Bazgayev threatens to use a weapon of mass destruction in an attack against a Russian target, but the FSB prevented the attack. In the 2019 film *Captain Hollywood*, the FSB investigates a terrorist attack that destroyed an apartment building in the city of Volgodonsk. The film's synopsis states that it was based on actual events, referring to the 1999 bombings of apartment buildings in the cities of Buynaksk, Moscow, and Volgodonsk. The film shows the FSB getting to the bottom of the attacks; however, as noted in chapter 4 above, those real-world attacks are highly controversial. The film appears to be the FSB's answer to the allegations of FSB complicity in those attacks.

Awards for literature have often focused on the Caucasus, Central Asia, and the Far East / China, areas where Soviet and Russian state security officers have gained prominence. The Soviet intelligence historian Filip Kovacevic assessed that the literature awards reflect an FSB goal of "counteract[ing] the existing negative social perceptions of Russian intelligence and establish[ing] a favorable narrative framework for its present and future activities based on the defense of Russian national interests and 'traditional' values defined in opposition to Western liberalism and consumerism."[18] The same statement could apply to all the other FSB arts and literature awardees.

The FSB awards include several remarkable awardees. Six-year-old Aleksandra Kondratyeva, who recorded a song about the glories of the FSB, was an honorable mention in 2015.[19] A 2008 literature honorable mention was Archpriest Nikolay Pogrebnyak, who published a book titled *Defeating Evil with Good: Patron Saints of Special Forces*. The book states, "Today, the spiritual traditions of the Russian army are being revived: cathedrals are being built, clergy seek to bring knowledge of the faith and provide prayer support to military personnel, those who risk their lives every day to guard the peace of their native land."[20]

Also among honorable mentions are two in Belarus, one in 2007 for a museum dedicated to Feliks Dzerzhinsky in the town of Petrilovichi, Belarus, where Dzerzhinsky lived as a child.[21] The other was a novel called *Notes of the "Black Colonel,"* a spy-versus-spy story from 1950s Germany. Its author, retired Belarusian KGB officer Sergey Trakhimenok, was an honorable mention for the FSB literature prize in 2012.[22]

Additionally, a second-place song award in 2011 went to Liliya Mkrtyan, a Russian border guard officer serving Armenia, who was recognized for her song honoring her fallen border guard comrades. Two 2012 honorable mentions in the visual arts category went to the children of FSB border guard officers in middle schools in Gyumri and Armavir, Armenia.

The FSB awards serve a similar function as, and even accentuate in many instances, the Hero of the Russian Federation Medal, providing a constant reminder to the Russian population of the glories of state security. Few other countries honor their internal security and border guards as often and enthusiastically as Russia does.

It is common to read interviews with serving senior FSB officers who support this honored image. During the Soviet era, it was unusual for a serving KGB officer to give public interviews. KGB director Vladimir Kryuchkov changed that somewhat during the glasnost period by appearing publicly. However, in the post-Soviet era, senior FSB officers, like Aleksandr Bortnikov, have given multiple interviews, often connected to state security anniversaries. The director of the Border Guard Service, Vladimir Kulishov, has given multiple media interviews, as has his deputy for the Coastal Defense Department. Interviews with various senior FSB officers also appear in the FSB's journal, *FSB: For and Against*, including one featuring the chief of Vympel. These public statements serve two purposes: to show senior FSB leaders as real people, and to allow them to communicate an FSB message directly to the FSB workforce and the public.

The front covers of many issues of *FSB: For and Against* feature anniversaries. As noted previously in the book, the years 2017 to 2022 provided numerous opportunities for the FSB to celebrate anniversaries: the founding of Soviet state security, military counterintelligence, border guards, SIGINT, and general counterintelligence. These anniversaries have drawn wide press coverage, interviews, celebrations, unveilings of new memorials, and the like. As the Russian government heavily exploits history to justify its current actions, these anniversaries are valuable moments for the FSB to join in this exploitation. The cover headline of the October 2020 issue of *FSB: For and Against* demonstrated the importance of history to the FSB: "Countering the Falsification of History."

The historiography of the Russian special services is a combination of selected episodes that show officers as the cream of society, the most loyal defenders of the fatherland, and the only hope for Russia's future. These episodes thus give Russian state security officers the ability to contrast themselves with those who oppose the state, either internally or externally, and to place themselves at the forefront of protecting the state from traitors. To preserve this history, the FSB and veterans' organizations sponsor what the FSB calls historical research. The Society for the Study of the History of Patriotic Special Services, which is associated with the FSB's Public Relations Center, publishes historical essays that analyze pre-Soviet, Soviet, and post-Soviet intelligence and state security activities. The FSB has also selectively released archival materials that support the FSB's message.[23] Numerous Russian authors have published books on Soviet/Russian state security history from the tsarist era to the present. The FSB's website has a section for FSB-approved books that support this historiography.

These public relations tools combine to present the heroic character of the FSB officer, biographies of leaders who portray ideal characteristics, and connections between the current time and the glorious past, especially the time of the VChK and World War II. They portray Russia as under siege by foreign countries—often the United States—and terrorists trying to wreck the country. They also claim that Russian state security services are always victorious; they catch terrorists and spies, protect the Russian people, and sometimes even save the MVD.

Publicity Effects

The effect of the FSB's arts awards on the Russian public is difficult to gauge. The recognition of so many people—over four hundred as of 2020, including youth—broadens the appeal of the awards. However, awardees often do not mention the award in public. For example, many of the documentary film awardees are available on the Internet, some with over a hundred thousand views on YouTube, but few mention that they are FSB award winners. That lessens the positive impact of the awards for the FSB. Nevertheless, as the award winners invariably portray Russian state security officers as the strongest, most patriotic, and self-sacrificing of all Russians, an explicit link to the FSB awards may not be necessary.

FSB-friendly local and national TV and Internet media channels broadly cover the heroic stories, unveilings of monuments, museum launchings, and the like. Consequently, the Russian public tends to view the FSB as an effective, powerful organization. A 2002 survey by the All-Russian Center for Studying Public Opinion (VTsIOM) found that 40 percent of Russians viewed the FSB as effective in fighting crime, compared with the MVD at only 26 percent. One-fourth of Russians felt that an increase in FSB influence is good for society, although financially successful respondents more often tended to feel the FSB's influence more personally.[24] In a 2010 VTsIOM poll, 44 percent of respondents considered the FSB to be an effective organization, the highest rating of any "power" agency.[25] In a 2019 Levada Center poll, Russian respondents placed the FSB as the third most influential organization in the Russian government, behind only Putin and the Army, although both Putin's and the FSB's ratings had fallen since 2017.[26] A survey in 2020 placed the Army as the most trusted Russian institution, the president second, and the FSB still third.[27]

Some of the public's trust in the early 2000s may be related to the lack of public information about the FSB, or possibly to indifference about or fear of expressing genuine opinions. At the same time as the FSB has pushed heroic information about itself, the agency has been publicly entangled in multiple corruption cases. However, the lack of media coverage and a lack of interest at least partially mitigate the negative impact of corruption revelations. When asked in 2007 whether they had heard of the "Three Whales" scandal (see below), in which FSB officers were accused of contraband and money-laundering activities, 81 percent of respondents said they had either never heard of the case or had difficulty answering the question, according to a Levada Center survey.[28]

In 2010, the Levada Center asked Russians what they thought about proposed legislation that would expand the FSB's authority. The legislation in question was an amendment to the law on the FSB that would return a KGB-era practice of issuing prophylactic warnings to suspects whom the agency perceived were about to commit a crime. It was intended to increase the FSB's ability to prevent crime, although it would authorize the FSB to pursue individuals who had not yet committed any crime. Two-thirds of respondents had never heard of the legislation, and 27 percent had heard only a little about it. Only 3 percent of Russians claimed to be following it closely. After the legislation was explained to respondents, 50 percent expressed concern that it would allow the FSB to violate the constitutional rights of citizens or that the FSB would use it to suppress opposition and independent media.[29]

This public lack of knowledge of or interest in the FSB allows the FSB to use history to its advantage while ignoring the darker side of Russian state security history, including purges, midnight knocks on the door, monitoring dissidents and defectors, extraconstitutional measures, deception and disinformation, and corruption, for which Soviet/Russian state security is notorious. Many Russian citizens know about that past, especially older Russians, and content about it is available, but it often comes from dissidents and oppositionist media organizations, which the FSB can paint as disloyal "foreign agents."

The International Memorial Foundation, a Russian human rights organization dedicated to providing accurate historical information about the Soviet past, has published a series of books based on archival records that reveal the darker side of Soviet state security. They include books about the Soviet Gulag system of forced labor camps, the structure and evolution of state security organizations, details of the Great Purge of the 1930s, early Bolshevik suppression of dissent, monitoring foreigners inside the Soviet Union, and so on. The Memorial Foundation has been declared a "foreign agent," along with other organizations that openly contradict the FSB's historical narratives, based on a Russian law that so labels organizations that receive foreign funding. Russian "foreign agent" laws have broadened in scope since their introduction in 2012, initially covering nongovernment organizations like the Memorial Foundation and expanding in 2017 to media organizations and individual journalists that report unflattering information about the FSB. In February 2022, not long after Russia initiated its invasion of Ukraine, the Russian Supreme Court ordered the International Memorial Foundation to close.[30] Many opposition and human rights groups face the same fate.

Foreign agent laws require nongovernmental and media organizations to prominently display a banner on their online materials that says, "This communication (material) is created and (or) distributed by a foreign media organization fulfilling the functions of a foreign agent and (or) by a Russian legal entity fulfilling the functions of a foreign agent." Russians' reactions to this banner are varied. Some view it as an intrusion into their right to think for themselves, and it has elicited small protests. Others, however, see it as a necessary measure to protect Russian society.[31] In

2016, Putin instructed the FSB during his annual speech to the FSB collegium to use counterintelligence resources to vigorously pursue foreign agents inside Russia, equating those who speak out against the Putin regime with foreign spies.[32]

Corruption within the FSB

However, the indifference of the Russian population does not completely protect the FSB from scrutiny. Aleksey Navalny, a vocal oppositionist to Putin, has produced and disseminated videos that sharply criticize Putin and the FSB. Navalny's videos about corruption draw millions of views, many more than FSB-awarded documentary films. A video released in January 2021, just after Navalny's arrest upon his return to Russia, showed Putin's palatial mansion and estimated the millions of rubles required to build it.[33] Navalny describes Putin's wealth as the biggest theft in the history of Russia and he claims that Putin is psychologically ill. In the video, Navalny's team portrays the FSB as complicit in protecting Putin's theft. The team claims to have conducted practically a covert operation to shake FSB and other law enforcement surveillance that would have prevented them from revealing the true nature of Putin's wealth. This video received over 120 million views worldwide, many of which were likely in Russia, as it was initially produced in Russian without subtitles.

Five other videos produced by Navalny's supporters had received over 20 million views each by June 2022.[34] One of them, released a month before the video about Putin's palace, directly implicated the FSB in organizing and conducting the operation to poison Navalny in 2020. Navalny claimed to have posed as an FSB employee and phoned a real FSB officer who was involved in the operation. The FSB officer openly discussed the operation over the phone and admitted his involvement in it.[35] This video, which was highly embarrassing for the FSB, was viewed nearly 30 million times worldwide.

As noted above, in 2007, most Russians paid little attention to media accounts of corruption within the FSB. That has likely gradually changed as FSB corruption scandals have broken in the media more often and with greater intensity. Navalny's popular videos are part of this increasing trend. The website kompromat.ru also provides searchable access to media reports of corruption within the Russian government, with many of those reports focusing on FSB officers. The accumulation of those reports has undoubtedly had an impact on the FSB's credibility and popularity.

The "Tri Kita" (Three Whales) Case

In 2001, the MVD initiated an investigation into customs fraud involving furniture imported into Russia. This was the case that VTsIOM polled Russians about in 2007. The furniture was imported at suppressed prices to reduce customs fees and was then sold in well-known furniture stores chains called "Tri Kita" (Three Whales) and "Grand." The owner of a parent company of Tri Kita was Yevgeniy Zaostrovtsev, a retired KGB general and the father of an FSB first deputy director at the time, Colonel General Yuriy Zaostrovtsev.

The fraud resulted in a loss of customs duties of about 50 million rubles to the Russian government. However, the connection to the FSB came not only in the conduct of the crime but also in conflicts between various investigative agencies that followed. The cases pitted the MVD and State Customs Committee against the FSB and General Prosecutor's Office.

Soon after the MVD opened its case, the MVD learned that Yevgeniy Zhukov, Yuriy Zaostrovtsev's assistant, was attempting to interfere in the case. The MVD questioned Zhukov, and just hours later, the General Prosecutor's Office intervened and demanded to take over the investigation, claiming that the MVD investigator had exceeded his authority.[36] Subsequently, the case was closed for "an absence of corpus delicti." The MVD investigator was put on trial, rather than the FSB perpetrators of the fraud. The presiding judge received pressure from the General Prosecutor's Office to convict the MVD officer but refused; that judge was subsequently dismissed.

Vladimir Putin inserted himself into the case and appointed an independent prosecutor in 2002 at the request of a State Duma investigative committee, which included former FSB director Nikolay Kovalev. However, after three years, the independent prosecutor had made little progress, which sources attributed to resistance from various agencies, especially the FSB. Because FSB officers were subjects of the fraud allegations and the company involved was connected to a senior FSB officer, the FSB had ample reason to obstruct the investigation. Finally, after General Prosecutor Vladimir Ustinov was promoted to minister of justice, a new general prosecutor reopened the case. In September 2006, after five years of investigation, the prosecutor ordered nineteen people administratively removed from their positions, including Zaostrovtsev and other senior FSB officers.[37]

The Tri Kita case shed light on the FSB's interference in the prosecutorial process, similar to the KGB's influence during the Soviet era. The FSB sheltered its own people from prosecution to prevent corruption within the FSB from becoming public. Nevertheless, Zaostrovtsev was eventually the highest-ranking FSB leader to suffer for it. Another investigation that spun off from the Tri Kita case, called the Chinese Contraband Case, showed a similar FSB tactic of manipulating an MVD investigation to hide the FSB connection to import violations.

The Kirill Cherkalin Fraud Cases

Over the time that elapsed between those cases in the early 2000s and 2019, several other FSB corruption cases were revealed in the Russian media. But the most publicized FSB corruption case broke in September 2019, when FSB colonel Kirill Cherkalin was arrested for taking bribes from bankers whose businesses he was responsible for regulating. In the words of a Russian journalist, Cherkalin became a "symbol of corruption in the FSB."[38] Cherkalin was the chief of the Second Section of Directorate K. His section was responsible for combating corruption in the Central Bank of Russia and providing counterintelligence support for the credit, financial, and banking sectors. He worked with FSB colonel Mikhail Gorbatov, who had previously worked in Directorate K but had been transferred to the Office of the President for Ensuring the Constitutional Rights of Citizens.

Gorbatov was acquainted with a businessman associated with the "Transportniy" commercial bank, who was looking for someone who could help keep the bank out of legal trouble. In 2013, Gorbatov recommended the businessman to Cherkalin, who offered to provide "cover" ("*крыша*") for the bank for a fee of $50,000 per month. The services that Cherkalin rendered for Transportniy included intervening with regulators' demands that the bank increase its reserve by 1.3 billion rubles (about $18.5 million) to cover high-risk lenders. The bank's owner could not come up with the money, so he contacted Cherkalin, who convinced the regulator to reduce the reserve amount to 522 million rubles (about $7.5 million).

After Cherkalin's arrest, he agreed to cooperate with investigators. Some analysts have connected his willingness to cooperate with the appointment of Sergey Korolev as FSB first deputy director in February 2021. Cherkalin had committed most of his financial crimes while Korolev was his supervisor in the Fourth Service. Cherkalin may have agreed to cooperate, hoping that his relationship with Korolev would protect him.[39] But Cherkalin's hope was in vain. Gorbatov and Cherkalin both admitted their guilt in court. Gorbatov was sentenced to four and a half years in prison, lower than the maximum sentence, because he provided testimony in the case and because he had served faithfully for over twenty years in the FSB, including time in the North Caucasus.[40] Cherkalin received an eleven-year prison sentence just two months after Korolev assumed his new position.[41]

In total, Cherkalin received $850,000 in bribes from Transportniy Bank over a year and a half. However, police identified goods estimated at 12 billion rubles ($185 million) in his possession, including five apartments, two dachas, and cash worth 800 million rubles, $72 million, and €8 million. Cherkalin had also apparently been involved in other types of embezzlement.

Investigation of Gorbatov led to another FSB colonel from Department K, Andrey Vasiliyev, who supported a separate effort to defraud investors. Vasilyev was acquainted with Sergey Glyadelkin, the part owner of an investment company that was financing the construction of high-cost condominiums in prestigious sections of Moscow.[42] Vasiliyev had initially become acquainted with Glyadelkin in connection with an earlier FSB investigation. When Vasiliyev renewed the acquaintance in 2011, he met Glyadelkin and two other FSB officers: Cherkalin and the deputy chief of Department K, Dmitriy Frolov. They threatened Glyadelkin with freezing the project if he did not remove himself from it. They convinced Glyadelkin to surrender his portion of the project to the remaining partners, who were also connected with FSB officers, with the promise that he would get his share when the project was over. However, rather than reimbursing Glyadelkin, the FSB officers took the money totaling about 500 million rubles for themselves. The investigation into this embezzlement did not surface until 2019.

The FSB Robbery Case

The Cherkalin case came on the heels of an even more embarrassing incident involving FSB officers, including several from the elite Alfa and Vympel units. In June 2019, a group of attackers was arrested for robbing a corrupt businessman en route to depositing 136 million rubles ($2.2 million) in cash into a bank. The attackers included offices from Alfa and Vympel and Department K. The officers received information about the planned deposit from investigative files and organized the robbery to look like an FSB raid. However, rather than arresting the businessman, they stole the money and divided it among themselves. Arrests initially included seven individuals, but the number of FSB suspects rose to fifteen after further investigation. One of the suspects from the Fourth Service had moved to another department within FSB headquarters but decided to take advantage of his insider knowledge to make money. He recruited the others into the crime, assuming that, because the businessman had obtained the money illegally in the first place, no one would inform the police. The police were informed, however, and the plot unraveled only a few weeks after the robbery. The perpetrators received from eight to ten years in prison.[43] The event was highly embarrassing for the FSB, making it appear that FSB officers were no better than the common criminals they were supposed to be catching.

These highly publicized cases have increasingly cast the FSB as a corrupt organization, undoubtedly making an impact on Russians' perceptions of the organization. However, the FSB still has the power to hide its employees' activities from public visibility. In May 2022, the Russian government personnel agency, Gossluzhba, published a list of 3,228 Russian government officials who had been fired from their jobs between July 4, 2018, and May 12, 2022, for "loss of confidence." The people on the list represent numerous government agencies across Russia, including regional ministers of health, culture, forestry and agriculture; the MVD; the Federal Drug Control Service; municipal officials across the country; and many other low-level officials. Not a single FSB case appears on the list, despite the publicity that several of the above-noted cases have received.[44] The list does, however, retain blank placeholders for 22 entries removed between December 2021 and May 2022. It cannot be determined with certainty that they relate to the FSB, but it is possible.

Conclusion

The FSB faces contradictory forces that pull its public reputation in two opposite directions. The FSB heroizes its officers by awarding them medals and glorifies its activities through arts and literature awards. However, a growing awareness of FSB officers' corruption and greed is beginning to counterweigh this reputation. While convoluted corruption cases involving esoteric banking laws do not resonate with Russians as much as the FSB's simple patriotic messages, increasingly frequent FSB corruption cases provide a counterpoint to the FSB's portrayal of its officers as the best of the best in Russian society. Navalny's compelling videos have drawn the Russian population's attention to corruption in the Russian government, including the FSB. The arrest of FSB Alfa and Vympel group special forces officers—the FSB's elite—for armed robbery compounds this impression. In 2016, a Levada Center survey found that 72 percent of Russians felt that official corruption was "a typical phenomenon, a manifestation of the degradation of Russian authorities," although that survey was asking about FSB arrests of other Russian government officials, not arrests of FSB officers themselves.[45]

The FSB has reacted by preventing certain stories from being widely broadcast inside Russia, but it has not blocked them entirely, as evidenced by the popularity of Navalny's videos and the opinions of the majority of Russians who see corruption as an inherent characteristic of their government. The FSB also labels anyone who expresses doubt in the FSB as "foreign agents," and in extreme cases—such as Aleksandr Litvinenko, Aleksey Navalny, and others—to target them for assassination. The FSB will need to confront this reality of corruption in the future as it faces additional pressures from the retirements of influential leaders and demographic decline in Russia.

Notes

1. "Gromov, Sergey Sergeyevich."
2. "Alekseyev, Aleksandr Ivanovich."
3. "Yevskin, Vyacheslav Mikhailovich."
4. "Romashin, Sergey Viktorovich."
5. "Shavrin, Sergey Ivanovich."
6. Makeyeva, "My School."
7. Makeyeva.

8. "Memorial Bust."
9. "Alekseyev, Aleksandr Ivanovich"; "Honored Citizens."
10. Soldatov and Borogan, *New Nobility*, 43.
11. Boltunov, *Gold Stars*, 3–22.
12. "Pismenniy, Vladimir Leonidovich."
13. "About Us."
14. Korenkov, *Military Counterintelligence*.
15. Zolotov, "'Death to Spies.'"
16. Waller, *Secret Empire*, 236; Shevchenko, "Who Was 'Miss KGB.'"
17. Mendel, "Miss KGB."
18. Kovacevic, "FSB Literati."
19. Kondratyeva, "FSB."
20. Pogrebnyak, *They Defeat Evil*.
21. State Cultural Institution, "Manor Museum.'"
22. Trakhimenok, *Notes*.
23. E.g., Vinogradov, Litvin, and Khristoforov, *VChK Archive*.
24. Golov, "MVD."
25. "Russians Consider the FSB."
26. "Public Opinion."
27. "In First Place."
28. "Scandal."
29. "United Russia Members."
30. "Russia's Supreme Court."
31. "Russians React."
32. "Putin Instructs FSB."
33. Navalny, "Putin's Palace."
34. "Most Popular Videos."
35. Navalny, "I Phoned My Killer."
36. Ushakov, Melnikova, and Kuleshov, "Broad Consumption Generals."
37. "'Three Whales' Case; "Siloviki Could Not Hush the 'Three Whales' Case"; Kiseleva, Sergeyev, and Fishman, "Whale." The phrase "кит и меч" is a play on the phrase "щит и меч" ("shield and sword"), by which the FSB is known.
38. Sergeyev, "FSB Colonel."
39. "Game of Thrones in Lubyanka."
40. Sergeyev, "FSB Colonel"; Sergeyev, "Money Was Brought to FSB Colonel."
41. "Russian Military Court Sentences Former Top Security Agent."
42. Senatorov, "One Criminal Case"; Mashkin, "Chekists."
43. "Seven FSB Employees Arrested"; "Number of FSB Employees"; "Money Stolen by FSB Attackers"; "Ex-FSB Spetnazovtsy."
44. Russian Federation, Gossluzhba, "Register."
45. "FSB Arrests."

7

Legacy, Impact, and Future

Since the dawn of the Putin era, the FSB has enjoyed much success in neutralizing both real and perceived threats to Russia. Although the FSB is not without critics and is subject to the demographic and economic decline that the rest of Russia is experiencing, Putin's patronage ensures that the FSB remains a powerful organization in pursuing Putin's national security priorities.

The FSB has a wide array of capabilities to perform its missions. Like the KGB, the FSB's tentacles reach nearly every corner of the Russian government and society. It is the primary inheritor of the KGB's legacy and the fear that accompanies it, which is still a significant factor in Russians' lives. With the addition of modern technology, the FSB is a potent organization designed to protect the ruling regime from any real or perceived threats.

In numerous cases, the FSB has used crises in Russia to increase its power. In the 1990s, the Russian government bolstered the FSB's counterterrorist authorities after serious terrorist attacks. This included expanding the FSB's counterterrorist structure and the return of special operations groups to the FSB, strengthening internal communications monitoring with SORM, creating a foreign intelligence capability, and re-creating an "ideological counterintelligence" capability and merging it with the fight against terrorists. The reorganization of 2003–4 returned SIGINT and border guards to the FSB. In the early 2000s, the FSB was strengthened to react to the "color revolutions" in post-Soviet states and to conduct assassinations. After mass demonstrations in 2011–12, the FSB was further empowered to pursue anti-Putin oppositionists. After Russia's invasion of Ukraine, the FSB requested further "prophylactic" powers to counter so-called Ukrainian neo-Nazi groups. Crises have been opportunities for the FSB to grow.

There is a direct descendancy—organizationally, culturally, and in personnel—from the KGB to the FSB. Each of the name changes that Russian state security has experienced since the dissolution of the Soviet Union came due to political decisions geared toward controlling state security functions. Eventually, these resources made their way to the FSB. However, there will soon be no former KGB officers left. The average age of the FSB's senior leadership is nearing seventy. That generation's departure will require a new generation of Russians raised in the chaos and corruption of the 1990s to run the service.

An indicator of what this might look like appeared in 2016, when a group of recent graduates of the FSB Academy paraded through the streets of Moscow in expensive Mercedes Benz SUVs, honking their horns and cheering and posing for a group photo with their faces—all males—fully visible (figure 7.1). The footage of the parade was transformed into a music video.[1]

The video elicited a highly negative reaction from the public and retired Russian officers, who considered it a gross violation of professionalism. The FSB leadership did not take the stunt well, either. The FSB announced a few weeks later that "principled personnel decisions have been taken toward the guilty individuals, changing the condition of their service. Severe disciplinary measures against the leadership of the academy, including the demotion of several leaders [and] their firing, will be taken."[2] While it is unlikely FSB Academy graduates will ever repeat such an episode, it is a possible indicator of the caliber of recruits available to the FSB over the coming decades.

Other indicators point to lower skill and education levels among FSB officers compared with the Soviet era. KGB veterans have noted the difference in quality. According to retired KGB general Aleksandr Mikhailov, KGB personnel in the 1970s and 1980s were exceptionally professional and well-educated. The KGB hired individuals with whatever training was needed: if the agency needed a physicist, it hired one;

Figure 7.1 Photograph of FSB Academy graduates from a 2016 video
Source: "Citizens Bearing No Resemblance to FSB Academy Graduates."

if a chemist was required, it hired a chemist. The bar of professionalism was high. Mikhailov lamented, "Today, that is not the case. To be honest, I can't understand how a graduate of the FSB Academy can provide security to a nuclear power station if he neither knows the working principles of that type of nuclear reactor nor even Ohm's law. True, that does not apply to the informatics and cryptography department. Other institutes envy our mathematicians."[3]

A Dossier Center source recounted an incident in which the chief of a regional FSB directorate wrote a monthly report and gave it to a local journalist, a former Soviet-era KGB officer, for publicity purposes. The officer had written the text so poorly that the journalist was forced to correct multiple errors before it was publication-ready. When the situation became publicly known, the FSB office offered to rehire the journalist into the FSB rather than replace the FSB leader who could not write. The journalist refused the offer but began to write the reports himself anyway.[4]

As the FSB portrays its officers as the best of the best in Russian society, incompetence and corruption continue to contradict that image. According to a Dossier Center source, if the FSB tried to catch every officer who commits extortion, takes bribes, offers brokering services, collects debts, or protects small illegal businesses, it would require the resources of the entire agency.[5] While petty local corruption is rampant and affects the lives of many Russians, major corruption cases, such as an FSB officer caught with hundreds of millions of dollars' worth of stolen goods in his apartment or FSB special forces officers robbing a corrupt banker, take an even greater toll on the organization's reputation.

The FSB's handling of terrorism also raises questions. Putin was elected president in 2000 based partially on his promise to eliminate terrorism in the country. The Russian government claims success in countering terrorism and proudly proclaimed in April 2009 that counterterrorism operations in Chechnya were complete.[6] Putin touts this stated success as a laudable accomplishment for his legacy, which is one reason domestic support for Putin is high. However, major terrorist incidents in Russia did not end with the declaration of victory in Chechnya. High-profile attacks have since occurred in Moscow, Saint Petersburg, and other Russian cities, as well as the crash of an airplane taking Russian vacationers returning to Saint Petersburg from the Egyptian Red Sea resort town of Sharm el-Sheikh in 2015, which killed all 224 passengers and crew members on board.[7]

The FSB has been able to recast those events to its advantage: according to Soldatov, the FSB used the 2015 airplane crash as a reason to lobby for greater surveillance and operational powers, such as the authority to use violence to prevent a terrorist attack.[8] In February 2021, Putin declared that 72 "terrorist crimes" had been thwarted in 2020, up from 57 in 2019, and that "in December last year, the last organized bandit group that was committing crimes on the territory of the Chechen Republic and Ingushetia was destroyed."[9] The statement did not mention how those "terrorist crimes" relate to the 2009 declaration of victory in Chechnya. The FSB plays a leading role in fulfilling Putin's promise of defeating terrorism, even though it mishandled terrorist incidents like the Dobrovka Theater hostage crisis, in which at least 170 hostages died, and the Beslan hostage crisis, in which over 300 people died, including over 180 children. These events were well documented outside Russia, but the journalists who detailed the FSB's counterterrorism mistakes have been silenced inside Russia.

The FSB's reported misassessment of a quick victory in Ukraine has likely taken a toll on the Russian leadership's trust in the agency. Western media reported that a Fifth Service officer, Igor Kovalenko, an Operational Information Department case officer who handled sources inside Ukraine, was so confident about Russia's prospects in Ukraine that he contacted a recruited agent in Kyiv a week before the invasion began in

February 2022 and said he had picked out an apartment for himself in Kyiv.[10] Western journalists also claimed that FSB officers, including Fifth Service director Sergey Beseda, were punished for the error that led to a more costly war in Ukraine than Putin had anticipated.

All these trends will affect the FSB's future and the trust the Russian people and leadership places in it. However, the weightiest impact on the future will come when Putin someday leaves the scene, even though he acts like that will never happen. Putin's departure could lead to three possible scenarios regarding the FSB: a longtime chekist in Putin's inner circle could take charge; a younger chekist could fill the position; or a nonchekist from another "power ministry" could take control and push the FSB aside.

The FSB could become the leading power in Russian society, as when Beriya assumed leadership of the Soviet Union in 1953 and unified state security and internal affairs into a single agency soon after Stalin's death, placing himself at its head. Yeltsin similarly attempted to unify state security and internal affairs in late 1991, but state security at the time had been turned into a monster, per Putin's words, and the merger never happened. The environment in Russia is more amenable to such a move today than it was in 1953 or 1991, especially if the FSB were to dominate the merged entity. Either of the past two FSB directors, Patrushev or Bortnikov, could fill the role that Beriya played in 1953. Both are as close to Putin as Beriya was to Stalin—both come from Putin's Leningrad KGB circle. Like Beriya, both have fulfilled tasks beyond just directing a state security agency. Patrushev has been the secretary of the Security Council since 2008, serving as a leading hard-line Putin loyalist in Russia's decision-making. Putin has dispatched Bortnikov, also in the decision-making inner circle, to handle delicate economic relations with countries like China and Pakistan.

If Putin were to die suddenly, as Stalin did, Patrushev and Bortnikov could potentially battle each other for the throne. However, both Patrushev and Bortnikov turned seventy-one in 2022. Neither has many more years of active service left than Putin, who turned seventy in 2022. Other, younger leaders may be more likely to pick up the mantle. FSB first deputy director Sergey Korolev, for example, is a decade younger than Patrushev or Bortnikov and is also a Saint Petersburg native with good connections, although there is no indication that he has the stature to replace Putin. Either way, the FSB would benefit from either an older or younger chekist taking charge of the country.

Another possibility could be that elites from a different "power ministry" could replace Putin. Such a scenario would be to the FSB's detriment. The FSB has made many enemies within the Russian ruling elite, just as Beriya did. Analogously, the FSB's rivals with the Ministry of Defense and Ministry of Internal Affairs could persuade other powerful elites to subordinate the FSB and prevent a chekist from taking charge, as happened with Beriya.

Although any of these scenarios—an older chekist, a younger chekist, or a nonchekist from another "power ministry"—is possible, Putin's departure will likely lead to a power struggle that will make an impact on the FSB. Consequently, it is in the FSB's interest to continue its propaganda campaign among the Russian people, keep its tentacles firmly ahold of rival Russian agencies, suppress negative information about the agency, stay close to Putin, and avoid missteps that might convince him to look elsewhere for an agency to handle his priorities. Self-survival will be the FSB's most urgent mission in the future.

Notes

1. "Citizens Bearing No Resemblance to FSB Academy Graduates."
2. "Russia's FSB Disciplines Future Officers."
3. Tsurygin, "Communist, Chekist, Occupier."
4. "Regional Directorates."
5. "Regional Directorates."
6. "Russia 'Ends Chechnya Operation.'"
7. "Russian Plane Crash."
8. Soldatov, "All-Encompassing Paranoia."
9. "Conference of the FSB Collegium."
10. Baker, "Top Russian Official."

Bibliography

"About Us" (О Нас). In *Герои Страны* (*Heroes of the Country*). https://warheroes.ru/about.asp.
Afonskiy, Artem. "Where a Man Doesn't Go: Women in the FSB Spetsnaz" (Там, где мужчина не пройдет: женщины в спецназе ФСБ). *TVZvezda*, November 26, 2017. https://tvzvezda.ru/news/201711261227-dmec.htm.
Albats, Yevgenia. *State Within a State: KGB and Its Hold on Russia Past, Present, and Future*. New York: Farrar, Straus & Giroux, 1994.
"Alekseyev, Aleksandr Ivanovich" (Алексеев, Александр Иванович). In *Герои Страны* (*Heroes of the Country*). https://warheroes.ru/hero/hero.asp?Hero_id=5198.
Allenova, Olga. "Only One Bomber Still Remains Free" (На свободе остался только один взрывник). *Kommersant*, December 10, 2002. www.kommersant.ru/doc/355437.
Alyarkinskaya, Natalya. "Nicknamed ZAO" (По Прозвищу ЗАО). *Moskovskie Novosti*, April 2, 2004. https://web.archive.org/web/20051128162216/ and www.mn.ru/issue.php?2004-12-32.
"Ambush Wounds 'Anti-Putin Plotter' and Kills Wife Near Kiev," BBC, October 31, 2017. www.bbc.com/news/world-europe-41811969.
"Analyst with Knowledge of Foreign Languages" (Аналитик со знанием иностранных языков). www.superjob.ru/resume/menedzher-proektov-10058546.html.
Anderson, Julie. "The Chekist Takeover of the Russian State." *International Journal of Intelligence and CounterIntelligence* 19, no. 2 (2006): 237–88.
Andrew, Christopher, and Oleg Gordievsky. *KGB: The Inside Story of Its Foreign Operations from Lenin to Gorbachev*. New York: HarperCollins, 1990.
Andreyev, Aleksandr. "There Are 44 Women in Russia with the Rank of General: We'll Tell What They Command" (В России 44 женщин в звании генерала: рассказываем, чем они командуют). Yakapitalist.ru, July 20, 2020. https://yakapitalist.ru/finansy/v-rossii-zhenshhin-generalov.

Anin, Roman. "Russo chekisto." *Novaya Gazeta*, August 22, 2013. https://novayagazeta.ru/articles/2013/08/23/56033-russo-chekisto.

———. "Who Arranged the Hunt for Navalny?" (Кто устроил охоту на Навального?). *Vazhnye Istorii*, September 19, 2020. https://istories.media/investigations/2020/09/17/kto-ustroil-okhotu-na-navalnogo/.

Arshanskiy, Roman. "An Army Without Intelligence Is Blind and Without Counterintelligence Is Defenseless" (Армия без разведки слепа, без контрразведки–беззащитна). *FSB: For and Against* 10, no. 3 (2010).

Balashov, Denis. "A Criminal Group of Engineers: How Spare Parts for a Fighter Jet Were Taken from a 'Rostec' Factory" (Преступное сообщество инженеров. Как с завода "Ростеха" вывозили запчасти для истребителя). Gazetu.ru, February 16, 2022. www.gazeta.ru/social/2022/02/16/14537593.shtml.

Ball, Desmond. *Soviet Signals Intelligence (SIGINT)*. Canberra: Australian National University, 1989.

Bakatin, Vadim. *Getting Rid of the KGB* (Избавление от КГБ). Moscow: Novosti, 1992.

Balmforth, Tom. "You Say Crimea, They Say Taurida." RFE/RL, January 21, 2015. www.rferl.org/a/crimea-russia-renaming-taurida/26806157.html.

Balmforth, Tom, and Maria Tsvetkova. "Russia Takes Down REvil Hacking Group at US Request—FSB." Reuters, January 14, 2022. www.reuters.com/technology/russia-arrests-dismantles-revil-hacking-group-us-request-report-2022-01-14/.

Barabanov, Ilya, and Vladimir Voronov. "Who Killed Litvinenko and Why" (Кто и Зачем Убил Литвиненко). *New Times*, February 12, 2007. https://newtimes.ru/articles/detail/3462.

Baranets, Viktor. "Why Did the FSB Descend Upon Defense Factories?" (Из-за чего ФСБ нагрянула на оборонные заводы?). *Komsomolskaya Pravda*, March 22, 2019. www.kp.ru/daily/26957.7/4010626/.

Barmin, Fedor. "Spetsnaz Opera" (Опера Спецназа). *Specnaz.ru*, 2021. www.specnaz.ru/article/?2021.

Barnes, Julian E. "Pentagon Computer Networks Attacked." *Los Angeles Times*, November 28, 2008. www.latimes.com/archives/la-xpm-2008-nov-28-na-cyberattack28-story.html.

Barron, John. *KGB: The Secret Work of Soviet Agents.* New York: Reader's Digest Press, 1974.

Barry, Ellen, and Michael Schwirtz. "Arrests and Violence at Overflowing Rally in Moscow." *New York Times*, May 6, 2012. www.nytimes.com/2012/05/07/world/europe/at-moscow-rally-arrests-and-violence.html.

Baryshnikov, Valentin. "The Second Service" (Вторая служба). *Svoboda*, August 31, 2017. www.svoboda.org/a/28705258.html.

Bateman, Aaron. "The KGB and Its Enduring Legacy." *Journal of Slavic Military Studies* 29, no. 1 (2016): 23–47.

Batyushin, N. S. *At the Origins of Russian Counterintelligence: A Collection of Documents and Materials* (У истоков русской контрразведки: Сборник документов и материалов). Moscow: Kuchkovo Pole, 2007.

BBC News Russian Service Telegram Channel. July 22, 2021. https://t.me/s/bbcrussian/18639.

Belov, Oleg. "A Quarter Century in the Organs: Nikolay Kovalev, Predecessor to

Vladimir Putin in the Post of FSB Director" (Четверть века в органах: Николай Ковалев, предшественник Владимира Путина на посту директора ФСБ). *Saint Petersburg Vedomosti*, August 6, 2021. https://spbvedomosti.ru/news/nasledie/chetvert-veka-v-organakh-nikolay-kovalev-predshestvennik-vladimira-putina-na-postu-direktora-fsb/.

Bennett, Gordon. *The Federal Security Service of the Russian Federation*. London: Conflict Studies Research Center, 2000.

———. *The Ministry of Internal Affairs of the Russian Federation*. London: Conflict Studies Research Center: 2000. www.files.ethz.ch/isn/96611/00_Oct.pdf.

Berls, Robert E., Jr. *The Roots of Russian Conduct*. Washington, DC: Nuclear Threat Initiative, 2021. www.nti.org/analysis/articles/special-report-the-roots-of-russian-conduct-test/.

Berman, Ilan, and J. Michael Waller, eds. *Dismantling Tyranny: Transitioning Beyond Totalitarian Regimes*. Lanham, MD: Rowman & Littlefield, 2006.

"Biography of Aleksandr Mikhailov" (Александр Михайлов, биография). Grani.ru, July 28, 2004. https://graniru.org/Politics/Russia/FSB/m.74621.html.

"The Biography of the New Chief of the UFSB for the Saratov Oblast Is Made Public" (Обнародована биография нового главы УФСБ по Саратовской области). *Vzglyad-Info*, September 25, 2013. www.vzsar.ru/news/2013/09/25/obnarodovana-biografiya-novogo-glavy-yfsb-po-saratovskoi-oblasti.html.

"The Birthday of the President of Our Club, Mikhail Vasilyevich Shekin" (День Рождения Президента Клуба Михаила Васильевича Шекина). Dinamo Volleyball Club, January 20, 2017. https://vcdynamo.ru/novosti-i-sobytiya/novosti-kluba/61379/.

Boltunov, M. E. *Gold Stars of "Alfa"* (Золотые звезды "Альфы"). Moscow: Kuchkovo Pole, 2009.

Borisov, Aleksandr, Aleksandr Malygin, and Roland Mulukayev. *Three Centuries of Russian Police* (Три века российской полиции). Moscow: Ripol Klassik, 2016.

"Bortnikov Announced That People Preparing to Attack Television Personality Solovyev Had Conducted Surveillance on Him" (Бортников заявил, что готовившие нападение на телеведущего Соловьева вели за ним слежку), TASS, April 25, 2022. https://tass.ru/proisshestviya/14468157.

"Bortnikov to Lose His Right Hand: General Smirnov's Contract Will Not Be Extended" (Бортников лишится правой руки: Генералу Смирнову не продляют контракт). Pasmi.ru, August 12, 2019. https://pasmi.ru/archive/239722/.

"Bortnikov: The Hope of Citizens of LNR and DNR to Live in Peace Will Be Realized by the Recognition of the Republics" (Бортников: Надежда граждан ЛНР и ДНР о жизни в мире будет реализована признанием республик). TASS, February 21, 2022. https://tass.ru/politika/13788747.

Bratersky, Alexander. "Patriarch Plants Church Near FSB School." *Moscow Times*, July 31, 2012. www.themoscowtimes.com/2012/07/31/patriarch-plants-church-near-fsb-school-a16678.

Burenkov, Mikhail. "Lessons from Russian Special Services" (Уроки русских спецслужб). *FSB: Za i Protiv* 3 (2016): 62–67. www.osfsb.ru/upload/iblock/668/6681728c6d648412be26601d23 ad6530.pdf.

"Cam Ran Military Base" (Военная база Камрань). TASS, February 15, 2015. https://tass.ru/info/1766807.

Chapple, Amos, and Kaisa Alliksaar. "Some Shall Pass: Russia's Bizarre Border Blip with Estonia." RFE/RL, September 20, 2019. www.rferl.org/a/estonias-strange-border-anomaly-with-russia/30174472.html.

Chebrikov, Viktor, ed. *The History of Soviet State Security Agencies: A Textbook* (История Советских Органов Государственной Безопасности: Учебник). Moscow: Dzerzhinskiy Higher Red Banner School of the Committee of State Security, 1977.

"Chekists Repulsed About 100 Thousand Attacks on the President's Site" (Чекисты отразили около 100 тысяч атак на сайт президента). *SecurityLab*, December 19, 2003. www.securitylab.ru/news/213418.php.

Chernukhin, Andrey. "A Stinger Stuck into Alexander Potkin" (В Александра Поткина вонзилось Жало). June 5, 2015. https://andreychernuhin.livejournal.com/201392.html.

"China-Russia Energy Cooperation." World Energy, September 18, 2019. www.world-energy.org/article/2343.html.

Chirgwin, Richard. "Swiss CERT Publishes Reveals Details of Defence Contractor Hack." *Register*, May 24, 2016. www.theregister.com/2016/05/24/anatomy_of_a_breach_swiss_cert_publishes_analysis_of_ruag_attack.

"Citizens Bearing No Resemblance to FSB Academy Graduates Organized a Parade of Gelandwagens in Moscow (21.06.16)" (Граждане, не похожие на выпускников Академии ФСБ, устроили парад на Gelandwagen в Москве [21.06.16]), *YouTube*, July 2, 2016. www.youtube.com/watch?v=liohDIOc8Fo.

Coalson, Robert. "The Close Ties Between Russia's Church and State." Modern Diplomacy, May 19, 2013. https://moderndiplomacy.eu/2013/05/19/the-close-ties-between-russias-church-and-state/.

"Colonel G. Drachev Appointed to the Position of Chief of the UFSB RF for the Pskov Oblast" (На должность начальника УФСБ РФ по Псковской области назначен полковник Г. Драчев). rbc.ru, November 28, 2006. www.rbc.ru/spb_sz/freenews/5592c40a9a79473b7f4bf46b.

Colton, Timothy J. *Yeltsin: A Life.* New York: Basic Books, 2008.

"The Commission Has Named Names: Pronichev, Anisimov, Tikhonov . . ." (Комиссия Назвала Фамилии: Проничев, Анисимов, Тихонов . . .). *Novaya Gazeta*, November 30, 2005. https://novayagazeta.ru/articles/2005/12/01/23607-komissiya-nazvala-familii-pronichev-anisimov-tihonov.

"Conference of the FSB Collegium of Russia" (Заседание коллегии ФСБ России). Kremlin.ru, February 24, 2021. www.kremlin.ru/events/president/news/65068.

Corera, Gordon. *Russians Among Us: Sleeper Cells, Ghost Stories, and the Hunt for Putin's Spies.* New York: William Morrow, 2020.

Corso, Molly. "Georgia: Russian Border Guards in Abkhazia, South Ossetia Pose New Challenge for Tbilisi." Eurasia Net, May 12, 2009. https://eurasianet.org/georgia-russian-border-guards-in-abkhazia-south-ossetia-pose-new-challenge-for-tbilisi.

"Countersanctions: How FSB Employees Tried to Poison Vladimir Kara-Mirza" (Контрсанкции: Как сотрудники ФСБ пытались отравить Владимира Кара-Мурзу). *Insider*, February 11, 2021. https://theins.ru/politika/239317.

Crowdstrike. *2019 Global Threat Report: Adversary Tradecraft and the Importance of Speed.* Sunnyvale, CA: Crowdstrike, 2020.

Cumming-Bruce, Nick, and Anton Troianovski. "A Russian Diplomat Resigns: 'Never Have I Been So Ashamed of My Country.'" *New York Times*, May 23, 2022. www.nytimes.com/2022/05/23/world/europe/russia-diplomat-un-geneva.html.

Darczewska, Jolanta. *Defenders of the Besieged Fortress: Notes on the Historical Legitimisation of Russia's Special Services*. Warsaw: Centre for Eastern Studies, 2018.

Dean, Aimen, Paul Cruikshank, and Tim Lister. *Nine Lives: My Time as MI6's Top Spy Inside Al-Qaida*. London: Oneworld, 2018.

Demidov, Anton. "Ex-FSB Investigators Receive Sentences for Extorting Bitcoins" (Экс-следователи ФСБ получили сроки за вымогательство биткоинов). Gazeta.ru, February 26, 2021. www.gazeta.ru/social/news/2021/02/26/n_15670562.shtml.

Denisenko, Petr. "A Native Kursk Leads the Lipetsk UFSB" (Липецкое УФСБ возглавил курянин). *Kommersant*, March 30, 2004. www.kommersant.ru/doc/461760.

"Deputy Director of the FSB Spoke in the UN about Russia's International Cooperation against Terrorism" (Замдиректора ФСБ рассказал в ООН о международном сотрудничестве России против терроризма). TASS, March 1, 2019. https://tass.ru/politika/6173438.

Deriabin, Petr, and Frank Gibney. *The Secret World*. New York: Doubleday, 1959.

Deych, Mark. "The Sinister 'Dulles Plan': The Machinations of an American Intelligence Chief or a Fake?" (Зловещий "план Даллеса": Происки шефа американской разведки или фальшивка?). *MK.ru*, January 20, 2005. www.mk.ru/editions/daily/article/2005/01/20/200843-zloveschiy-plan-dallesa.html.

"Directorate 'M.'" Dossier Center.

"Director of the UFSB for Ingushetia Koryakov Removed from His Position" (Руководитель УФСБ по Ингушетии Коряков отстранен от должности). Prague Watchdog, February 2, 2005. www.watchdog.cz/?show=000000-000005-000004-000087&lang=2.

Dixon, Robyn. "Chechen War Propels Putin to Front Ranks." *Los Angeles Times*, January 1, 2000. www.latimes.com/archives/la-xpm-2000-jan-01-mn-49592-story.html.

Dolgov, Anna. "Appointment of Ex-KGB Agent to Strengthen Russian Security Service." Associated Press, July 27, 1998.

Donetsk DNR News Donbass Russia Novorossiya. "Eternal Glory to the Hero!" (Вечная Память Герою!). *VKontakte*, June 19, 2022. https://vk.com/wall-50332460_3334349.

Dossier Center. *The Lubyanka Federation: How the FSB Determines the Politics and Economy of Russia* (Лубянская Федерация: Как ФСБ определяет политику и экономику России). Dossier Center, 2022. https://fsb.dossier.center/.

Duhamel, Luc. *The KGB Campaign Against Corruption in Moscow, 1982–1987*. Pittsburgh: University of Pittsburgh Press, 2010.

Dunlop, John. *The Moscow Bombings of September 1999: Examinations of Russian Terrorist Attacks at the Onset of Vladimir Putin's Rule*. Stuttgart: Ibidem-Verlag, 2012.

Ebon, Martin. *KGB: Death and Rebirth*. Westport, CT: Praeger, 1994.

Eckel, Mike. "Chiefs of Three Russian Intelligence Agencies Travel to Washington." RFE/RL, February 1, 2018. www.rferl.org/a/russia-spy-chiefs-washington/29010324.html.

———. "In Moscow Treason Trial, A Major Scandal for Russian Security Agency." RFE/RL, February 27, 2019. www.rferl.org/a/russia-hacker-mikhailov-stoyanov-fsb-scandal-for-russian-security-agency/29794092.html.

———. "Two Decades On, Smoldering Questions About the Russian President's Vault to Power." RFE/RL, August 7, 2019. www.rferl.org/a/putin-russia-president-1999-chechnya-apartment-bombings/30097551.html.

"Eduard Chernovoltsev, Head of the Scientific and Technical Service of the Federal Security Service of the Russian Federation." InfoForum.ru. https://infoforum.ru/greetings/eduard-chernovoltsev.

Ermolov, Viktor. "The Head of the FSB Fifth Service Gave a Speech at a Cemetery; He Had Earlier Been Reported to Be Under Arrest" (Глава Пятой Службы ФСБ Выступил С Речью На Кладбище; Ранее Писали О Его Аресте). *Glavnaya Stranitsa*, April 29, 2022. https://befreeinrussia.com/2022/глава-пятой-службы-фсб-выступил-с-речь/.

Escritt, Thomas. "German Court Accuses Russia of 'State Terrorism' over 2019 Berlin Park Murder." Reuters, December 15, 2021. www.reuters.com/world/europe/german-court-convicts-russian-2019-berlin-park-murder-2021-12-15/.

"EU Targets Russian Officials in Sanctions List." Reuters, July 25, 2014. www.reuters.com/article/uk-ukraine-crisis-eu-sanctions/factbox-eu-targets-russian-officials-in-sanctions-list-idUKKBN0FV02Q20140726.

"Ex-FSB Officer and 'Kaspersky Laboratory' Manager Convicted of State Treason" (Экс-сотрудника ФСБ и топ-менеджера "Лаборатории Касперского" осудили за госизмену). BBC Russian Service, February 29, 2019. www.bbc.com/russian/news-47367728.

"Ex-FSB Spetnazovtsy Vladimir Urusov and Khetag Margiyev Are Sentenced for Robbing a Businessman" (Экс-спецназовцы ФСБ Владимир Урусов и Хетаг Маргиев осуждены за разбойное нападение на бизнесмена). Region15.ru, January 24, 2022. https://region15.ru/eks-spetsnazovtsy-fsb-vladimir-urusov-i-hetag-margiev-osuzhdeny-za-razbojnoe-napadenie-na-biznesmena/.

"The Family of the 'FSB Supply Chief,' Gutseriyev and 'Krost,' and the History of the 'VollyGrad,' Where Putin Visited Today" (Семья "завхоза ФСБ," Гуцериев и Крост: история "Волей Града," в котором побывал сегодня Путин). *Open Media*, August 16, 2019. https://openmedia.io/news/semya-zavxoza-fsb-guceriev-i-krost-rasskazyvaem-istoriyu-volej-grada-v-kotorom-pobyval-segodnya-putin/.

"The Fatal KGB Rank" (Смертельная рана КГБ). *Argumenty i Fakty*, August 15, 1991. https://archive.aif.ru/archive/1625139.

"Federal State Public Enterprise 'Social Welfare Service'" (Федеральное Государственное Казенное Учреждение "Служба Социально-Бытового Обеспечения"), Audit-It.ru. www.audit-it.ru/contragent/1037710006410_fgku-ssbo.

Fedor, Julie. "Chekists Look Back on the Cold War: The Polemical Literature." *Intelligence and National Security* 26, no. 6 (2011): 842–63.

———. *Russia and the Cult of State Security: The Chekist Tradition, from Lenin to Putin.* London: Routledge, 2011.

Feldschreiber, Jared. "Russia Convicts Estonian Border Guard Eston Kohver." UPI, August 19, 2015. www.upi.com/Top_News/World-News/2015/08/19/Russia-convicts-Estonian-border-guard-Eston-Kohver/8811439986450/.

Felshtinskiy, Yuriy, and Aleksandr Litvinenko. "The FSB Is Blowing Up Russia" (FSB

Взрывает Россию). *Novaya Gazeta*, August 27, 2001. http://2001.novayagazeta.ru/nomer/2001/61n/n61n-s00.shtml. This article is a preview of their book *Blowing Up Moscow: Terror from Within*. New York: SPI Books, 2002.

Fesenko, Anatoliy, and Nikolay Milovsorov. "Determination of the Primary and Minor Components of Gold Alloys in Forensic Research" (Определение основных и неосновных компонентов сплавов золота при криминалистическом исследовании). *Russian Chemical Journal* 44, no. 4 (2002): 81–87.

Fischer, Ben B., ed. *Okhrana: The Paris Operations of the Russian Imperial Police*. Washington, DC: CIA Center for the Study of Intelligence, 1997.

"Friendship Order Presented to Russian Security Leaders." *Vietnam Pictorial*, December 3, 2017. https://vietnam.vnanet.vn/english/tin-van/friendship-order-presented-to-russian-security-leaders-165201.html.

Fronin, Vladislav. "FSB Highlights" (ФСБ расставляет акценты). *Rossiyskaya Gazeta*, December 19, 2017. https://rg.ru/2017/12/19/aleksandr-bortnikov-fsb-rossii-svobodna-ot-politicheskogo-vliianiia.html.

"FSB." Dossier Center.

FSB. "Process for Admission into the Service" ("Порядок Поступления на Службу"). FSB.ru. http://www.fsb.ru/fsb/supplement/employ/doc1.htm.

———. (ФСБ). *Belov List*. No date. https://spisokbelov.wordpress.com/фсб-2/.

"FSB Arrests." Levada Center, September 5, 2016. www.levada.ru/en/2016/09/05/fsb-arrests/.

"FSB Border Guard Service: To Avoid Casting a Shadow on Your Vacation, Check Your Fines with the Bailiff" (Погранслужба ФСБ: Чтобы не омрачить вылет в отпуск, проверьте свои штрафы у приставов). Interfax, April 9, 2019. www.interfax.ru/interview/657472.

"The FSB Conducted a Massive Special Operation Against 'Jehovah's Witnesses' Across All of Russia" (ФСБ провела по всей России масштабную спецоперацию против "Свидетелей Иеговы"). Lenta.ru, November 24, 2010. https://lenta.ru/news/2020/11/24/iegova/.

"FSB Created a National Center for Cyber Defense" (ФСБ создала национальный центр кибербезопасности). CNews.ru, September 10, 2018. www.cnews.ru/news/top/2018-09-10_v_rossii_sozdan_natsionalnyj_tsentr_po_kompyuternym.

"FSB Directorate 'M.'" Agentura.ru.

"The FSB Has Uncovered an Underground Network Amongst Illegal Immigrants" (ФСБ раскрыла подрывную сеть в среде нелегальных мигрантов). RBC.ru, May 30, 2013. www.rbc.ru/society/30/05/2013/570409759a7947fcbd4498a6.

"FSB Officers Revealed a Cell of Jehovah's Witnesses in Sevastopol, Opened a Criminal Case" (Сотрудники ФСБ раскрыли ячейку Свидетелей Иеговы в Севастополе, Возбуждено уголовное дело). TASS. https://tass.ru/obschestvo/6510396.

"The FSB Rendered Harmless a Group of Religious Extremists in Omsk" (ФСБ обезвредила в Омске группу религиозных экстремистов). *Novye Izvestia*, April 2, 2021. https://newizv.ru/news/incident/02-04-2021/bolshuyu-gruppu-religioznyh-ekstremistov-zaderzhali-v-omske.

"FSB Report about the Prevention of Terrorist Acts in the Armed Forces of Russia" (В ФСБ рассказали о предотвращении терактов в Вооружённых силах России). *Moskovskiy Komsomolets.ru*, December 18, 2018. www.mk.ru/incident/2018/12/18/v-fsb-rasskazali-o-predotvrashenii-teraktov-v-vooruzyonnykh-silakh-rossii.html.

"FSB Reported on the Level of Security at the Upcoming Confederations Cup" (ФСБ отчиталась об уровне безопасности на предстоящем Кубке конфедераций). *RIA Novosti*, June 6, 2017. https://ria.ru/20170606/1495919008.html.

"The FSB Reports of 70 Million Cyberattacks on Objects of the RF Information Infrastructure over a Year" (ФСБ сообщила о 70 млн кибератаках на объекты информационной структуры РФ за год). Interfax, January 24, 2017. www.interfax.ru/russia/546767.

"The FSB's Licensing Center" (Центр Лицензирования ФСБ). Center for the Security of Information Systems. https://xn--90ao1ar.xn--p1ai/tsentr-litsenzirovaniya-fsb/.

"'FSB Spetsnaz': Who Is Behind the Cases Against Ulyukaev and Other High-Ranking Officials" ("Спецназ ФСБ": Кто стоит за делами против Улюкаева и других высокопоставленных чиновников). TVRain.ru, November 15, 2016. https://tvrain.ru/articles/spetsnaz_fsb-421082/.

"The FSB Stopped the Activities of Religious Extremists" (ФСБ пресекла деятельность религиозных экстремистов). News.ru, June 3, 2022. https://news.ru/regions/fsb-presekla-deyatelnost-religioznyh-ekstremistov/.

"The FSB Stopped the Activities of Religious Extremists in Yekaterinburg" (ФСБ пресекла деятельность религиозных экстремистов в Екатеринбурге). *Izvestia*, September 22, 2021. https://iz.ru/1225460/2021-09-22/fsb-presekla-deiatelnost-religioznykh-ekstremistov-v-ekaterinburge.

"The FSB Structure Warned of Cyberattacks in Light of US Statement" (Структура ФСБ предупредила об угрозе кибератак в свете заявлений США). Interfax, January 22, 2021. www.interfax.ru/russia/746316.

"FSB Will Apply the Developments of Siberian Scientists" (ФСБ Применит Разработки Сибирских Ученых). *Navigator*, July 13, 2012. https://navigato.ru/stati/publication/fsb-primenit-razrabotki-sibirskih-uchenih.

"The FSB Will Check Participants in the Privatization of a Company" (ФСБ проверит участвующие в приватизации компании), RBC.ru, August 12, 2014. www.rbc.ru/economics/12/08/2014/5704208f9a794760d3d40a2d.

Gabowitsch, Mischa. *Protest in Putin's Russia*. Malden, MA: Polity Press, 2017.

Galeotti, Mark. "Putin's Hydra: Inside Russia's Intelligence Services." European Council on Foreign Relations, May 2016.

———. *Russian Security and Paramilitary Forces Since 1991*. New York: Osprey, 2013.

"A Game of Thrones in Lubyanka." Warsaw Institute, March 24, 2021. https://warsawinstitute.org/game-thrones-lubyanka/.

Garthoff, Raymond. *Soviet Leaders and Intelligence: Assessing the American Adversary during the Cold War*. Washington, DC: Georgetown University Press, 2015.

Gavrilov, Yevgeniy. "Ukraine Wants to Question FSB General Who Was in Ukraine on 20–21 February" (Украина хочет допросить генерала ФСБ, находившегося в Украине 20–21 февраля). ZN.ua, April 4, 2014. https://zn.ua/POLITICS/ukraina-hochet-doprosit-generala-fsb-nahodivshegosya-v-ukraine-20-21-fevralya-142656_.html.

Genzlinger, Neil. "Eduard Limonov, Russian Writer and Dissident, Dies at 77." *New York Times*, March 17, 2020. www.nytimes.com/2020/03/17/books/eduard-limonov-dead.html.

"The German in the Safronov Case: Who Is Demuri (Dieter) Voronin / Russia and Russians: A View from Europe." *Time.News*, November 5, 2021. https://time.news/the-german-in-the-safronov-case-who-is-demuri-dieter-voronin-russia-and-russians-a-view-from-europe-dw/.

Gerts, Irina. "FSB Detains a Sevastopol Resident for Inciting Extremism and Disrespect for Religion" (ФСБ задержала севастопольца за призывы к экстремизму и неуважение к религии). *Komsomolskaya Pravda*, March 24, 2022. www.crimea.kp.ru/daily/27396/4591993/.

Goldfarb, Alexander, and Marina Litvinenko. *Death of a Dissident: The Poisoning of Alexander Litvinenko and the Return of the KGB*. New York: Free Press, 2007.

Golov, A. A. "MVD or FSB: Which Class's Interests Do Special Services Represent?" (МВД или ФСБ? Интересы Какого Класса Представляют Спецслужбы?). Levada Center, 2002. www.levada.ru/2002/10/22/mvd-ili-fsb-interesy-kakogo-klassa-predstavlyayut-spetssluzhby/.

Goode, Paul. "Russia and Digital Surveillance in the Wake of COVID-19." PONARS Eurasia Policy Memo 650, May 2020. www.ponarseurasia.org/russia-and-digital-surveillance-in-the-wake-of-covid-19/.

Gorlenko, Sergey. *From the KGB to the FSB: Opera Notes* (От КГБ до ФСБ. Записки опера). Moscow: Avka-Term, 2015.

Gorokhova, T. A., Yu. A. Fedorov, L. I. Savvateyeva, and V. A. Kobylyanskiy. "Drug Simulator for Training Detection Dogs to Detect Drugs" (Имитатор наркотических веществ для тренировки розыскных собак на обнаружение наркотиков). Patent number RU2160529C1, December 20, 2000. https://patents.google.com/patent/RU2160529C1/ru.

"Gromov, Sergey Sergeyevich" (Громов, Сергей Сергеевич). In *Герои Страны* (*Heroes of the Country*). https://warheroes.ru/hero/hero.asp?Hero_id=9666.

"Guys from Alfa: How the Elite Spetsnaz of the FSB of Russia Works" (Ребята из "Альфы": Как работает элитный спецназ ФСБ России). *RIA Novosti*, July 29, 2019. https://ria.ru/20190729/1556911713.html.

"Hackers Try to Break into Ministry's Sites" (Хакеры пытаются взломать министерские сайты). *Vslukh*, June 15, 2006. https://vsluh.ru/novosti/obshchestvo/khakery-pytayutsya-vzlomat-ministerskie-sayty_84773/.

Haidar, Suhasini. "Afghanistan: CIA Chief, Russian Security Head in Delhi." *The Hindu*, September 7, 2021.

Hall, Steven L. "Intelligence Sharing with Russia: A Practitioner's Perspective." Carnegie Endowment for International Peace, February 14, 2017. https://carnegieendowment.org/files/2-14-17_Stephen_Hall_Intelligence_Sharing.pdf.

Halpin, Tony. "Gunmen Kill Seven Women in Russian Sauna." *The Times* (London), August 14, 2009.

Hammond, Andrew. "Becoming a Russian Intelligence Officer." Interview with Janosh Neumann, International Spy Museum Spycast, August 2, 2022. https://thecyberwire.com/podcasts/spycast/550/transcript.

Higgins, Andrew. "Chat Group Becomes Target of Moscow's Wrath as Security Crackdown Widens." *New York Times*, August 6, 2020. www.nytimes.com/2020/08/06/world/europe/russia-extremisim-chat-group-sentence.html.

———. "Tensions Surge in Estonia Amid a Russian Replay of Cold War Tactics." *New

York Times, October 5, 2014. www.nytimes.com/2014/10/06/world/europe/estonia-russia-cold-war-eston-kohver-border.html.

Hill, Fiona, and Clifford Gaddy. *Mr. Putin: Operative in the Kremlin.* Washington, DC: Brookings Institution Press, 2015.

Hoffman, David, and Walter Pincus. "American Accused of Spying." *Washington Post*, December 1, 1999. www.washingtonpost.com/wp-srv/WPcap/1999-12/01/068r-120199-idx.html.

"Honored Citizens" (Почётные граждане). Ukhta City District. https://mouhta.ru/gorod/pgr/.

"How Was the KGB-FSB Analysis Service Created" (Как создавалась аналитическая служба КГБ-ФСБ). *Zen*, September 15, 2020. https://zen.yandex.ru/media/vestnikpolit/kak-sozdavalas-analiticheskaia-slujba-kgbfsb-5f60ea59249b32282b0547f5.

"Idea of US Threat to Russia Is 'Ludicrous'—Rice." Reuters, April 26, 2007. www.reuters.com/article/idUSL26606311.

"Individual Proprietor Sablin Anatoliy Anatolyevich" (ИП Саблин Анатолий Анатольевич). ERGInf.com. https://egrinf.com/ip9713982.

"In First Place, the Army; In Second, the President; in Third, the FSB" (На Первом Месте—Армия, На Втором—Президент, На Третьем—ФСБ). Levada Center, March 29, 2021. www.levada.ru/2021/03/29/na-pervom-meste-armiya-na-vtorom-prezident-na-tretem-fsb/.

"The Internet Got a New Guardian in the FSB" (У интернета появился новый куратор в ФСБ). RBC.ru, July 28, 2017. www.rbc.ru/technology_and_media/28/07/2017/5979f6339a7947102993ac64.

"Investigative Section for Especially Important Cases" (Следственная часть по особо важным делам). *Shield and Sword*, 2022. https://shieldandsword.mozohin.ru/VD3462/nkvd4143/structure/sledchast.htm.

Ivanov, Anatoliy. *Eternal Call* (*Вечный Зов*). Moscow: Sovremennik, 1972.

Ivashkina, Darya. "Border Guards Days in 2023: History and Tradition of the Holiday" (День пограничника в 2023 году: История и традиции праздника). *Semya*, no date. www.kp.ru/family/prazdniki/den-pogranichnika/.

Ivshina, Olga. "Cargo 200: What Is Known About Russian Army Losses in Ukraine at the Beginning of July" (Груз 200: Что известно о потерях российской армии в Украине к началу июля). BBC Russian Service, July 8, 2022. www.bbc.com/russian/features-62087305.

Jahn, Egbert. "The Castling of Presidential Functions by Vladimir Putin." In *International Politics: Political Issues Under Debate*, vol. 1. Berlin: Springer, 2015.

"Journalist, Activist, and 'Patriot': Who Have the Poisoners from FSB NII-2 Killed?" (Журналист, активист, "патриот"—кого убивали отравители из НИИ-2 ФСБ?). *Insider*, January 27, 2021. https://theins.ru/politika/238673.

"Journalist Christo Grozev Named the Diplomat Who Died in the FRG the Son of a General" (Журналист Христо Грозев назвал погибшего в ФРГ дипломата сыном генерала). RBC.ru, November 5, 2021. www.rbc.ru/rbcfreenews/618542479a794767f5bec744.

Juurvee, Ivo, and Lavly Perling. *Russia's Espionage in Estonia: A Quantitative Analysis of Convictions*. Tallinn: International Center for Defense and Security, 2019.

"Kalimatov, Alikhan Maksharipovich" (Калиматов, Алихан Макшарипович). In

Герои Страны (*Heroes of the Country*), 2022. https://warheroes.ru/hero/hero.asp?Hero_id=13214.

Kaliyev, Roustam. "Can 'Power Ministries' Be Reformed?" *Perspective* 13, no. 1 (2002). https://open.bu.edu/handle/2144/3603.

Kalugin, Oleg. *The View from Lubyanka: The "Case" of a Former KGB General* (*Вид с Лубянки: «Дело» бывшего генерала КГБ*). Moscow: РИК, 1990.

Kaluzhskaya, Mariya. "Ten Years Without Starvoytova" (Десять лет без Старовойтовой). Grani.ru, November 20, 2008. https://graniru.org/Politics/Russia/m.144242.html.

Kanev, Sergey, Roman Anin, and Sergey Sokolov. "Lubyankans on the Rublevka" (Лубянские на Рублевке). *Novaya Gazeta*, July 26, 2015. https://novayagazeta.ru/inquests/69336.html.

Karavashkin, Vitaliy. *Who Betrayed Russia?* (*Кто Предал Россию?*). Moscow: AST, 2008.

"'Kaspersky Laboratory' Told of the Arrest of a Senior Manager" ("Лаборатория Касперского" рассказала об аресте топ-менеджера). BBC Russian Service, January 25, 2017. www.bbc.com/russian/news-38742660.

"KGB Passes Secrets Back to US." *New York Times*, December 14, 1991.

Khlobustov, Oleg. *August 1991: Where Was the KGB?* (*Август 1991 г. Где был КГБ?*). Moscow: Litres, 2022.

———. "Once Again on the 'Notorious Dulles Plan' (Еще раз о "Пресловутом Плане Даллеса"). In *Труды Общества изучения истории отечественных спецслужб* (*Proceedings of the Society for the Study of Patriotic Special Services*). Moscow: Kuchkovo Pole, 2006.

Kirillova, Kseniya. "'For Faith and the Fatherland': How Russian Special Services Use 'Nontraditional' Confessions" ("За веру и Отечество": как российские спецслужбы используют "нетрадиционные" конфессии). *SlavicSac*, February 3, 2020. www.slavicsac.com/2020/02/03/russian-special-services/.

Kiseleva, Yelena, Nikolay Sergeyev, and Mikhail Fishman. "The Whale and the Sword: The FSB Is Caught Smuggling" (Кит и меч: ФСБ попалась на контрабанде). *Kommersant*, September 14, 2006. www.kommersant.ru/doc/704751.

Klimenko, Valentin. *Notes of a Counterintelligence Officer: A View from the Inside on the KGB and CIA Conflict, and Other Things . . .* (*Записки контрразведчика: Взгляд изнутри на противоборство КГБ и ЦРУ, и не только . . .*). Moscow: Mezhdunarodnye Otnosheniya, 2018. http://loveread.ec/contents.php?id=85044.

Knight, Amy. *Russia's New Security Services: An Assessment*. Washington, DC: Library of Congress, 1994.

———. *Spies Without Cloaks: The KGB's Successors*. Princeton, NJ: Princeton University Press, 1996.

Knobel, Beth. "Putin's Spies Were Watching Us." *Columbia Journalism Review*, January 31, 2022. www.cjr.org/first_person/putins-spies-were-watching-us.php.

Kokurin, Aleksandr, and Nikita Petrov. *Lubyanka: VChK-OGPU-NKVD-NKGB-MGB-MVD-KGB 1917–1960* (*Лубянка: ВЧК-ОГПУ-НКВД-НКГБ-МГБ-МВД-КГБ 1917–1960*). Moscow: International Democracy Foundation, 1997.

Kolomytseva, Tamara. "My Son Is Not a Criminal!" (Мой Сын—Не Преступник!). Zavtra.ru, March 30, 1998. https://zavtra.ru/blogs/1998-03-3115letter.

Kolpakidi, Aleksandr. *Special Services of the Russian Empire: A Unique Encyclopedia*

(*Спецслужбы Российской Империи: Уникальная энциклопедия*). Moscow: Yauza, 2010.
Kondratyeva, Aleksandra. "FSB of Russia" (ФСБ России). YouTube. www.youtube.com/watch?v=-HujKRx_ypE.
Korenkov, Sergey, ed. *Military Counterintelligence of the FSB 1918–2003.* Moscow: ACT Moskovskiy Poligrapicheskiy Dom, 2004.
Korybko, Andrew. "Indian Fears: Is Russia Joining Pakistan China in CPEC?" Global Village Space, February 25, 2017. www.globalvillagespace.com/indian-fears-is-russia-joining-pakistan-china-in-cpec/.
Kouzminov, Alexander. *Biological Espionage: Special Operations of the Soviet and Russian Foreign Intelligence Services in the West.* London: Greenhill Books, 2005.
Kovacevic, Filip. "The FSB Literati: The First Prize Winners of the Russian Federal Security Service Literature Award Competition, 2006–2018." *Intelligence and National Security* 34, no. 5 (2019): 637–53.
———. "How KGB Spied on Foreign Journalists and Diplomats in the 1960s Lithuania." *Chekist Monitor*, October 10, 2021. https://thechekistmonitor.blogspot.com/2021/10/KGB-Spying-ForeignVisitors-Lithuania.html.
Kozyrev, Andrei. *The Firebird: The Elusive Fate of Russian Democracy.* Pittsburgh: University of Pittsburgh Press, 2019.
Krasnov, Vladislav. *Soviet Defectors: The KGB Wanted List.* Stanford, CA: Hoover Institution Press, 1985.
"Kryuchkov, Vladimir Vladimirovich" (Крючков, Владимир Владимирович). Labyrinth Data Base, no date. https://labyrinth.ru/content/card.asp?cardid=73928.
Kucera, Joshua. "Pashinyan Proposes Russian Border Guards for Entire Armenia-Azerbaijan Border." Eurasia Net, July 30, 2021. https://eurasianet.org/pashinyan-proposes-russian-border-guards-for-entire-armenia-azerbaijan-border.
Kudryavtsev, Nikolay. "General's Family Crashed with Flashers" (Семья генерала разбилась с мигалкой). Gazeta.ru, October 8, 2009. www.gazeta.ru/auto/2009/10/08_a_3270878.shtml.
Kudryavtseva, Darya, and Kirill Mikhailov. "Sechin's Spetsnaz: Who Has Power to Send Ministers and Governors to Prison" (Сечинский спецназ: У кого есть власть сажать министров и губернаторов). *Current Time*, November 16, 2016. www.currenttime.tv/a/28119857.html.
Kulikov. Vladislav. "Russian Border Guards Leave Tajikistan" (Российские пограничники покидают Таджикистан). *Rossiyskaya Gazeta*, July 13, 2005. https://rg.ru/2005/07/13/tadjikistan.html.
"Kupryazhkin Aleksandr Nikolayevich—Biography" (Купряжкин Александр Николаевич—биография). VIPerson.ru, February 6, 2022. http://viperson.ru/people/kupryazhkin-aleksandr-nikolaevich.
Kuzovnikova, Lyudmila. "Development of a Complex and Research into a Method of Remote Detection and Identification of Traces of Explosives on the Surface of Objects Under the Influence of IR Laser Radiation" (Разработка Комплекса и Исследование Метода Дистанционного Обнаружения и Идентификации Следов Взрывчатых Веществ на Поверхности Объектов при Воздействии Лазерного Излучения Ик-Диапазона). Dissertation for Tomsk National Research Institute, 2018. https://earchive.tpu.ru/bitstream/11683/52857/1/thesis_tpu-2018-77.pdf.

"The Laboratory: How Employees from FSB NII-2 Tried to Poison Aleksey Navalny" (Лаборатория: Как сотрудники НИИ-2 ФСБ пытались отравить Алексея Навального). *Insider*, December 14, 2020. https://theins.ru/politika/237705.

Lapin, Denis, Olga Pavlova, Bianca Britton, and Sarah Dean. "Film Director Oleg Sentsov and MH17 Suspect Among Those Freed in Russia-Ukraine Prisoner Swap." CNN, September 7, 2019. www.cnn.com/2019/09/07/europe/ukraine-russia-prisoner-swap-intl/index.html.

Latvian State Security Service. *Annual Report on the Activities of the Latvian State Security Service in 2018*. Riga, April 2019. https://vdd.gov.lv/uploads/materials/2/en/annual-report-2018.pdf.

Lee, Victor Robert. "Satellite Images: A (Worrying) Cuban Mystery." *Diplomat*, June 8, 2018. https://thediplomat.com/2018/06/satellite-images-a-worrying-cuban-mystery/.

Leshchenko, Oleksandr. "Зачем 20 февраля в Киев прибыл генерал ФСБ, причастный к отделению Абхазии и Южной Осетии от Грузии?" (Why Did an FSB General, Who Was Involved in Separating Abkhazia and South Ossetia from Georgia, Come to Kyiv on 29 February?). *Fakty*, April 10, 2014. https://fakty.ua/179850-tak-zachem-vse-taki-dlya-vstrechi-s-viktorom-yanukovichem-20-fevralya-v-kiev-pribyl-general-polkovnik-fsb-prichastnyj-k-otdeleniyu-abhazii-i-yuzhnoj-osetii-ot-gruzii.

Lezina, Evgenia. "Dismantling the State Security Apparatus: Transformations of the Soviet State Security Bodies in Post-Soviet Russia." In *Memory of Nations: Democratic Transition Guide—The Russian Experience*. Prague: CEVRO Institute, 2017.

"List of Russians Convicted of 'State Treason'" (Список россиян, осужденных по статье "Госизмена" 1997–2020 гг). *Novaya Gazeta*, May 28, 2021. https://novayagazeta.ru/articles/2021/05/28/spisok-rossiian-osuzhdennykh-po-state-gosizmena-1997-2020-gg.

Litvinova, Vera. "Olga from Spetsnaz" (Ольга из Спецназа). *Spetsnaz*, January 31, 2019. www.specnaz.ru/articles/268/22/3155.htm.

Litvrinm. Twitter post, April 25, 2022. https://twitter.com/litavrinm/status/1518635734252593153.

"Lovyrev Yevgeniy Nikolayevich" (Ловырев Евгений Николаевич). Moscow Institute of Aviation, no date. https://history.mai.ru/personalities/item.php?id=113822.

"A Major Staff 'Purge' Is Under Way in the FSB Because of the 'Chinese Contraband' Case" (В ФСБ готовится крупная кадровая "чистка" из-за дела о "китайской контрабанде"). Newsru.com, September 12, 2006. www.newsru.com/russia/12sep2006/cleanup.html.

Makeyeva, Aleksandra. "My School Carries His Name" (Моя школа носит его имя). Secondary school assignment written for Secondary School Number 3, Yuzhno-Sakhalinsk, Russia, 2015. https://infourok.ru/issledovatelskaya-rabota-po-kraevedeniyu-dlya-uchastiya-v-konferencii-shkolnikov-shag-v-buduschee-moya-shkola-nosit-ego-imya-ser-3372989.html.

Makutina, Maria. "The FSB Did Not Find 'State Department Cookies'" (ФСБ не нашла "печенек госдепа"). Gazeta.ru, January 14, 2013. www.gazeta.ru/politics/2013/01/14_kz_4923549.shtml.

Manenkov, Kostya. "Russian, Tajik Troops Hold Joint Drills Near Afghan Border." AP News, October 22, 2021. https://apnews.com/article/afghanistan-asia-pacific-russia-europe-moscow-d7188856178da0a4c785fea62bd8e980.

"A Man from 'Aeroflot' Has Arrived to the Leadership of the FSB SEB" (В руководство СЭБ ФСБ пришел человек из "Аэрофлота"). Pasmi.ru, April 12, 2020. https://pasmi.ru/archive/265337/.

Marten, Kimberly. "The 'KGB State' and Russian Political and Foreign Policy Culture." *Journal of Slavic Military Studies* 30, no. 2 (2017): 131–51.

Mashkin, Sergey. "Chekists Stole Skyscrapers" (Чекисты воровали высотками). *Kommersant*, November 6, 2019. www.kommersant.ru/doc/4149137.

Matishak, Martin. "Biden Says He Told Putin US Will Hack Back Against Future Russian Cyberattacks." *Politico*, June 16, 2021. www.politico.com/news/2021/06/16/biden-putin-russia-cyberattacks-494888.

"Memorial Bust of Vyacheslav Yevskin in Anapa" (Памятник-бюст Вячеславу Евскину в Анапе). RusTeam Media, August 1, 2016. https://rus.team/landmarks/pamyatnik-byust-vyacheslavu-evskinu-v-anape.

"Memorial to the Defenders of the Fatherland and to the Workers in the Rear Opened in Kaspiysk" (Мемориал защитникам Отечества и труженикам тыла открыли в Каспийске). *Diktant Pobedy*, November 14, 2021. https://диктантпобеды.рф/news/memorial-zashchitnikam-otechestva-i-truzhenikam-tyla-otkryli-v-kaspiyske.

Mendel, David. "Miss KGB 1990 Became a Popular Prostitute" (Мисс КГБ-90 стала популярной проституткой). *Livejournal*, October 18, 2020. https://david-mendel.livejournal.com/379206.html.

Mendez, Antonio, and Jonna Mendez. *The Moscow Rules: The Secret CIA Tactics That Helped America Win the Cold War.* New York: Hachette, 2019.

Mendyukov, A. V., S. G. Shilova, and E. N. Shmatov, eds. *Who Is Who: The Elite of the Russian Federation—Handbook* (*Кто есть кто: Статусная элита Российской Федерации—Справочник*). Moscow: Litres, 2022.

"Menshchikov, Vladislav Vladimirovich" (Меньщиков, Владислав Владимирович). *TASS Encyclopedia*. https://tass.ru/encyclopedia/person/menschikov-vladislav-vladimirovich.

Meshchanskiy Regional Court of the City of Moscow. Case number 2A–144/2022, February 16, 2022. www.mos-gorsud.ru/rs/meshchanskij/cases/docs/content/339ea0f0-a4e6-11ec-8591-19b107172aa8.

"Method for Marking and Identifying a Material Object." Patent registered August 31, 2007. https://easpatents.com/patents/shekin-mihail-vasilevich.

"The Military Journalist Is Now Unnecessary: The Trial of Ian Safronov" (Военный журналист, сейчас ненужный: Процесс против Ивана Сафронова). RFE/RL, April 4, 2022. www.svoboda.org/a/voenniy-zhurnalist-seichas-ne-nuzhniy-process-protiv-ivana-safronova/31784627.html.

"Minister of Regional Development Slyunyaev Leads 'Olympstroy' Supervisory Committee" (Министр регионального развития Слюняев возглавил набсовет "Олимпстроя"). *Vedomosti*, November 7, 2012. www.vedomosti.ru/management/news/2012/11/07/glava_minregiona_slyunyaev_vozglavil_nabsovet_olimpstroya.

Ministry of Defense of Ukraine, Main Intelligence Directorate. "Сотрудники ФСБ России участвующие в преступной деятельности страны-агрессора на территории Европы" (Russia FSB Employees Participating in Criminal Activity of the Aggressor Country on European Territory). March 28, 2022. https://gur.gov

.ua/content/sotrudnyky-fsb-rossyy-uchastvuiushchye-v-prestupnoi-deiatelnosty-stranyahressora-na-terrytoryy-evropy.html.

"Money Stolen by FSB Attackers Belonged to Assyrian Businessman" (Похищенные налетчиками из ФСБ деньги принадлежали ассирийским бизнесменам). *RBK*, August 12, 2019. www.rbc.ru/society/12/08/2019/5d4cd72b9a7947db471405d4?from=from_main.

"Most Popular Videos on the YouTube Channel of Alexei Navalny as of June 2022, by Number of Views Worldwide." *Statista*, June 2022. www.statista.com/statistics/1202972/most-popular-videos-by-alexei-navalny/.

Mzareupov, Valentin. "Оперативно-техническое управление" (Operational Technology Directorate). *Shield and Sword*, 2022. https://shieldandsword.mozohin.ru/kgb5491/structure/OTU.htm.

"A Nationalist in Russia Received a Life Sentence" (В России националист получил пожизненный срок). Apostrophe.ua, July 24, 2015. https://apostrophe.ua/news/world/2015-07-24/v-rossii-natsionalist-poluchil-pojiznennyiy-srok/30578.

Navalny, Aleksey. "I Phoned My Killer; He Confessed" (Я позвонил своему убийце; Он признался). YouTube, December 21, 2020. https://youtu.be/ibqiet6Bg38.

———. "Putin's Palace: History of the World's Largest Bribe." YouTube, January 19, 2021. https://youtu.be/ipAnwilMncI.

Neuman, Scott. "American Paul Whelan, Held in Russia on Spy Charges, Is Sentenced to 16 Years." NPR, June 15, 2020. www.npr.org/2020/06/15/876966569/american-paul-whelan-held-in-russia-on-spy-charges-is-sentenced-to-16-years.

"A New Chief, Colonel Tataurov, in the RU FSB for Archangelsk Oblast" (В РУ ФСБ России по Архангельской области новый начальник–полковник Татауров). March 6, 2013. www.echosevera.ru/news/2013/03/06/5923.html.

"A New Directorate of the FSB TsSN Was Established on Crimea" (В Крыму было создано новое управление ЦСН ФСБ). *Zen*, July 22, 2020. https://zen.yandex.ru/media/vms/v-krymu-bylo-sozdano-novoe-upravlenie-csn-fsb-5f18956d21e997324ad596b7.

"New Job Is Like Coming Home—New Russian Security Head." BBC Monitoring, July 27, 1998.

"Newsline—April 6, 1999." RFE/RL, April 6, 1999. www.rferl.org/a/1141878.html.

Nikolskaya, Polina, and Darya Korsunskaya. "Russian Ex-minister Ulyukayev Jailed for Eight Years over $2 Million Bribe." Reuters, December 15, 2017. www.reuters.com/article/us-russia-ulyukayev-verdict/russian-ex-minister-ulyukayev-jailed-for-eight-years-over-2-million-bribe-idUSKBN1E90SN.

"Nine Terrorist Crimes Were Prevented in Siberia in Four Years" (В Сибири за четыре года предотвратили девять террористических преступлений). TASS, April 12, 2022. https://tass.ru/proisshestviya/14352033.

"Number of FSB Employees in the Robbery Case Has Risen to 15" (Число сотрудников ФСБ по делу о разбое увеличилось до 15). Interfax, July 9, 2019. www.interfax.ru/russia/668465.

Nurshayeva, Raushan. "Russian Border Guards' Return to Tajikistan 'Not on Agenda': Official." Reuters, November 11, 2015. www.reuters.com/article/us-russia-tajikistan-border/russian-border-guards-return-to-tajikistan-not-on-agenda-official-idUSKCN0T10BY20151112.

Orlov, Sergey. "The Unweak Sex: FSB Colonel Tells about the Work of Women in the Special Services" (Неслабый пол: Полковник ФСБ рассказала о работе женщин в спецслужбах). *Versiya*, February 16, 2020. https://versiya.info/politika/army/142350.

Osborn, Andrew, and Pavel Polityuk. "Russia Fires on and Seizes Ukrainian Ships Near Annexed Crimea." Reuters, November 25, 2018. www.reuters.com/article/us-ukraine-crisis-russia/russia-blocks-ukrainian-navy-from-entering-sea-of-azov-idUSKCN1NU0DL.

Osborne, Charlie. "Russian APT Turla Targets 35 Countries on the Back of Iranian Infrastructure." *Zero Day*, October 21, 2019. www.zdnet.com/article/russian-apt-turla-targets-35-countries-on-the-back-of-iranian-infrastructure/.

Ostroukh, Andrey. "Russia's Putin Signs NGO 'Foreign Agents' Law." Reuters, July 21, 2012. www.reuters.com/article/us-russia-putin-ngos/russias-putin-signs-ngo-foreign-agents-law-idUSBRE86K05M20120721.

Ostroukh, Andrey, and Andrius Sytas. "Estonia Decries Detention of Diplomat in Russia." Reuters, July 6, 2021. www.reuters.com/world/europe/russia-detains-estonian-diplomat-st-petersburg-ifax-2021-07-06/.

Pandis, Robert. *Cheka: The History, Organization and Awards of the Russian Secret Police & Intelligence Services 1917–2017*. Saint Pete Beach, FL: Imperial House Antiques, 2017.

"Patrushev: Special Services Will Do Everything in Order to Catch the Diplomats' Murderer" (Патрушев: Спецслужбы сделают все, чтобы поймать убийц дипломатов). Vesti.ru, June 8, 2008. www.vesti.ru/article/2268481.

"Personnel" (Кадры). *Kommersant*, October 4, 2002. www.kommersant.ru/doc/344261.

Pertsev, Andrey. "Vladislav Menshchikov Took the Lead of the FSB Counterintelligence Service" (Службу контрразведки ФСБ возглавил Владислав Меньщиков). *Kommersant*, April 7, 2015. www.kommersant.ru/doc/2703485.

Petukhov, N. A., and A. S. Mamykin. *Law Enforcement and Judicial Organizations of Russia* (Правоохранительные и Судебные Органы России). Moscow: Russian State University of Justice, 2019.

"Pismenniy, Vladimir Leonidovich" (Письменный, Владимир Леонидович). In *Heroes of the Country*. https://warheroes.ru/hero/hero.asp?Hero_id=14824.

Pleasance, Chris. "Russia Has Fired 'About Eight' Generals for Failing to 'Complete the Task' of Taking Ukraine in Days, Kyiv Official Claims—as Putin Rages over FSB Failures." *Daily Mail*, March 10, 2022. www.dailymail.co.uk/news/article-10598315/Ukraine-war-Putin-fires-eight-generals-rages-FSB-battlefield-failures.html.

Pogrebnyak, Nikolay. *They Defeat Evil with Good: Patron Saints of Special Forces* (*Победившие зло добром: Святые, покровители сил специального назначения*). Moscow: Planeta, 2008.

"The Political Significance of Sects: In Armenia and Elsewhere" (Политическое значение сект: В Армении и не только). RVS.ru, March 3, 2021. https://rvs.su/statia/politicheskoe-znachenie-sekt-v-armenii-i-ne-tolko.

Popov, N. F., A. N. Linkov, N. B. Kurachenkova, and N. V. Baycharov. *The Method of Identifying Persons by Phonograms of Russian Speech Using the Automated "Dialect" System: A Guide for Experts* (Методика идентификации Лиц по *фонограммам русской речи на автоматизированной системе "Диалект": Пособие для экспертов*). V/ch 34435. Moscow: Forensic Laboratory, 1995.

Porter, Tom. "A Senior Russian Official Was Sent to a Notorious Moscow Jail in Retribution for Poor Ukraine Intel, Expert Says." *Business Insider*, April 8, 2022. www.businessinsider.com/russia-fsbs-beseda-in-prison-after-ukraine-intel-failings-soldatov-2022-4.

President of Russia. Order 621, July 11, 2013. http://pravo.gov.ru/proxy/ips/?docbody=&nd=102166734&rdk=0.

———. Order 1280, December 20, 1995. www.kremlin.ru/acts/bank/8615.

———. Order 2233, December 21, 1993. www.kremlin.ru/acts/bank/5109.

———. Resolution 870, July 11, 2004.

———. Resolution N1618-r, July 20, 2019. https://sudact.ru/law/rasporiazhenie-pravitelstva-rf-ot-20072019-n-1618-r/.

"The Prosecutor General's Office Was Denied the Confiscation of the Assets of the Ex-FSB Officer." *Time.News*, February 18, 2022. https://time.news/the-prosecutor-generals-office-was-denied-the-confiscation-of-the-assets-of-the-ex-fsb-officer/.

"Public Opinion: The Influence of the Kremlin and the FSB Is Falling in Russian Life" (Опрос социологов: Влияние Кремля и ФСБ на жизнь россиян снижается). RFE/RL, March 4, 2019. www.svoboda.org/a/29801948.html.

Pushkarskaya, Anna. "'Even the Cook in a Military Unit': Who and For What Is the FSB Proposing to Include in a New Listing of Foreign Agents?" ("Даже повариха военной части": Кого и за что ФСБ предлагает включать в новый реестр иностранных агентов). BBC, July 22, 2021. www.bbc.com/russian/news-57896066.

Putin, Vladimir. "Annual Address to the Federal Assembly of the Russian Federation." Kremlin.ru, April 25, 2005. http://en.kremlin.ru/events/president/transcripts/22931 (in English) and http://kremlin.ru/events/president/transcripts/22931 (in Russian).

———. "Being Strong: Why Russia Needs to Rebuild Its Military." *Foreign Policy*, February 21, 2012. https://foreignpolicy.com/2012/02/21/being-strong/.

———. "Congratulations on Security Service Workers' Day" (Поздравление с Днём работника органов безопасности). Kremlin.ru, December 20, 2020. www.kremlin.ru/events/president/news/64681.

———. "Gala Dedicated to State Security Agencies Workers' Day" (Торжественный вечер, посвящённый Дню работника органов безопасности). Kremlin.ru, December 20, 2014. www.kremlin.ru/events/president/news/47269.

———. "Russia on the Threshold of a New Millennium" (Россия на рубеже тысячелетий). *Nezavisimaya Gazeta*, December 30, 1999. www.ng.ru/politics/1999-12-30/4_millenium.html.

"Putin Began Purges Against the FSB 5th Service" (Путин начал репрессии против 5-й службы ФСБ). Meduza.io, March 11, 2022. https://meduza.io/feature/2022/03/11/putin-nachal-repressii-protiv-5-y-sluzhby-fsb-imenno-ona-nakanune-voyny-obespechivala-prezidenta-rossii-dannymi-o-politicheskoy-situatsii-v-ukraine.

"Putin Instructs FSB to Push Ahead with Operations Against Foreign Agents in Russia." TASS, April 21, 2016. https://tass.com/politics/871663.

"Putin Names First Deputy Director of the FSB" (Путин назначил первого заместителя директора ФСБ). RBC.ru, March 4, 2021. www.rbc.ru/politics/04/03/2021/603fff959a7947e7196b264c.

"Putin Stopped the Privatization of UK 'Rosnano' After an FSB Signal" (Приватиза́ция

УК "Роснано" была остановлена Путиным после сигнала ФСБ). Interfax, April 17, 2018. www.interfax.ru/russia/608954.

"Putin Thanks Trump for Foiling New Year Attacks." BBC, December 29, 2019. www.bbc.com/news/world-europe-50941754.

"Rajnath Meets Russian Intel Chief: 'Unfriendly Forces' Trying to Disrupt Ties, Say India, Russia Teams." *Express*, March 25, 2017. https://indianexpress.com/article/india/rajnath-meets-russian-intel-chief-alexander-bortnikov-india-russia-teams-4584488/.

Reevell, Patrick. "Before Navalny, a Long History of Russian Poisonings." ABC News, August 26, 2020. https://abcnews.go.com/International/navalny-long-history-russian-poisonings/story?id=72579648.

"Regional Directorates." Dossier Center.

Renz, Bettina. "The Russian Power Ministries and Security Services." In *Routledge Handbook of Russian Politics and Society*, edited by Graeme Gill and James Young. Abingdon, UK: Routledge, 2012.

Republic of Karelia. "New Memorial in Memory of the Great Patriotic War Opens in Karelia" (Новый мемориал в память о Великой Отечественной войне открылся в Карелии). September 25, 2020. https://gov.karelia.ru/news/25-09-2020-novyy-memorial-v-pamyat-o-velikoy-otechestvennoy-voyne-otkrylsya-v-karelii/

Richelson, Jeffrey. *The Sword and the Shield: Soviet Intelligence and Security Apparatus*. Cambridge, MA: Ballinger, 1986.

Riehle, Kevin. "Post-KGB Lives: Is There Such a Thing as a Former Chekist?" *International Journal of Intelligence and CounterIntelligence*, June 13, 2022. doi:10.1080/08850607.2022.2064201.

———. *Russian Intelligence: A Case-Based Study of Russian Services and Missions Past and Present*. Washington, DC: NI Press, 2022.

"The Rise and Fall of an FSB-Run Money-Laundering Empire." *Bell*, August 3, 2019. https://thebell.io/en/the-rise-and-fall-of-an-fsb-run-money-laundering-empire/.

"Romashin, Sergey Viktorovich" (Ромашин, Сергей Викторович). In *Герои Страны* (*Heroes of the Country*). https://warheroes.ru/hero/hero.asp?Hero_id=5137.

Rubinkovich, Oleg. "Counterintelligence Officers Transitioned from Bribery to Fraud" (Контрразведчиков перевели из взяточников в мошенники). *Kommersant*, January 23, 2018. www.kommersant.ru/doc/3527421.

"Russia: The FSB Branches Out." Stratfor, May 16, 2008. https://worldview.stratfor.com/article/russia-fsb-branches-out.

"Russia: FSB Detains Ukrainian Diplomat Over Classified Information." DW.com, April 17, 2021. www.dw.com/en/russia-fsb-detains-ukrainian-diplomat-over-classified-information/a-57235737.

"Russia 'Ends Chechnya Operation.'" BBC, April 16, 2009. http://news.bbc.co.uk/2/hi/europe/8001495.stm.

"Russian Accused of Chechen Assassination Plot Stands Trial in Germany." Reuters, June 15, 2022. www.reuters.com/world/europe/russian-accused-chechen-assassination-plot-goes-trial-germany-2022-06-15/.

"Russian Border Guards' Presence on Border with Turkey Important for Armenia—Premier." TASS, July 26, 2018, https://tass.com/world/1014872.

"Russian Counterintelligence Marks Its 100th Jubilee" (Российская контрразведка отмечает 100-летний юбилей). TASS, May 6, 2022. https://tass.ru/obschestvo/14560347.

"Russian Ex-Minister Ulyukayev Gets Eight Years for Bribery." BBC, December 15, 2017. www.bbc.com/news/world-europe-42365041.

Russian Federation. Federal Law 15-FZ, March 7, 2005.

———. Federal Law 35-FZ, June 3, 2006.

———. Federal Law 40-FZ, April 3, 1995; amended in Federal Law 424-FZ, December 8, 2011.

———. Federal Law 86-FZ, June 30, 2003. www.consultant.ru/document/cons_doc_LAW_42941/.

———. Federal Law 97-FZ, May 7, 2013. http://kremlin.ru/acts/news/18073.

———. Federal Law 187-FZ, July 26, 2017. www.consultant.ru/document/cons_doc_LAW_220885/.

———. Gossluzhba. "Register of Persons Fired in Connection with Loss of Confidence" (Реестр лиц, уволенных в связи с утратой доверия). https://gossluzhba.gov.ru/reestr.

———. Interdepartmental Order, December 10, 1996. www.projects.innovbusiness.ru/pravo/DocumShow_DocumID_47510.html.

———. Interdepartmental Order, December 2, 2005. http://voenprav.ru/doc-4334-1.htm. An appendix listing the names of agency representatives is located at http://voenprav.ru/doc-4334-5.htm.

———. Ministry of Energy. Order 22, March 14, 2014. www.bigpowernews.ru/photos/0/0_6dkc8HVEDyGRJTgbnORyxeB4K0i2ACSg.pdf.

———. Ministry of Sport. Order 84, January 28, 2015. https://studylib.ru/doc/2004821/prikaz---komitet-po-fizicheskoj-kul._ture-i-sportu.

———. National Antiterrorism Committee. "Состав Национального антитеррористического комитета" (Staff of the National Antiterrorism Committee). http://nac.gov.ru/sostav.html.

———. Order 465, September 14, 2007; amended November 9, 2021. https://base.garant.ru/12156445/53f89421bbdaf741eb2d1ecc4ddb4c33/.

———. Order 628, September 10, 2014. http://pravo.gov.ru/proxy/ips/?docbody=&prevDoc=102358203&backlink=1&&nd=102865975.

"Russian Justice Ministry Expands 'Foreign Agents' List to Include Navalny Foundation." RFE/RL, December 26, 2020. www.rferl.org/a/russian-justice-ministry-expands-foreign-agents-list-to-include-navalny-foundation/31019932.html.

"Russian Mercenaries in the War in Eastern Ukraine" (Российские наемники в войне на Востоке Украины). *One Ukraine, One Country*, November 2014. www.gpu.com.ua/content/rossiiskie-naemniki-v-voine-na-vostoke-ukrainy.

"Russian Military Court Sentences Former Top Security Agent to Prison for Massive Fraud." RFE/RL, April 23, 2021. www.rferl.org/a/russia-fsb-general-cherkalin-sentenced-for-fraud-/31218449.html.

"Russian Official: We Are Working on Reopening Cuba, Vietnam Bases." Voice of America, October 7, 2016. www.voanews.com/europe/russian-official-we-are-working-reopening-cuba-vietnam-bases.

"Russian Plane Crash: What We Know." BBC, November 17, 2015. www.bbc.com/news/world-middle-east-34687990.

"Russian Poet Dmitry Bykov Targeted by Navalny Poisoners." *Bellingcat*, June 9, 2021. www.bellingcat.com/news/2021/06/09/russian-poet-dmitry-bykov-targeted-by-navalny-poisoners/.

"A Russian Representative Will Lead SCO Antiterrorism Operations" (Антитеррористические операции ШОС будет курировать представитель России). Regnum.ru, December 16, 2015. https://regnum.ru/news/2040110.html.

"'The Russians Are Panicking': An FSB Analysis Base Was Destroyed in Melitopol, According to the Mayor" ("У росіян паніка": У Мелітополі було знищено базу аналітиків ФСБ—Мер). Focus.ua, December 12, 2022. https://focus.ua/uk/voennye-novosti/540590-u-rossiyan-panika-v-melitopole-byla-unichtozhena-baza-analitikov-fsb-mer.

"Russians Consider the FSB the Most Effective of Power Organizations" (Россияне считают ФСБ самым эффективным из силовых ведомств). *Vedomosti*, September 6, 2010. www.vedomosti.ru/lifestyle/news/2010/09/06/vciom_rossiyane_schitayut_fsb_samym_effektivnym_silovym.

"Russian Security Chief Accuses Murdered MP's Family of Impeding Inquiry." BBC Monitoring, December 29, 1998.

"Russians React to 'Foreign Agent' Media Law." RFE/RL, November 15, 2017. www.rferl.org/a/russia-media/28855967.html.

"Russia's 'Big Brother' Law Enters into Force." *Moscow Times*, July 1, 2018. www.themoscowtimes.com/2018/07/01/russias-big-brother-law-enters-into-force-a62066.

"Russia's Former Anticorruption Police Chief Sentenced to 22 Years for Corruption." RFE/RL, April 27, 2017. www.rferl.org/a/russia-anticorruption-police-chief-jailed/28455482.html.

"Russia's FSB Disciplines Future Officers Over SUV Parade Stunt." RFE/RL, July 14, 2016. www.rferl.org/a/russia-fsb-future-officers-disciplined-parade-stunt/27858804.html.

"Russia's Supreme Court Approves Liquidation of International Memorial." *Memorial*, February 28, 2022. www.memo.ru/en-us/memorial/departments/intermemorial/news/690.

Russo, Gus, and Eric Dezenhall. *Best of Enemies: The Last Great Spy Story of the Cold War*. New York: Twelve–Hachette, 2018).

Ryumshin, Vitaliy. "Pervert and Destroy: How the 'Dulles Plan,' One of the Most Famous Fakes, Appeared" (Извратить и развалить: как появился "план Даллеса," один из самых известных фейков). *Post News*, April 7, 2022. https://postnews.ru/a/8460.

"Salaries in the FSB in 2022" (Зарплата в ФСБ в 2022 году). Visasam.ru, May 8, 2022. https://visasam.ru/emigration/rabota/zarplata-fsb.html.

Saradzhyan, Simon, and Carl Schreck. "NGOs a Cover for Spying in Russia." Global Research, May 13, 2005. www.globalresearch.ca/ngos-a-cover-for-spying-in-russia/139.

Satter, David. *Darkness at Dawn: The Rise of the Russian Criminal State*. New Haven, CT: Yale University Press, 2003.

"The SBU Intercepted 'Surkov's Temniki' for Militants" (СБУ перехватила "темники Суркова" для боевиков). *Ukrainskaya Pravda*, February 27, 2015. www.pravda.com.ua/rus/news/2015/02/27/7059983/.

"Scandal in the FSB" (Скандал в ФСБ). Levada Center, October 30, 2007. www.levada.ru/2007/10/30/skandal-v-fsb/.

"Scandal in Moscow's FSB." Warsaw Institute, July 11, 2017. https://warsawinstitute.org/scandal-in-moscows-fsb/.

Schmidt, Michael S. "FBI Chief Not Invited to Meeting on Countering Violent Extremism." *New York Times*, February 19, 2015. www.nytimes.com/2015/02/20/us/politics/fbi-chief-not-invited-to-meeting-on-extremists.html.

"Security During the Olympics Will Be Unnoticeable, Promises the FSB" (Безопасность во время Олимпиады в Сочи будет незаметной, обещает ФСБ). *RIA Novosti*, October 2, 2013. https://ria.ru/20131002/967293668.html.

Seddon, Max. "Putin and the Patriarchs: How Geopolitics Tore Apart the Orthodox Church." *Financial Times*, August 21. 2019. www.ft.com/content/a41ed014-c38b-11e9-a8e9-296ca66511c9.

"Sedov, Alexei." In *Putin's List*. www.spisok-putina.org/en/personas/sedov-2/.

Senatorov, Yuriy. "'Chekists' Agree to Cooperate with Investigation" ("Чекисты" согласились со следствием). *Kommersant*, September 26, 2017. www.kommersant.ru/doc/3421563.

———. "Colonels Retained Everything but Freedom" (Полковники сохранили все, кроме свободы). *Kommersant*, April 11, 2018. www.kommersant.ru/doc/3599572.

———. "FSB Officers Were Not Fined for Taking a Bribe" (Офицеров ФСБ не стали штрафовать за взятку). *Kommersant*, April 3, 2018. www.kommersant.ru/doc/3592240.

———. "One Criminal Case United Three FSB Colonels" (Трех полковников ФСБ объединило одно уголовное дело). *Kommersant*, July 5, 2019. www.kommersant.ru/doc/4020246.

"A Senior Officer of the FSB Special Purpose Center Liquidated in Ukraine" (В Украине ликвидировали топ-офицера центра спецназначения ФСБ). *Unian*, August 7, 2022. www.unian.net/war/v-ukraine-likvidirovali-top-oficera-centra-specnazacheniya-fsb-foto-novosti-vtorzheniya-rossii-na-ukrainu-11932605.html.

"Senior Officers Invited to the Kremlin on the Occasion of Their Appointment to High-Level Positions and the Conferral of Senior Military (Special) Ranks" (Высшие офицеры, приглашенные в Кремль по случаю их назначения на вышестоящие должности и присвоения им высших воинских (специальных) званий). Kremlin.ru, March 9, 2007. www.kremlin.ru/supplement/3110.

Sergeyev, Nikolay. "A Corruption Fighter Has Been Transferred to Economics" (Борца с коррупцией перебросили на экономику). *Kommersant*, April 24, 2018. www.kommersant.ru/doc/3612803.

———. "FSB Colonel Took Bribes at the Lubyanka" (Полковник ФСБ брал взятки на Лубянке). *Kommersant*, September 30, 2019. www.kommersant.ru/doc/4110327.

———. "Money Was Brought to FSB Colonel in a Rolls-Royce" (Деньги полковнику ФСБ завозили на Rolls-Royce). *Kommersant*, October 29, 2019. www.kommersant.ru/doc/4141390.

Sergeyev, Sergey. "From SEB—to Deputies" (Из СЭБа—в замы). *Kommersant*, March 4, 2021. www.kommersant.ru/doc/4713238.

Sergeyev, Sergey, and Oleg Rubnikovich. "The FSB Takes Its Own" (ФСБ своих берет). *Kommersant*, April 19, 2019. www.kommersant.ru/doc/3947618.

Sergeyev, Sergey, and Yuriy Syun. "FSB Economic Security Becomes Its Own" (Экономическая безопасность ФСБ станет собственной). *Kommersant*, June 11, 2016. www.kommersant.ru/doc/3011906.

"Service for Operational Information and International Relations (SOIiMS)" (Служба оперативной информации и международных связей [СОИиМС]). Agentura.ru, 2022. https://agentura.ru/profile/federalnaja-sluzhba-bezopasnosti-rossii-fsb/sluzhba-operativnoj-informacii-i-mezhdunarodnyh-svjazej-soiims/.

"'Services to Society as a Whole': What Is Known about the Biysk Institute from the Investigation of Navalny's Poisoning" ("Услуги обществу в целом": Что известно о бийском институте из расследования отравления Навального). *Tayga*, December 15, 2020. https://tayga.info/162670.

"Seven FSB Employees Arrested in Robbery Case" (Семерых сотрудников ФСБ арестовали по делу о разбое). BBC, July 5, 2019. www.bbc.com/russian/news-48883915.

"'Shaltai Boltai' and Colonel Mikhailov" ("Шалтай-Болтай" и полковник Михайлов). Dossier Center, 2021, https://fsb.dossier.center/mikhaylov/.

Shashkov, Aleksandr. "The Chief of the Border Guard Service: Every Day, 6,000 Illegal Immigrants Try to Come to the RF" (Глава Погранслужбы ФСБ: Ежегодно в РФ стремятся попасть 6 тыс. нелегальных мигрантов). TASS, May 27, 2020. https://tass.ru/interviews/8557449.

"Shavrin, Sergey Ivanovich" (Шаврин, Сергей Иванович). In *Герои Страны* (*Heroes of the Country*). https://warheroes.ru/hero/hero.asp?Hero_id=7787.

Shchegolev, K. A. *Who Is Who in Russia: Executive Branch—Who Rules Modern Russia* (*Кто есть кто в России: Исполнительная власть—Кто правит современной Россией*). Moscow: Astrel, 2007.

"Shekin, Mikhail Vasilyevich" (Шекин, Михаил Васильевич). In *Persona RF: Who Is Who in Russia*. https://whoiswhopersona.info/archives/42037.

Shevchenko, Nikolay. "Who Was 'Miss KGB' Who Won a Secret Beauty Contest in 1990?" *Russia Beyond*, June 5, 2020. www.rbth.com/history/332286-miss-kgb-russia-1990.

Shirokorad, Aleksandr. *Secret Operations of Tsarist Special Services, 1877–1917* (*Секретные операции царских спецслужб, 1877–1917 гг.*). Moscow: Beche, 2016.

Shironin, Vyacheslav. *Agents of Perestroika: The Declassified KGB Dossier* (*Агенты перестройки: Рассекреченное досье КГБ*). Moscow: Eksmo Algoritm, 2010.

———. *KGB-CIA: The Secret Origins of Perestroika* (*КГБ-ЦРУ: Секретные пружины перестройки*). Moscow: Yaguar, 1997.

———. *Under the Cover of Counterintelligence: The Secret Rationale of Perestroika* (*Под колпаком контрразведки: Тайная подоплека перестройки*). Moscow: Paleya, 1996.

Shulipa, Yuriy. *How Putin Kills Abroad* (*Как Путин убивает за рубежом*). Vilnius: International Center for Civic Initiatives "Our Home," 2021.

Sinelschikova, Yekaterina. "Sergei Ivanov: Who Is the Official Putin Has Just Fired?" *Russia Beyond*, August 15, 2016. www.rbth.com/politics_and_society/2016/08/15/sergei-ivanov-who-is-the-official-putin-has-just-fired_621223.

Sinodov, Yuriy. "Dirty Hands" (Грязные руки). Roem.ru, July 18, 2011. https://roem.ru/18-07-2011/120190/gryaznye-ruki/.

Sipher, John, Steven L. Hall, Douglas H. Wise, and Marc Polymeropoulos. "Trump Wants the CIA to Cooperate with Russia—We Tried That; It Was a Disaster." *Washington Post*, June 15, 2020. www.washingtonpost.com/outlook/2020/07/15/cia-russia-putin-trump/.

"Sirotkin Igor Gennadyevich" (Сироткин Игорь Геннадьевич). RusTeam Media, June 21, 2020. https://rus.team/people/sirotkin-igor-gennadevich.

Skak, Mette. "Russian Strategic Culture: The Role of Today's Chekisty." *Contemporary Politics* 22, no. 3 (2016): 324–41.

"The SK Denies Information About the Arrest of FSB General Sergey Beseda" (В СК отрицают информацию об аресте генерала ФСБ Сергея Беседы). RTVI, April 15, 2022. https://rtvi.com/news/v-sk-otritsayut-informatsiyu-ob-areste-generala-fsb-sergeya-besedy/.

Sokolov, Maksim. "Colonel Yushekov Threatened General Stepashin" (Полковник Юшенков погрозил генералу Степашину). *Kommersant*, June 30, 1994. www.kommersant.ru/doc/82513.

Sokolova, Yekaterina. "Where Does the Money for Expensive 'Velvet Revolutions' Come From?" (Откуда берутся средства на дорогие "бархатные революции?"). CentrAsia.org, December 18, 2004. https://centrasia.org/newsA.php?st=1103342580.

Sokut, Sergey. "Defense of Identity, Society, and State" (Защита Личности, Общества, и Государства). *Nezavisimaya Gazeta*, November 20, 1998.

Soldatov, Andrei. "All-Encompassing Paranoia." *Russian Social Science Review* 58, no. 1 (2017): 60–68.

———. "Analysis in State Security Organs" (Аналитика в органах госбезопасности). Nomad.su. https://nomad.su/?a=5-200510270107.

———. "How Many Intelligence Services Do We Have? In Russia, Even the Counterintelligence Officers Are Spies" (Сколько у нас разведок? В России шпионят даже контрразведчики). *Versiya*, June 10, 2002; republished on Agentura.ru. http://archive.agentura.ru/dossier/russia/people/soldatov/skolko/.

———. "How a Renegade 'Middle Eastern Mafia' Invented Modern Russian Espionage." *Daily Beast*, June 13, 2021. www.thedailybeast.com/how-a-renegade-middle-eastern-mafia-invented-modern-russian-espionage.

———. "Putin Has Finally Reincarnated the KGB." *Foreign Policy*, September 21, 2016. https://foreignpolicy.com/2016/09/21/putin-has-finally-reincarnated-the-kgb-mgb-fsb-russia/.

———. "The Untold Story of How Vladimir Putin Created His Own Foreign Intelligence Service to Shore Up His Standing in Post-Soviet Russia." *Daily Beast*, August 30. 2021. www.thedailybeast.com/inside-vladimir-putins-shadowy-army-of-global-spies.

Soldatov, Andrei, and Irina Borogan. *The New Nobility: The Restoration of Russia's Security State and the Enduring Legacy of the KGB*. New York: PublicAffairs, 2010.

———. "Putin Began Purges Against the FSB Fifth Service" (Путин начал репрессии против 5-й службы ФСБ). *Meduza*, March 11, 2022. https://meduza.io/feature/2022/03/11/putin-nachal-repressii-protiv-5-y-sluzhby-fsb-imenno-ona-nakanune-voyny-obespechivala-prezidenta-rossii-dannymi-o-politicheskoy-situatsii-v-ukraine.

———. *The Red Web: The Struggle Between Russia's Digital Dictators and the New Online Revolutionaries*. New York: PublicAffairs, 2015.

Soldatov, Andrei, and Irina Borogon, eds. "Federal Security Service of Russia (FSB)" (Федеральная служба безопасности России [ФСБ]). https://agentura.ru/profile/federalnaja-sluzhba-bezopasnosti-rossii-fsb.

Soshnikov, Andrey. "'Turn Off the Internet in a Small Country': Hackers Tell of a New Cyberweapon Ordered by the FSB" ("Отключить интернет в небольшой стране": Хакеры рассказали о новом кибероружии, заказанном ФСБ). BBC Russian Service, March 18, 2020. www.bbc.com/russian/news-51951933.

Sotnikov, Matvey. "The Ambassador of 'Alfa' (Полпред "Альфы"). Specnaz.ru, July 31, 2018. www.specnaz.ru/articles/262/22/3007.htm.

"A Spy from the Russian FSB Detained in Lithuania" (В Литве задержали шпиона из российской ФСБ). *TCH*, May 4, 2015. https://tsn.ua/ru/svit/v-litve-zaderzhali-shpiona-iz-rossiyskoy-fsb-423802.html.

"Staff Changes in the FSB After a Series of Loud Arrests" (В ФСБ произошли кадровые перестановки после серии громких арестов). Lenta.ru, May 17, 2019. https://lenta.ru/news/2019/05/17/komkov/.

Standish, Reid. "Interview: Why the 'Failure' of Russian Spies, Generals Is Leading to 'Apocalyptic' Thinking in the Kremlin." RFE/RL, May 8, 2022. www.rferl.org/a/russia-ukraine-war-setbacks-strategy-generals-putin/31839737.html.

Stanley, Alessandra. "Yeltsin Signs Peace Treaty with Chechnya." *New York Times*, May 13, 1997.

Starkov, Boris. *Охотники на Шпионов: Контрразведка Российской Империи 1903–1914* (*Spy Hunters: Counterintelligence in the Russian Empire 1903–1914*), Saint Petersburg: Piter, 2006.

State Cultural Institution. "Manor Museum 'Dzerzhinovo.'" http://dzerzhinovo.museum.by/.

Stavitskiy, V. A., ed. *Lubyanka: Providing the State's Economic Security* (*Лубянка: Обеспечение Экономической Безопасности Государства*). Moscow: Kuchkovo Pole, 2005 (vol. 1) and 2006 (vol. 2).

Steele, Jonathan. "Chechens Rounded Up in Moscow." *Guardian*, September 17, 1999. www.theguardian.com/world/1999/sep/18/russia.chechnya.

Stewart, Will. "Putin's Billionaire Former Son-in-Law Escapes Sanctions Misery in Russia to Fly to Dubai to Celebrate His 40th Birthday with Wealthy Daughter of FSB General." *Daily Mail*, March 27, 2022. www.dailymail.co.uk/news/article-10656747/Russias-youngest-billionaire-Putins-playboy-former-son-law-triggers-scandal-sanctions.html.

Stone, Oliver. *The Putin Interviews*. New York: Hot Books, 2017.

Sukhotin, Andrey. "The Gray Beards Begin and Win" (Серые начинают и выигрывают). *Novaya Gazeta*, June 21, 2019. https://novayagazeta.ru/articles/2019/06/21/80973-serye-nachinayut-i-vyigryvayut.

"Sverdlov Court Recognized the 'Dulles Plan' as Extremist Material" (Свердловский суд признал "план Даллеса" экстремистским материалом). RBC.ru, June 5, 2015. www.rbc.ru/rbcfreenews/5571d5199a7947c17716512a.

"Swiss Defence Ministry Foils Cyberattack." Reuters, September 15, 2017. www.reuters.com/article/swiss-cyber-attacks/swiss-defence-ministry-foils-cyber-attack-idUSL5N1LW3VQ.

Sychev, Vladimir. "One Hundredth Anniversary of the Organs of State Security" (100 лет органам государственной безопасности). *Natsionalnaya Oborona*, no. 12 (December 2017): 82–94. https://2009-2020.oborona.ru/includes/periodics/armedforces/2017/1212/154823117/detail.shtml.

Talbott, Strobe. *The Russia Hand: A Memoir of Presidential Diplomacy.* New York: Random House, 2002.

Tarasov, Ivan. *Police of Russia: History, Laws, and Reforms* (Полиция России: История, законы, реформы). Moscow: Knizhniy Mir, 2011.

Taylor, Brian D. *State Building in Putin's Russia. Policing and Coercion after Communism.* Cambridge: Cambridge University Press, 2011.

Terentyev, Mikhail. "The 'Order to the Ugrian Voevods' of 16 May 1512" ("Наказ угорским воеводам" от 16 мая 1512 года). *Voenno-Istoricheskiy Zhurnal,* January 21, 2019. http://history.milportal.ru/nakaz-ugorskim-voevodam-ot-16-maya-1512-goda/.

"Those Convicted in Russia of Espionage on Behalf of Foreign Powers: A Reference" (Осужденные в России за шпионаж в пользу иностранных государств: Справка). *RIA Novosti,* July 7, 2010. https://ria.ru/20100707/252841303.html.

"Tikhonov, Aleksandr: Leader of the FSB Spetsnaz Operations during the Terrorist Attack at Dubrovka and the Terrorist Attack in Beslan" (Тихонов, Александр: Руководитель операций спецназа ФСБ во время теракта на Дубровке и теракта в Беслане). Lenta.ru. https://lenta.ru/lib/14163199/.

"Tikhonov, Aleksandr Yevgenyevich" (Тихонов, Александр Евгеньевич). In *Герои Страны* (*Heroes of the Country*). https://warheroes.ru/hero/hero.asp?Hero_id=11262.

Topol, Sergey. "'Alpha' Shot to Kill" ("Альфа" стреляла на поражение). *Kommersant,* December 23, 1997. www.kommersant.ru/doc/189990.

"Top Russian FSB Official Has Multiple Underworld Ties." OCCRP.org, April 12, 2021. www.occrp.org/en/investigations/istories-top-russian-fsb-official-has-multiple-underworld-ties.

Trakhimenok, Sergey. *Notes of the "Black Colonel"* (Записки "черного полковника"). Minsk: Literatura and Iskusstvo, 2012.

"Tribute to the Ancestor's Deeds: Laying Flowers and Wreaths at the Memorial to Counterintelligence Personnel in Moscow" (Дань подвигам предков: У мемориала военным контрразведчикам в Москве возложили цветы и венки). TVZvezda.ru, May 8, 2022. https://tvzvezda.ru/news/202259321-DBmts.html.

Trifonov, Vladislav. "Medical Equipment Taken Out in Two Cadillacs" (Медоборудование вывезли на двух Cadillac). *Kommersant,* April 11, 2022. www.kommersant.ru/doc/5304324.

"Trump Putin Call: CIA Helped Stop Russia Terror Attack." BBC, December 17, 2017. www.bbc.com/news/world-europe-42386258.

Tsurygin, Vladislav. "Communist, Chekist, Occupier" (Коммунист, чекист и оккупант). *Zavtra,* September 23, 2018. https://zavtra.ru/blogs/trizhdi_general.

UK Government. *The Litvinenko Inquiry: Report into the Death of Alexander Litvinenko.* London: UK Government, 2016. https://assets.publishing.service.gov.uk/government/uploads/system/uploads/attachment_data/file/493860/The-Litvinenko-Inquiry-H-C-695-web.pdf.

"United Russia Members Introduced Amendments to the Law on the FSB" (Единороссы внесли в Госдуму поправки в закон о ФСБ). *RIA Novosti,* September 13, 2010. https://ria.ru/20100913/275330117.html.

"The Unit 'Smerch' of the FSB" (Подразделение "Смерч" ФСБ). In *About the FSB*, no date. https://o-fsb.ru/podrazdelenie-smerch-fsb/.

"Unprecedented Instance: The FSB Openly Interfered in the Work of Government toward MPS Reform" (Беспрецедентный случай: ФСБ открыто вмешалась в работу правительства по реформе МПС). Polit.ru, January 14, 2002. https://m.polit.ru/news/2002/01/14/568479/.

US Central Intelligence Agency. "Use of Dogs by Soviet Border Troops." May 6, 1964. CIA Reading Room, Document CIA-RDP82-00046R000300290008-9.

"US Coast Guard, Russian Border Guard Patrolled Maritime Boundary Line." *Sea Power*, January 28, 2021. https://seapowermagazine.org/u-s-coast-guard-russian-border-guard-patrolled-maritime-boundary-line/.

US Cybersecurity and Infrastructure Security Agency. "Russian State-Sponsored and Criminal Cyber Threats to Critical Infrastructure." May 9, 2022. www.cisa.gov/uscert/ncas/alerts/aa22-110a.

US Department of Justice. "Four Russian Government Employees Charged in Two Historical Hacking Campaigns Targeting Critical Infrastructure Worldwide." Press release, March 24, 2022. www.justice.gov/opa/pr/four-russian-government-employees-charged-two-historical-hacking-campaigns-targeting-critical.

———. "Justice Department Announces Court-Authorized Disruption of Snake Malware Network Controlled by Russia's Federal Security Service." Press release, May 9, 2023. www.justice.gov/opa/pr/justice-department-announces-court-authorized-disruption-snake-malware-network-controlled.

———. "Russian Cyber-Criminal Sentenced to 14 Years in Prison for Role in Organized Cybercrime Ring Responsible for $50 Million in Online Identity Theft and $9 Million Bank Fraud Conspiracy." Press release, November 30, 2017. www.justice.gov/opa/pr/russian-cyber-criminal-sentenced-14-years-prison-role-organized-cybercrime-ring-responsible.

———. "US Charges Russian FSB Officers and Their Criminal Conspirators for Hacking Yahoo and Millions of Email Accounts." Press release, March 15, 2017. www.justice.gov/opa/pr/us-charges-russian-fsb-officers-and-their-criminal-conspirators-hacking-yahoo-and-millions.

US Department of State. "Department of State Actions in Response to Russian Harassment." December 29, 2016. https://2009-2017.state.gov/r/pa/prs/ps/2016/12/266145.htm.

———. "Moscow and the Peace Movement: The Soviet Committee for the Defense of Peace." *Foreign Affairs Note*, May 1987. https://books.google.com/books?id=fPBFpeAxa6cC

"US Embassy Diplomat Caught at Moscow Opposition Demonstration." *RT*, November 2, 2009. www.youtube.com/watch?v=pMII_PMGo00.

"US Fails to Persuade Russia to Support Missile Defense Expansion in Europe." Voice of America, November 1, 2009. www.voanews.com/a/a-13-2007-04-20-voa7/347819.html.

US government. "Unclassified Summary of Information and Handling Prior to the April 15, 2013, Boston Marathon Bombings." April 10, 2014. https://oig.justice.gov/reports/2014/s1404.pdf.

US National Counterintelligence and Security Center. *Foreign Economic Espionage in Cyberspace.* Washington, DC: US National Counterintelligence and Security Center, 2018.

Ushakov, V. N., ed. *Legal Regulation of the Activities of the Federal Security Service to Ensure the National Security of the Russian Federation* (Правовое регулирование деятельности федеральной службы безопасности по обеспечению национальной безопасности Российской Федерации). Moscow: Eksmo Education, 2006.

Ushakov, Valeriy, Anastasiya Melnikova, and Andrey Kuleshov. "Broad Consumption Generals" (Генералы Широкого Потребления). *Novaya Gazeta*, October 1, 2006. https://novayagazeta.ru/articles/2006/10/02/27720-generaly-shirokogo-potrebleniya.

"The USSR's Intellectual Spetsnaz: How Captured Diplomats Were Saved in Lebanon" (Интеллектуальный спецназ СССР: Как спасли захваченных в Ливане дипломатов). *RIA Novosti*, October 30, 2020. https://ria.ru/20201030/spetsnaz-1582201570.html.

Ustinova, Tanya. "Russia Detains Romanian Diplomat for Spying." Reuters, August 16, 2010. www.reuters.com/article/uk-russia-romania-espionage/russia-detains-romanian-diplomat-for-spying-idUKTRE67F39220100816.

Varyvdin, Maksim. "Counterintelligence Has Not Followed an Eastern European Path" (Контрразведка не пошла по восточноевропейскому пути). *Kommersant*, March 26, 1994. www.kommersant.ru/doc/74594.

Vavilova, Elena, and Andrey Bronnikov. *The Woman Who Can Keep Secrets* (Женщина, которая умеет хранить тайны). Moscow: Eksmo, 2020.

Velichko, Valeriy. *From Lubyanka to the Kremlin: Secret Missions* (От Лубянки до Кремля: Секретные Миссии). Moscow: Akva-Term, 2013.

"'V' for 'Vympel': FSB's Secretive Department 'V' Behind Assassination of Georgian Asylum Seeker in Germany," *Bellingcat*, February 17, 2020. www.bellingcat.com/news/uk-and-europe/2020/02/17/v-like-vympel-fsbs-secretive-department-v-behind-assassination-of-zelimkhan-khangoshvili/.

Vinogradov, Egor. "The 'For Honest Elections' Movement Began a New Series of Protests" (Движение "За честные выборы" начало новую серию протестов). *Deutsche Welle* (in Russian), March 6, 2012.

Vinogradov, V., A. Litvin, and V. Khristoforov, eds. *The VChK Archive: A Collection of Documents* (Архив ВЧК: Сборник Документов). Moscow: Kuchkovo Pole, 2007.

Volchek, Dmitry. "'All of Russia Was at Stake in This Game': Who Blew Up the Apartment Buildings in 1999?" RFE/RL, September 19, 2019. www.rferl.org/a/who-blew-up-moscow-apartment-buildings-1999/31033208.html.

Vyshenkov, Yevgeniy. "Main Editor of Arrests Korolev" (Главред арестов Королев). Fontanka.ru, July 19, 2016. www.fontanka.ru/2016/07/19/132/.

Waller, J. Michael. "The KGB and Its Successors under Gorbachev and Yeltsin: Russian State Security and Elusive Civil Controls" Dissertation for Boston University, 1993.

———. "The KGB Legacy in Russia." *Problems of Post-Communism* 42, no. 6 (1995).

———. "Russia: Death and Resurrection of the KGB." *Demokratizatsiya* 12, no. 3 (2004): 333–55.

———. *Secret Empire: The KGB in Russia Today.* Boulder, CO: Westview Press, 1994.

Walsh, Nick Paton. "Russia Says 'Spies' Work in Foreign NGOs." *Guardian*, May 13, 2005. www.theguardian.com/world/2005/may/13/russia.nickpatonwalsh.

Walther, Ulf. "Russia's Failed Transformation: The Power of the KGB/FSB from Gorbachev to Putin." *International Journal of Intelligence and Counterintelligence* 27 (2014): 666–86.

"Warned Against State Treason: The FSB Took an Unusual Measure Toward a Former Worker of a Defense Factory" (Предостерегли от Госизмены: ФСБ Приняла Необычные Меры к Экс-Работнику Оборонного Завода). *Vladimir Tsargrad TV*, December 16, 2021. https://vladimir.tsargrad.tv/news/predosteregli-ot-gosizmeny-fsb-prinjala-neobychnye-mery-k-jeks-rabotniku-oboronnogo-zavoda_463584.

Weir, Fred. "Russia Arrests US Diplomat Accused of Spying." *Christian Science Monitor*, May 14, 2013. www.csmonitor.com/World/Europe/2013/0514/Russia-arrests-US-diplomat-accused-of-spying.

White, Stephen, and Ol'ga Kryshtanovskaya. "Public Attitudes to the KGB: A Research Note." *Europe-Asia Studies* 45, no. 1 (1993): 169–75.

Williams, Matthias. "Moldova Sees Russian Plot to Derail Money-Laundering Probe." Reuters, March 15, 2017. www.reuters.com/article/us-moldova-russia-insight-idUSKBN16M1QQ?il=0.

Winter, Tom. "Russia Warned US About Tsarnaev, But Spelling Issue Let Him Escape." NBC News, March 25, 2014. www.nbcnews.com/storyline/boston-bombing-anniversary/russia-warned-u-s-about-tsarnaev-spelling-issue-let-him-n60836.

"Woman Generals in Russia" (Женщины-генералы в России). Cyclowiki.org, May 26, 2021. https://cyclowiki.org/wiki/Женщины-генералы_в_России.

Worthington, Peter. "Worthington's Top Secret Story: The Untold Story of Olga's Defection, Part 1." *Toronto Sun*, May 10, 2014.

Yarovoy, Arkadiy. *Farewell, KGB* (Прощай, КГБ). Moscow: Olma Press, 2001.

Yegorov, Aleksandr, and Ilya Bulavinov. "Andrey Nikolayev: There Will Be No Unification of the FPS and FSB" (Андрей Николаев: Объединения ФПС и ФСБ не будет). *Kommersant*, February 3, 1998. www.kommersant.ru/doc/14054.

"Yeltsin Appoints 'Permanent' Members of Russian Security Council." ITAR-TASS, November 20, 1998.

"Yeltsin Humiliates Gorbachev: Transcript of Russian Federation Duma Session with USSR, President Gorbachev." TASS, August 23, 1991. https://soviethistory.msu.edu/1991-2/the-august-coup/the-august-coup-texts/eltsin-humiliates-gorbachev/.

"Yevskin, Vyacheslav Mikhailovich" (Евскин, Вячеслав Михайлович). In *Герои Страны* (*Heroes of the Country*). https://warheroes.ru/hero/hero.asp?Hero_id=7578.

Yezhov, Sergey. "Russian Federation Is My Middle Name: How the Daughter of the Head of FSB Counterintelligence Hid Her Elite Real Estate" (Российская Федерация—мое второе имя; Как дочь главы контрразведки ФСБ спрятала свою элитную недвижимость). *Insider*, August 7, 2020. https://theins.ru/korrupciya/pod-zaschitoi-rossiiskoi-federatsii-kak-doch-glavy-kontrrazvedki-fsb-spryatala-svou-elitnuu-nedvizhimost.

Zavarzin, Petr. *"The Okhranka": Reminiscences of a Leader of the Protection Directorate* (*"Охранка": Воспоминания руководителей охранных отделений*). Moscow: New Literary Review, 2004.

———. *The Work of the Secret Police: Reminiscences of a Corps Commander* (*Работа тайной полиции: Воспоминания генерала корпуса*). Moscow: Direct Media, 2018.

———. *The Work of the Secret Police: Reminiscences of a Corps Commander* (*Работа тайной полиции: Воспоминания генерала корпуса*). Moscow: V. Sekayev, 2020.

Zdanovich, Aleksandr, ed. *Proceedings of the Society for the Study of the History of Patriotic Special Services* (*Труды Общества изучения истории отечественных спецслужб*). 3 vols. Moscow: Kuchkovo Pole, 2006 and 2007.

Zhirinovskiy, Vladimir. *Order, Prosperity, and Security! Election Program for the Post of President of Russia for Candidate V. V. Zhirinovskiy* (*Порядок, достаток, безопасность! Предвыборная программа кандидата на пост Президента России В. В. Жириновского*). Moscow: Liberal Democratic Party of Russia, 1996.

Zhukov, Aleksandr, and Konstantin Kuteynikov. "Automation of the Entry Points on the RF Border" (Автоматизация Пропускных Пунктов на Границе РФ). *Mining Information-Analytic Bulletin*, 2005. https://cyberleninka.ru/article/n/14882596.pdf.

Zolotov, Andrei, Jr. "'Death to Spies' and Thousands of Others." *Moscow Times*, May 28, 2003. www.themoscowtimes.com/2003/05/28/death-to-spies-and-thousands-of-others-a238196.

Index

Abdurakhmanov, Mokhmad, 86
Activity Support Service (SOD) (Seventh Service), 57, 62, 117, 122
Afghanistan, 14, 40, 53, 77, 109, 114, 124, 133, 134
Agentura.ru, 3, 42, 46, 58, 59, 61, 73, 91, 109
Akuyeva, Amina, 90
Alekseyev, Aleksandr, 137
All-Russian Extraordinary Commission for Combating Counterrevolution and Sabotage, 5, 79
All-Russian Federation of Volleyball (VFV), 123
Almaz-Antey, Joint Stock Company, 118
Alpatov, Sergey, 44, 56, 117, 120–21
Ames, Aldrich, 32
Amin, Hafizullah, 139
Analysis and Coordination Department (subordinate to the PS), 52
"The Anatomy of a Protest," 98
Andreyev, Valentin Grigoryevich, 40
Andropov, Yuriy, 10, 35, 39, 46, 60, 106, 107, 140
Antiterrorist Center of the Commonwealth of Independent States, 130
apartment building bombings, 1999, 112–13, 142
assassinations, 33, 40, 48, 82, 85–86, 100, 114, 139, 152, 155
Aviation Directorate (UA), 60, 62, 139

Bakatin, Vadim, 12–13, 25, 129
Barannikov, Viktor, 13–16, 25, 111
Barsukov, Mikhail, 40, 108–9
Batyushin, Nikolay, 7–8
Belan, Aleksey, 93
Beletskiy, Stepan, 7
Beliy, Nikita, 88
Belov, Aleksandr, 82
Beriya, Lavrentiy, 13, 26, 158–59
"Berzerk Bear" (aka "Dragonfly," "Energetic Bear," and "Crouching Yeti"), 93
Beseda, Sergey, 47, 97, 117, 121–22, 133, 158
Beslan hostage crisis, 84–85, 125, 157
Bezrukov, Andrey, 24
Bezverkhniy, Aleksandr, 75–78, 131
Biysk Institute for Problems of Chemical-Energy Technologies, 100
Bolshakova, Kseniya, 75
Bolyukh, Anatoly, 133
Bondarev, Boris, 73
Bondarev, Sergey, 73
Border Control Department (DPK), 53, 95
Border Guard Service (PS), 8–9, 21, 51–53, 60, 62, 90–91, 92, 94–95, 99, 105, 114, 116, 117, 130–31, 134, 139–40, 143
Border Protection Department, 52
Borogan, Irina, 3, 59, 81, 113, 121, 122, 138

Bortnikov, Aleksandr, 43, 49, 55, 87, 107–8, 115, 117, 126, 132, 134, 143, 158
Bubenin, Vitaliy, 139, 141
Budennovsk hostage crisis, 37, 84, 108
Burlutskiy, Grigoriy, 53
Bykov, Andrey, 91

Capital Construction Directorate (UKS), 57
Captain Hollywood, 142
Center for Communications Security (TsBS), 49
Center for Information Defense and Special Communications (Eighth Center), 48–49, 96–97
Center for Information Security (TsIB) (Center 18), 31, 33–34, 74–75, 93, 96, 98, 100, 132
Center for Licensing, Certification, and Defending State Secrets (TsLSZ), 61
Center for Operational Technical Measures (TsOTM) (Center 12), 50, 60
Central Intelligence Service of the USSR, 13
Central Physical Fitness Center (TsSFP) (Fourteenth Center), 58
Central Scientific Research Institute for Special Research (subordinate to the KGB), 48, 50
Central Scientific Research Institute of Special Technology (Tenth Center), 49–50
Chechnya, 46, 60, 62, 84–86, 90, 109–10, 112, 113–14, 116, 137–38, 141–42, 157
chekist mind-set, 1, 18, 22–25, 69, 132
Cherkalin, Kirill, 87, 149–51
Chernovoltsev, Eduard, 117, 123
China, 32, 62, 77–78, 95, 97, 118, 134, 139, 141–42, 149, 158
Chronopay, 75
Chubais, Anatoliy, 80
"Club of Plant Lovers," 82–83
Coast Guard Department, 52, 66, 97, 143
color revolutions, 89, 121, 155
Commandant Directorate, 58
Committee for Defending the USSR State Border and Unified Command of Border Forces, 13
Committee for the Defense of USSR State Borders, 51
Contract and Legal Directorate (DPU), 57–58
Control Service, 54, 117, 126

Counterintelligence Directorate (UKR) (Smersh), 42, 139–40, 141
Counterintelligence Section (KRO), 19, 31
The Cry of the Owl, 141
Cuba, 121, 133

Daerbayev, Rafael, 95
Danilov, Ruslan, 83
Decision to Liquidate, 141
Dedyukhin, Igor, 111
Defeating Evil with Good: Patron Saints of Special Forces, 142
Department for Combating Terrorism, 37
Department for Counterintelligence Operations (DKRO), 31–33, 35, 70–74, 90, 98
Department of Economic Security (DEB), 43
Department of Military Counterintelligence (DVKR), 35, 41–43, 54, 62, 64, 70, 75–77, 117, 120, 131, 139
Deryabin, Petr, 78
Dinamo women's volleyball club, 122
Directorate "A" (Alfa), 39–40, 64, 84–85, 109, 124, 138–39, 140, 141, 151
Directorate "K" (Kavkaz), 39, 41
Directorate "K" (subordinate to the SEB), 30, 32, 43–45, 82, 87–88, 149–50
Directorate "M," 25, 54–56, 88, 124
Directorate "P" (subordinate to the SEB), 43–44
Directorate "R." *See* Radio Counterintelligence Directorate
Directorate "S" (Smerch), 39–41
Directorate "T" (subordinate to the SEB), 43–44, 86
Directorate "T" (Taurida), 39, 41
Directorate "V" (Vympel), 39–40, 84–85, 137–40, 143, 151–52
Directorate for Combating International Terrorism (UBMT), 37
Directorate for Combating Terrorism and Political Extremism (UBTPE), 37–38
Directorate for Coordination of Analysis and Counterintelligence Activities (UKAKD), 31, 33, 72, 90, 97–98
Directorate for Facility Security, 31, 35
Directorate for Operational-Technical Measures (UOTM), 50, 60–61, 91–92
Directorate for Orders and Deliveries

of Weapons, Military, and Special Equipment, 50
Directorate for Protecting the Constitutional Order (UZKS), 37–38
Directorate for Support Programs (UPS), 58–59
Directorate for the Defense of the Constitutional Order (Directorate "Z"), 36–37
Directorate of Information Support for Operational-Investigative Activities (UIOORD), 31, 33–34, 98
Directorate of Special Measures (USM), 35
Directorate of Special Operations (USO), 40
Dokuchayev, Dmitriy, 74–75, 93
Dorofeyev, Aleksey, 56
Dossier Center, 3, 39, 56, 57, 75, 81, 87, 88, 95, 121, 125, 156
Dubrovka Theater hostage crisis, 64, 71, 84–85, 138
Dulles Plan, 23–24
Dzerzhinskiy, Feliks, 44, 106, 142

Economic Counterintelligence Service (also called Economic Security Service) (SEB) (Fourth Service), 43–45, 78–80, 82, 86, 117
Electronic Intelligence and Communications Center (TsRRSS) (Center 16), 61, 92–94
Eleventh Center (Special Technology Center), 49, 50, 99–100

Farmakovskaya, Olga, 71
Federal Agency for Government Communications and Information (FAPSI), 20–21, 34, 48–49, 114, 133
Federal Counterintelligence Service (FSK), 16, 20, 43, 48, 51, 59, 108–9, 112, 124, 137
Federal Protection Service (FSO), 14, 20, 109
Federal Security Agency (AFB), 13
Federal Tax Police Service, 92, 116, 119
Felshtinskiy, Yuriy, 113
Feoktistov, Oleg, 88
Fetisov, Andrey, 123, 133
Fifth Service. *See* Service for Operational Information and International Relations
Filimonov, Roman, 75
Finance-Economic Directorate (FEU), 57

Fomchenkov, Georgiy, 74
Foreign Intelligence Service (SVR), 14, 19–20, 32, 43, 46, 47, 48, 53, 66, 73, 84, 132
Fourth Service. *See* Economic Counterintelligence Service
Frolov, Dmitriy, 150
FSB foreign liaison, 2, 47, 129–33
FSB: For and Against, 7, 76

Gavrilov, Viktor, 44
General Prosecutor's office, 148
Gerasimov, Andrey, 75, 96
Glyadelkin, Sergey, 150
Golitsyn Border Institute, 52
Golushko, Nikolay, 15–16
Gorbachev, Mikhail, 10, 12–13, 24, 26, 36
Gorbachev, Viktor, 97
Gorbatov, Mikhail, 149–50
Gordievsky, Oleg, 7
"Granitsa" Publishing House, 52
Gromkov, Yevgeniy, 73
Gromov, Sergey, 136–37
GT/PROLOGUE (CIA cryptonym), 32
Gurtopov, Aleksandr, 73

Hero of the Russian Federation Award, 85, 89–90, 110, 124, 136–39, 141, 143

India, 134
Information-Analysis Directorate (IAU), 45–47, 97
InformInvestGroup, 100
Institute of Coastal Defense, 58
Institute of Cryptography, Communications, and Informatics (IKSiI), 58
Internal Security Directorate (USB) (Ninth Directorate), 31–32, 54, 56, 88, 112, 116, 118, 120
International Cooperation Directorate (UMS), 45, 47–48, 129–31
International Memorial Foundation, 146
Interrepublic Security Service (MSB), 13, 40
Investigative Directorate (SU), 32, 59
Ivanov, Sergey, 47

Jehovah's Witnesses, 83

Kadyrov, Ramzan, 86, 114
Kalimatov, Alikhan, 89–90
Kalugin, Oleg, 7

Index

Kara-Murza, Vladimir, 100
Kaspersky Laboratories, 74–75
KGB Analysis Directorate, 46
KGB Chief Directorate of Border Guards, 13, 19, 51
KGB Eighth Chief Directorate, 21, 49, 61
KGB Fifth Directorate, 2, 13, 20, 35–38, 46, 59, 81, 83, 109
KGB First Chief Directorate, 13–14, 19–20, 46, 48, 110, 139
KGB Ninth Directorate, 14, 109
KGB Operational Technology Directorate (Directorate OT), 48
KGB Second Chief Directorate, 19, 31, 61, 110
KGB Sixteenth Directorate, 20–21, 61, 133
KGB Sixth Directorate, 20, 43
KGB Third Chief Directorate, 19–20, 41–42, 76, 114
Khangoshvili, Zelimkhan ("Tornike"), 85
Kharaberyush, Aleksandr, 90
Khodorkovsky, Mikhail, 3
Khokhlov, Nikolay, 100
Khoperskov, Grigoriy, 138
Khramov, Oleg, 133
Khrushchev, Nikita, 26
Kirill, Patriarch, 11
Kiriyenko, Sergey, 110
Klimova, Natalya, 64
Kohver, Eston, 91
Komkov, Aleksey, 32
kompromat.ru, 147
Kondratyeva, Aleksandra, 142
Korenkov, Sergey, 131
Korolev, Sergey, 32, 42, 115–16, 117, 118, 120, 150, 158
Kouzminov, Alexander, 40
Kovalenko, Igor, 157
Kovalev, Nikolay, 6, 109–10, 111, 112, 148
Kozlov, Evald, 139
Kozyrev, Andrey, 73
Krivoshlyapov, Viktor, 33–34
Kryuchkov, Vladimir Aleksandrovich (KGB Chairman), 12, 26, 36, 143
Kryuchkov, Vladimir Vladimirovich, 55–56, 117, 123–24, 126
Kulishov, Vladimir, 95, 116–17, 143
Kupryazhkin, Aleksandr, 117–18

Latyš, Martin, 86
Lavrishchev, Aleksey, 73–74
Lefortovo Investigative Detention Center (SIZO), 59–60, 122
Limonov, Eduard, 81
Litvinenko, Aleksandr, 100, 113–14, 152
Lovyrev, Yevgeniy, 117, 122, 133

Main Directorate for Communications Security, 49
Main Directorate for Protection (GUO), 14, 20, 39
Main Directorate of State Security (GUGB), 106
Malofeyev, Konstantin, 96
Material-Technical Supply Directorate (UMTO), 57
Mayorova, Yekaterina (Katya), 140
Menshchikov, Vladislav, 117–19
Mikhailov, Aleksandr, 46–47, 155–56
Mikhailov, Sergey, 74–75, 78, 93, 96, 132
Militant Organization of Russian Nationalists (BORN), 38
Military Construction Directorate (VSU), 57
Military Medical Directorate (VMU), 57
Ministry of Internal Affairs (MVD), 12, 13, 16, 25, 40, 46, 48, 54–55, 59, 66, 78, 84, 88–89, 92, 106–7, 108, 109, 114, 120, 136, 138, 141, 145, 148–49, 151
Ministry of Security (MB), 14–17, 19–20, 40, 43, 48, 51, 59, 106, 124
Ministry of Security and Internal Affairs (MBVD), 13, 106
Mkrtyan, Liliya, 143
Moscow Institute of New Information Technologies (MINIT), 58
Movement Against Illegal Immigration (DPNI), 38
Murashov, Nikolay, 97

National Antiterrorist Committee (NAK), 53
National Bolshevik Party (NBP), 81
National Coordination Center for Computer Incidents (NKTsKI), 49
Navalny, Aleksey, 2, 81–82, 98, 147, 152
Nazarenko, Lyudmila, 64
Nemtsov, Boris, 82
Neumann, Janosh (aka Aleksey Artamonov), 88
Nikolayev, Andrey, 51
Notes of the "Black Colonel," 142
Novichok, 82
Nurgaliyev, Rashid, 55

Okhrana, 7
Operational Information Department (DOI) (of the Fifth Service), 45, 47, 133, 157
Operational Investigative Directorate (ORU) (of the Second Service), 37, 39
Operational-Investigative Directorate (of the Border Guard Service), 52
Operational-Organizational Department (of the Border Guard Service), 52
Ordered to Destroy: Operation Chinese Casket, 141
Organizational Analysis Directorate (of the NTS), 49, 50
Organizational-Analytical Directorate (of the Fourth Service), 43–44
Organizational and Personnel Service (SOKR) (Sixth Service), 30–31, 56–57, 117, 122
Organizational-Operational Directorate (of the Second Service), 37, 39
Organizational-Operational Directorate (of the TsSN), 39, 41
Osmayev, Adam, 90
Ostroukhov, Viktor, 11

Pakistan, 134, 158
Pasko, Grigioriy, 138
Patrushev, Nikolay, 43, 55, 71, 85, 96–97, 111–14, 124, 126, 134, 138, 140, 158
People's Commissariat of State Security (NKVD), 13, 15, 106
Pismenniy, Vladimir, 139
Pogrebnyak, Nikolay, 142
Primakov, Yevgeniy, 16, 73
Pronichev, Vladimir, 124
prophylactic activities, 87, 108, 145, 155
Public Relations Center (TsOS), 58, 144
Pushkarenko, Aleksey, 111
Pushkarev, Igor, 88
Putin, Vladimir, 2, 8–9, 11, 16–19, 21–23, 24–25, 26, 29, 37, 40, 43, 47, 51, 54–55, 71–72, 76, 80, 82, 85, 88, 89, 90, 96, 97, 105, 107–8, 110–16, 119, 123, 132, 133, 145, 147–48, 154, 157–59

Radio Counterintelligence Directorate (Directorate "R"), 61, 98
Repkin, Aleksey, 87
Reznev, Aleksey, 50
Rogozin, Dmitriy, 86
Romashin, Sergey, 137

Romashin, Viktor, 137
Roshchupkin, Aleksandr, 33, 72
Roskosmos, 44, 86
Rosnano, 44, 80
Rostec, 44, 86–87
Russian National Guard (Rosgvardiya), 43, 53, 76
Russian Orthodox Church, 11, 83
Rutskoy, Aleksandr, 15

Sablin, Anatoliy, 115, 117, 124
Safronov, Ivan, 86–87
Savelev, Anatoliy, 110
Savva, Mikhail, 125
Science and Technology Service (NTS), 48–51, 82, 99–101, 114, 117, 123, 133
Scientific Research Institute of Intelligence Problems, 48
Scientific Research Institute-1 (NII-1) (Special Technology), 50, 99–100
Scientific Research Institute-2 (NII-2) (Criminal Forensics Institute), 50, 100
Scientologists, 83
Sechin, Igor, 54, 88
Sechin's Spetsnaz (Sixth Service) (subordinate to the Internal Security Directorate (54, 88)),
Second Service. *See* Service for Defense of the Constitutional Order and Combatting Terrorism
Seconded Personnel Section (APS), 56–57
Security Council of Russia, 47, 53, 97, 105, 111, 115
Sedov, Aleksey, 117, 119–20
Seleznev, Roman, 75
Serdyukov, Anatoliy, 42, 116
Service for Defense of the Constitutional Order and Combatting Terrorism (SZKSiBT) (Second Service), (35, 117)
Service for Operational Information and International Relations (SOIiMS) (Fifth Service), 45–48, 70, 71, 72, 89–90, 97, 117, 121, 133, 157–58
Sevastyanov, Konstantin, 73–74
Seventh Service. *See* Activity Support Service
"Shaltay-Boltay" ("Humpty Dumpty"), 75
Shamalov, Kirill, 123
Shanghai Cooperation Organization (SCO), 130
Shapoval, Maksim, 90

Shavrin, Sergey, 137
Shaytanov, Valeriy, 90
Shekin, Mikhail, 117, 122–23
Shoigu, Sergey, 75
signals intelligence (SIGINT), 20–21, 61, 106, 133, 143, 154
Sirotkin, Igor, 117–18
Sixth Service. *See* Organizational and Personnel Service
Sixth Service (subordinate to the Internal Security Directorate) (Sechin's Spetsnaz), 31, 54, 88–89
Skorokhodov, Sergey, 34, 75
Sobchak, Anatoliy, 110
Social Welfare Service (SSBO), 57, 115, 117, 124
Society for the Study of the History of Patriotic Special Services, 144
Soldatov, Andrey, 3, 35, 59, 81, 89, 113, 121, 122, 157
Special Purpose Center (TsSN), 30, 37, 39–43, 84–85, 117, 124, 138, 140
Special Section (OO), 42
Special Service (Cryptography), 61
Special Technology Center (Eleventh Center), 49–50, 99–100
Spiridonova, Olga, 64–65
Spirin, Oleg, 40
Starovoytova, Galina, 111
State Customs Committee, 66, 148
State (Federal) Drug Control Service, 46, 66, 119–20, 123, 151
State Maritime Inspectorate, 52
State Political Directorate (GPU), 106
State System for Detecting, Warning, and Liquidating the Consequences of Computer Attacks (GosSOPKA), 96
Stepashin, Sergey, 16–17, 25, 107, 108, 111
Stoyanov, Ruslan, 74–75
Strauss, Robert, 129
Sugrubov, Denis, 88–89
Syromolotov, Oleg, 73
Sysoyev, Yevgeniy, 130
System of Operational-Investigative Measures (SORM), 60, 91–92, 154

Three Days Before Spring, 141
"Three Whales" scandal, 145, 148
Tikhomirova, Yuliya, 123
Tikhon, Metropolitan, 11
Tikhonov, Aleksandr, 117, 124, 138

Tikhonova, Katerina, 123
Trakhimenok, Sergey, 142
"Transportniy" commercial bank, 149–50
Tsarnayev, Tamerlan, 131
Tyukov, Anatoliy, 56

Ugryumov, German, 138
Ukraine, 3, 15, 33, 41, 45, 56, 62–63, 72–73, 78, 83, 84, 89, 90, 91, 93, 95, 97, 108, 121, 122, 130, 132–33, 141, 146, 155, 157–58
Ulyukayev, Alexey, 88
Umarov, Mamikhan, 85
Unified State Political Directorate (OGPU), 15, 108
Ustinov, Vladimir, 148

"Vanguard of Red Youth," 81
Vasiliyev, Andrey, 150
Vavilova, Yelena, 24
Venomous Bear (aka Turla), 92
Vertyazhkin, Aleksey, 56
Vidmanova, Yelena, 98
Vietnam, 130, 133–34
VolleyGrad, 123
Voronin, Demuri, 86
Vorontsov, Dmitriy, 44
Vrublevskiy, Pavel, 74

Worthington, Peter, 71

Yanukovich, Viktor, 121, 132–33
Yarovaya law, 92
Yarovaya, Irina, 92
Yeltsin, Boris, 6, 10, 12–15, 17, 18, 21, 39–40, 59, 106–9, 111, 112, 113, 158
Yevskin, Vyacheslav, 137
Yuryev, Nikolay, 76, 117, 120
Yuryeva, Aleksandra, 120

Zadorina, Anastasiya, 123
Zaostrovtsev, Yevgeniy, 148–49
Zaostrovtsev, Yuriy, 148
Zavarzin, Petr, 7–8
Zhalo, Aleksey, 38, 82, 133
Zhirinovskiy, Vladimir, 6
Zhomov, Aleksandr, 32
Zhukov, Yevgeniy, 148
Zotov, Gennadiy, 81
Zubkov, Viktor, 116

About the Author

Kevin P. Riehle is a lecturer in intelligence and security studies at Brunel University London. He spent over thirty years in the US government as a counterintelligence analyst studying foreign intelligence services, and he finished his government career as an associate professor of strategic intelligence at the National Intelligence University. He previously taught at the University of Mississippi Center for Intelligence and Security Studies. He received a PhD in war studies from King's College London, an MS in strategic intelligence from the Joint Military Intelligence College, and a BA in Russian and political science from Brigham Young University. He has written on a variety of intelligence and counterintelligence topics, focusing on the history of Soviet and Eastern Bloc intelligence services. In 2020, his first book—*Soviet Defectors: Revelations of Renegade Intelligence Officers, 1924–1954*—was published by Edinburgh University Press. His second book, *Russian Intelligence: A Case-Based Study of Russian Services and Missions Past and Present*, was published by the National Intelligence Press in 2022. His articles have appeared in a variety of peer-reviewed journals, including *Intelligence and National Security*, *International Journal of Intelligence and CounterIntelligence*, *Cold War History*, and *Journal of Intelligence History*; and he has appeared in interviews by various media organizations and by the International Spy Museum.